READING AND WRITING WITH CONFIDENCE

READING AND WRITING WITH CONFIDENCE

Carol Kanar

HOUGHTON MIFFLIN COMPANY   Boston   New York

Senior Sponsoring Editor: Mary Jo Southern
Senior Associate Editor: Ellen Darion
Senior Project Editor: Fred Burns
Production/Design Coordinator: Jill Haber
Senior Manufacturing Coordinator: Priscilla Abreu
Marketing Manager: Nancy Lyman

Cover design: Diana Coe
Cover image: Tate Gallery, London/Art Resource, NY

Acknowledgments for reprinted material appear on page 301.

Printed in the U.S.A.

Library of Congress Catalog Card Number: 97-78236

ISBN 0-395-71865-1

1 2 3 4 5 6 7 8 9—QF—02 01 00 99 98

BRIEF CONTENTS

CONTENTS

Intro for [handwritten annotation]

PREFACE

Good reading and writing depend on a student's recognition and application of several essential concepts common to each process: main idea, details, organization, purpose, audience, tone, inferences, and conclusions. These concepts represent critical choices readers and writers make all the time. *Reading and Writing with Confidence* is not merely a reading text with writing exercises nor simply a writing text with readings. It is a combined reading and writing text that borrows chapters from *The Confident Reader 2* and *The Confident Writer,* teaching students to become better readers at the same time.

An underlying theme of the book is that students must see themselves as both readers and writers. As writers, their goal is to effectively communicate their ideas. As readers, their goal is to follow an author's ideas and to comprehend the information or message communicated. My goal in writing this text is to help students develop the skills needed to successfully and confidently meet the reading and writing demands of college, work, and life.

SPECIAL FEATURES OF THE TEXT

Focus on Process and Skill

Reading and Writing with Confidence teaches reading and writing as processes to be developed and controlled and as skills to be mastered and applied.

Integration of Skills

Although each chapter focuses on one or two skills such as finding a main idea of writing a topic sentence, there is much cross-referencing, interweaving, and reinforcement of skills covered in other chapters. This approach models the reading and writing processes themselves in which skills are integrated and often applied simultaneously.

Transference of Skills

Many students who seem to achieve success in a reading or writing class fall back into bad habits when required to read or write in their other courses. To promote the transference of skills, *Reading and Writing with Confidence* contains reading selections and excerpts from a variety of sources: periodicals, fiction, non-fiction, textbooks, and others, so that students gain practical reading and writing experience with materials and ideas they are likely to encounter in their other college courses and in the world beyond the classroom as well.

Organization and Content

Chapters 1 and 2 lay the foundation for confident reading and writing. Chapters 3 through 10 are organized according to the five choices that connect reading and writing. (See the chart on the inside front cover.)

Chapter 1 describes the reading and writing processes and explains how students can take control of these processes to achieve successful outcomes. Chapter 2 helps students develop the vocabulary skills necessary to improve reading comprehension and to make good word choices for writing.

Chapter 3 explains how to find stated and implied main ideas in paragraphs and longer reading selections such as essays and textbook chapters. Chapter 4 addresses how to write a topic sentence and a thesis statement.

Chapter 5 covers types of details and levels of development to look for in reading. Chapter 6 explains how to select and arrange details in writing.

Chapters 7 and 8 focus on three organizational principles of reading and writing: unity, coherence, and organizational pattern. For example, students learn how to recognize transitions and thought patterns in reading and how to use organizational patterns in their writing.

Chapter 9 covers purpose, audience, and tone in reading and writing. Students learn that the choices writers make about purpose and tone determine how the audience responds. They also learn the importance of audience awareness and to see themselves not only as members of a reading audience having certain expectations but as writers who must also consider the expectations of their readers. Although purpose, audience, and tone can be difficult concepts for students to grasp, *Reading and Writing with Confidence* approaches them in a pragmatic way that will expand students' reading comprehension and writing options.

Chapter 10 shows students how to make inferences from their reading and how to write effective conclusions that have implications for readers.

The appendix explains how students can edit their papers for several common sentence errors and contains an editing checklist, which is a chart students can use to keep track of their errors and watch their improvement.

CHAPTER FEATURES

Reading and Writing with Confidence has a strong visual appeal and a student-friendly tone. Figures, diagrams, annotated excerpts, and integrated exercises break up the text. In addition, *Reading and Writing with Confidence* has several unique features that make it a practical text for instructors and students alike.

Thinking First

Each chapter opens with three thought-provoking questions framed to focus students' attention on the chapter's major concepts. This feature, as its name suggests, is designed to help students develop the habit of thinking before they read.

Backgrond Check

The background check follows the chapter introduction and is the pre-reading activity for the chapter-opening reading selection. This feature helps students establish a context for reading, assess their prior knowledge, and make predictions about what the selection covers.

Vocabulary Check

The vocabulary check lists difficult words from the chapter-opening reading selection with paragraph numbers and definitions. The purpose of this feature is to alert students to words that may give them difficulty so that they can familiarize themselves with their definitions before reading.

Chapter-Opening Reading Selection

Students need ideas to think and write about. The reading selections provide content for reading practice and serve as a springboard for writing. The readings are interesting, thought-provoking, and represent a wide range of sources. A headnote preceding each selection provides information about the author and may contain a clue about the selection's content.

Thinking Critically

This post-reading activity checks students' comprehension and provides a structure that enables them to think critically about the reading selection. Thinking Critically consists of six parts: (1) Main Idea; (2) Details; (3) Organization; (4) Purpose, Audience, Tone; (5) Inferences and Conclusions; (6) Making Connections. These parts reflect the book's overall organizational plan.

Thinking About Process

This feature encourages students to think about their own reading and writing processes and to discover practical ways to apply the skills they are learning.

Thinking It Over

Thinking It Over is an interactive summary and review. This feature helps students test their recall of chapter concepts by completing several fill-in-the-blank statements.

Topics for Writing

Near the end of each chapter is a list of suggested topics and a checklist for revision. Some topics are generated from the chapter-opening essay; others are more general but still related to chapter content. Most chapters contain a topic suitable for academic writing. The revision checklist reminds students to revise and edit their paragraphs or essays for content, organization, and grammar.

Reflections on Reading and Writing

This final chapter activity encourages students to reflect on what they have learned and the progress they are making. The reflections can be used as a journal activity or as a communication channel between instructor and student.

INSTRUCTIONAL SUPPORT

Instructor's Resource Manual   The manual provides teaching suggestions for each chapter, sample syllabi for a sixteen or ten-week course, and an answer key.

Newsweek Subscription   A ten-week subscription card may be shrink-wrapped with the text for a nominal fee.

Expressways Second Edition Software   Available in IBM and Macintosh versions, *Expressways* is an interactive software program that provides a tutorial review of key writing strategies and a broad range of writing activities to guide students through the writing process.

The Dictionary Deal   *The American Heritage College Dictionary* may be shrink-wrapped with the text at a substantial savings.

ACKNOWLEDGMENTS

I am grateful to the many instructors who asked for a book that connects reading and writing, and to Nancy Lyman and Mary Jo Southern who suggested that I write it. I thank everyone involved with this project, especially Ellen Darion, Fred Burns, Kate O'Sullivan, and Christian Zabriskie. No writer works alone, and I am indebted to the Houghton Mifflin family of editors and others for the parts they played in the development and production of *Reading and Writing with Confidence*. I also thank my husband, Stephen P. Kanar, for his continued support.

Most of all, I thank my students. If not for them, I would never have been moved to write.

—Carol Kanar

READING AND WRITING WITH CONFIDENCE

Chapter 1

Getting Ready to Read and Write

THINKING FIRST

- *What do reading and writing have in common?*
- *Why are reading and writing essential skills?*
- *How can I improve my reading and writing?*

Reading and writing are two closely related processes that require you to participate actively and think critically. Many of the skills that help you read efficiently also help you write successfully. Both processes can be improved by using proven learning techniques such as reading systems and writing strategies. Reading and writing are shared experiences. Writers write for an audience. When you read, you are a member of that audience. When you write, your readers are the audience.

Reading and writing not only are essential skills for success in all your courses, but they have a practical application beyond college as well. Effective reading and writing are two of the communication skills that today's employers expect of employees, and these skills are predicted to become even more important in the workplace of the twenty-first century. It is hard to imagine a job that does not require some reading and writing. At some point in your working life, you may have to fill out invoices; write reports; develop projects; read manuals, blueprints, or contracts; or conduct research and summarize your findings in a written report.

Reading and writing are essential parts of many people's personal lives as well as their working lives. They may read or write for entertainment or self-expression. Many turn to books, newspapers, and periodicals as their main sources of information. Others use their reading and writing skills to search for information and entertainment on the Internet and to communicate with others online. Reading and writing may play some of these roles in your life, or you may think of other ways you use these important skills.

Finally, reading requires you to make sense of a writer's choices. Writing requires you to make choices of your own. To read and write with confidence, you must know what the choices are. This chapter begins with an overview of the reading and writing processes and concludes with the choices upon which reading and writing depend.

BACKGROUND CHECK

Before reading the following essay, check your knowledge and assumptions about the U.S. space program.

1. Do the names *Challenger* and *Christa McAuliffe* mean anything to you? What do you know about them?

2. What is your opinion about space travel in general and about U.S. expenditures on the space program?

3. If you had the opportunity to travel in a future space shuttle mission, would you? Why or why not?

4. Based on your survey of the title, author information, and first two paragraphs, what do you expect to follow?

5. What else do you know or think about the topic?

There Had Been a Death in the Family
Mike Pride

This essay is about a teacher, Christa McAuliffe, who became an astro-naut, and about her death in the Challenger *explosion and her legacy of courage and inspiration. The essay appeared in* Newsweek.

VOCABULARY CHECK

incredible (1)	unbelievable
odyssey (2)	journey, quest
catechism (3)	basic principles of Christianity
deadpan (4)	expressionless, matter-of-fact
vibrant (4)	lively, energetic
advocate (5)	support, defend
consoled (9)	comforted
resilient (10)	able to recover
traversed (11)	moved across or through
subtle (11)	not obvious

1   In the journal I keep, the entry for July 20, 1985, begins: "Yesterday was an incredible day to be editor of the local paper." The day before at the White House, Christa McAuliffe, from my hometown, Concord, N.H., had been named the teacher in space. Near the end of my jour-nal entry is this quotation from her: "I think the students will say that an ordinary person is contributing to history, and if they can make that connection, they are going to get excited about history and about the future."

2   Christa made the future—space—an area we covered in the small newspaper I edit. From before that July day until the moment she dis-appeared in a pink-white puff on the newsroom television screen, we helped her neighbors follow her odyssey. Last week we had a differ-ent job. There had been a death in the family, and we groped, with our readers, for what it meant.

3   Christa made Concord proud. The people in our city saw in her

the best that we have to offer. Concord is a family town, and it cares about education. A mother, a wife and a teacher, Christa spoke out for her profession. She was robust and confident; she played volleyball and loved the outdoors. She was a volunteer in a city that seems at times to be run by volunteers. She also taught what Roman Catholics used to call a catechism class. She let no one forget that when she was growing up, teaching was one of the few fields open to women. She was a role model, bringing home the message again and again: if I can do this, think what you can do.

And she became a media darling. In front of a semicircle of TV cameras, she would describe deadpan how the shuttle's toilet worked. The people of Concord, of course, knew that Christa was not performing for the media. The camera didn't lie, and Christa didn't act. This was the real *her.* Whether she was waving Paul Giles's baton to conduct Nevers' Band—it dates back to the Civil War—or chatting with her son's hockey teammates at the Everett Arena, she was the same vibrant, positive person the rest of America saw on TV.

Crazy about Christa: It is assumed in our society that people who capture the nation, as Christa had, go on to fame and fortune. Those who knew her best knew that Christa had no such intention. She would have used her celebrity to advocate causes she believed in, but she could hardly wait to get back to her classroom at Concord High. She had chosen the profession and chosen Concord, and her selection as teacher in space had done nothing but affirm those choices.

If Christa liked Concord, Concord was crazy about Christa. It made her the grand marshal in a parade. It gave her a day. Her high school sent her off to Houston with a banner that read "Good luck from the Class of '86 . . . Mrs. McAuliffe . . . Have a blast!" A committee made big plans for her homecoming. New Year's Eve, the city featured ice sculptures of rocket ships and stars on the New Hampshire State House lawn.

Bob Hohler, our paper's columnist, became Christa's shadow, sending back dispatches from Washington, Houston, and, finally, Cape Canaveral. Her beaming face graced our front page countless times, floating weightless during training, dwarfed by *Challenger* before an earlier launch, grinning with her husband, Steve. Her story always seemed too good to be true, and too American. No one is really the girl next door. No one rides in a parade down Main Street on a bright, sunny Saturday afternoon. No one equates a modern venture with the pioneers crossing the plains in Conestoga wagons.

In the journal I keep, the entry for Jan. 28, 1986, begins: "What a tragic day for Concord." Tears have flowed in my city for days—long, wearying days. Words have flowed, too, in verse, in letters to the editor, on radio talk shows.

Intense and Personal: All the media people who have interviewed 9
me and others at the newspaper want to know how it feels here. Our
pain is more intense and personal, I tell them, but we know we are
not alone; nearly everyone I know was consoled by a call from someone. Ordinary people, the kind McAuliffe's mission had intended to
reach, have called from out of the blue. One man from Alberta,
Canada, told me that his family felt terrible and needed to speak with
someone here because if they felt that bad, we must feel much
worse.

I thought at first that Christa's death would be hardest on the 10
children. They had learned all about the shuttle, and in an age without heroes, they had found one in her. Most had witnessed the dread-
ful moment. Yet times like these remind us that children are resilient.
Age robs us of the instinct to go forward without a backward glance.
I even suspect now that we have tried too hard to make our children
feel what we want them to feel. It is the adults in Concord who still
have swollen eyes and stricken looks. They comprehend what was
lost, and what was lost was a part of them. It is not a myth to say that
everyone in town knew Christa. She was easy to meet, easy to talk to.
Even those who never had the chance felt as though they had.

Since we picked up Christa McAuliffe's trail, our town has tra- 11
versed from the green, fertile days of midsummer to the cold heart of
winter. The subtle daily changes of nature have played tricks on us;
sometimes, at this time of year, it can seem as if summer might never
come again.

Many people have compared Christa's death with the assassina- 12
tion of John F. Kennedy, the inspiration of her youth. There are differences, but for the people of Concord—even for the nation as a
whole—the comparison is valid. She stood for what was best in us at
a time when we wanted to believe that the American spirit was reborn. That makes her death hard.

THINKING CRITICALLY

Main Idea

1. Author Mike Pride's topic is Christa McAuliffe's death. His point
   is that her death has had a profound effect on the people of Concord and the nation. Which sentence in the second paragraph
   states this point in slightly different words?

Details

2. The main idea of the third paragraph is stated in the first sentence. What examples support the main idea? What facts support the main idea of the sixth paragraph?

Organization

3. Pride organizes his details into two major sections. The first explains the town's pride in McAuliffe; the second explains its sorrow at her death. Each section begins with a journal entry. Find the two sections and explain how each helps to show the effect of McAuliffe's death.

Purpose, Audience, Tone

4. Why do you think Pride wrote the essay? Use evidence from the essay to support your answer.

5. Who is Pride's audience, and how can you tell?

Inferences and Conclusions

6. In the last paragraph, Pride says that McAuliffe "stood for what was best in us at a time when we wanted to believe that the American spirit was reborn." He suggests that this quality is what makes the comparison between McAuliffe and John F. Kennedy valid. Why? What other public figure can you think of, either from recent times or the past, who has this quality and who is a hero?

Making Connections

Christa McAuliffe was an everyday hero because she was a person like most of us: a good citizen with a family and a job. As a teacher, she was dedicated and creative, and her efforts earned her the honor of being selected as the first teacher to travel in outer space. To get on board *Challenger* took courage and hope. That is what made McAuliffe a hero, not that the flight ended in tragedy. Write about a man or woman you think is an everyday hero, someone you know who has courage and hope and who stands for what is best in us.

HOW THE READING AND WRITING PROCESSES COMPARE

Reading is a process that occurs in the mind. Writing is a process that occurs both in the mind and on paper or computer screen. Both processes involve the interaction of many skills. Both processes can be broken down into steps for purposes of explaining and understanding them. For example, whether you are reading or writing, what you do *before, during,* and *after* can make all the difference in whether the outcome is successful. The outcome of the reading process is comprehension. The outcome of the writing process is a finished product: a paragraph, an essay, or other piece of writing.

Reading and writing are *recursive* processes. Although we can break them down into basic steps (things to do before, during, and after reading or writing) the steps do not always occur in order, and they may *recur* or be repeated at any point in the process. Figure 1.1 compares the reading and writing processes. Before reading about each process in detail, see Figure 1.1 for an overview.

THE READING PROCESS AND OUTCOME

When asked how they read, many students answer, "I start at the beginning and read to the end." When asked to describe their reading problems, many students respond in one of the following ways:

"I have trouble concentrating."

"I get bored easily."

"I don't like to read."

"I enjoy reading, but I can't seem to remember what I read."

"The vocabulary, especially in science, is hard for me."

If you find yourself agreeing with any of these comments, you may not be reading as effectively as you could. The outcome of reading is comprehension. To improve your reading, you need to understand the reading process so that you can control the outcome.

Understanding the Process

Why is it not a good idea to "start at the beginning and read to the end?" This method of reading ignores two facts of human learning and

FIGURE 1.1

Comparing the Reading and Writing Processes: Three Steps

THE READING PROCESS

1. BEFORE READING

Preread: Check background. Explore your knowledge, experience, and assumptions about the author's topic.

Read with a purpose: Know why you are reading and determine what you need to find out.

Choose a reading system: Use SQ3R (survey, question, read, recite, review) or another appropriate strategy.

2. DURING READING

Read actively: Ask questions. Look for an organizational pattern. Mark your text. Monitor comprehension.

Repeat prereading activities as needed.

3. AFTER READING

Review your work: Reread any notes, underlining, or marking, and recite material/concepts you need to learn. Make study guides (charts, diagrams, outlines) for difficult material.

Repeat steps 1 and 2 as needed.

THE WRITING PROCESS

1. BEFORE WRITING

Prewrite: Choose a topic and think about it. Explore your knowledge, experience, and assumptions about your topic.

Write with a purpose: Make preliminary decisions about main or central idea, purpose, audience, organization, and tone.

Choose a writing strategy: Use one of several strategies to generate ideas about your topic that you may be able to use as details.

2. DURING WRITING

Write actively: Plan to write more than one draft (copy). Make final decisions about choice of details and organizational pattern.

Repeat prewriting activities as needed.

3. AFTER WRITING

Review your work: Read your draft and revise for content, organization, and style. Edit to find and correct errors.

Repeat steps 1 and 2 as needed.

memory. For one thing, most people lose concentration without a break. Second, the mind works better when it is actively processing information. If you read from first word to last word without stopping to question or think about what you read, you are reading passively. Passive reading leads to loss of concentration, boredom, and forgetting. Active reading involves you in the process, puts you in control, and keeps you interested.

Exercise 1.1 To determine how actively you read, check the statements that apply to you.

1. I read textbook chapters from beginning to end without stopping. _____

2. I stop reading to look at figures, charts, or other graphics and try to relate them to the rest of the chapter. _____

3. When I get confused, I mark the passage or make a note to ask about it later. _____

4. I usually have trouble deciding what is important in a textbook chapter or other assigned reading. _____

5. I often see a connection between what I read in textbooks and my life or course content. _____

6. I rarely underline, mark, or make notes when I read. _____

7. I can't decide what I should underline or mark. _____

8. Even if I'm not interested in what I'm reading, I am still able to decide what is important. _____

9. My only reason for reading a textbook chapter is that the instructor has assigned it. _____

10. I usually have a purpose for reading—something I want to know or need to find out. _____

If you checked statements 2, 3, 5, 8, and 10, then you are probably already reading actively. If you checked statements 1, 4, 6, 7, and 9, then you may need to learn some strategies that will help you gain control of your reading process.

The three steps of the reading process illustrated in Figure 1.1 are the key to active reading. Review them now before reading the next section.

Step 1: Before you read, take time to think about what you are going to do. When you have an assignment, do not start cold. Prereading activities motivate you and prepare you for successful comprehension. Begin by thinking about the topic. Ask yourself, "What do I already know about this?" Build background for the reading by examining your assumptions about the topic. What are your opinions, beliefs, or feelings about it? What experiences or knowledge do you bring to the topic? By checking your background before you read, you establish a context for reading that helps you relate new information to what you already know.

Read with a *purpose* in mind. Know what your instructor expects. Determine *why* you are reading and *what* you need to find out. Figure 1.2 illustrates some typical reading assignments and purposes.

FIGURE 1.2

Reading Assignments and Purposes

READING ASSIGNMENTS	PURPOSES
a chapter in a math textbook	to learn a concept such as the properties of 0; to learn an operation such as how to factor
a chapter on the circulatory system from a biology textbook	to learn the parts and functions of the system
a handout from your psychology professor on the memory process	to understand the stages of memory and how the memory processes information
an essay from an English composition textbook	to analyze the writer's strategy
a journal article on the costs and problems involved in a paper mill's conversion to a nonpolluting filtering system	to see how an environmental regulation is applied in a real-life situation

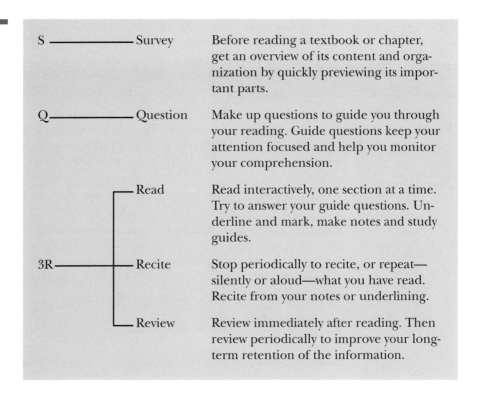

FIGURE 1.3

The SQ3R System

S ———————— Survey — Before reading a textbook or chapter, get an overview of its content and organization by quickly previewing its important parts.

Q———————— Question — Make up questions to guide you through your reading. Guide questions keep your attention focused and help you monitor your comprehension.

Read — Read interactively, one section at a time. Try to answer your guide questions. Underline and mark, make notes and study guides.

3R——— Recite — Stop periodically to recite, or repeat— silently or aloud—what you have read. Recite from your notes or underlining.

Review — Review immediately after reading. Then review periodically to improve your long-term retention of the information.

Choose a reading system. Reading systems cause you to read actively. If you have no system, you may fall into a passive reading habit. A classic system, one you may have tried, is SQ3R. Figure 1.3 briefly explains the steps.

A *survey* of a book or chapter is a quick preview of its content and organization. Surveying before reading helps you predict what a book or chapter covers. As you survey, check your background to recall what you already know about the author's topic. To survey a chapter, follow these steps. First, read the title, introductory section or first paragraph, and any learning goals or objectives that may be listed. This will tell you what the topic is and what the author expects you to learn. Second, look over the major headings or subheadings. These tell you how the chapter is organized. Third, look for graphic aids (charts, diagrams, pictures) and key terms (words in italics, boldface, or a second color). Graphic aids often simplify difficult processes, and key terms are essential to your understanding of concepts. Fourth, read the summary for a restatement of the author's central idea and conclusions. Finally, briefly note what kind of questions or problems are at the end of the chapter. Knowing in advance what questions you will be asked or what problems you may have to solve may help you pinpoint where to look for the answers when you do your careful reading.

Exercise 1.2   Select a textbook chapter you have been assigned to read for one of your courses. Practice reading with SQ3R by completing the items that follow.

1. Write the title and page numbers of the chapter you have selected.

    _____

2. Survey the chapter. Based on your survey, what does the chapter cover? What are you expected to know or be able to do after reading the chapter?

    _____

    _____

3. Choose one section to read. Write the heading of the section on the first line below. Write two guide questions about the heading on the next two lines.

    _____

    _____

    _____

4. Read the section you chose for item 3. Underline what you think are the important ideas to remember. On the lines below, write the answers to your guide questions for item 3. If you cannot answer your guide questions, explain why.

    _____

    _____

    _____

5. Suppose you were being tested on this chapter. What information from the section you chose for items 3 and 4 would you recite or review to prepare for the test?

Step 2: Read actively. Read one section at a time. Ask questions to guide your reading. Turn headings into questions, and look for the answers as you read. Headings focus your attention on the main ideas of the sections that follow. In fact, if you were to list a chapter's headings in order on a sheet of paper, you would have an outline of the chapter. Paying attention to headings and asking questions keeps you on track, shows you how a chapter is organized, and helps you follow the author's line of reasoning.

Asking questions is one way to read actively. Highlighting, underlining, making notes in the margin, or taking notes on paper are other ways. To mark your text effectively, read first. Read one section or paragraph at a time. Then go back and mark key ideas. To identify the key ideas, ask yourself three questions:

1. What is this paragraph or section about? (topic)

2. What do I need to know about the topic?

3. What details will help me remember?

The following example may give you an idea of where to look for the key ideas and how to mark them.

Topic

Main idea

The moorhen is a bird common to Florida that has several interesting characteristics. For one thing, it has a ① unique appearance. The moorhen is smaller than a chicken, with black and white feathers and a red beak. Specially adapted feet enable the moorhen to walk on water, figuratively speaking. The long toes help spread the bird's weight over plants such as water hyacinths and grasses. ② How moorhens live is also of interest. They nest and raise their young on floating islands of vegetation near the shores of lakes. They feed on insects

Three important characteristics

and other organic matter. ③ <u>Characteristic, too, is the sound</u> <u>the moorhen makes,</u> which is almost like a human cry yet not unpleasant. In the evening, the moorhen's cry—another voice in summer's symphony— blends with the chirping of crickets and the croaking of frogs.

> **STUDY TIP:**   *Do not wait until the last minute to read an assignment. Plan ahead. Allow yourself plenty of time to read, mark, and review a chapter before class.*

Step 3: After reading, review what you have read. It is important to review immediately so that you combat forgetting. Combining recitation with review improves memory because it opens another sensory pathway into your brain: reciting information aloud activates your sense of hearing. Reading over your notes, underlining, and marking activate your visual sense. Reviewing may help you discover what you have retained and what you need to relearn.

An important point to keep in mind is that reviewing does not mean rereading. The purpose of a review is to determine what you know and what you still need to learn. Rereading is inefficient because it keeps you from focusing on the concepts or ideas that are giving you trouble. The purpose of marking your text is to keep you from having to reread. If you have marked your text effectively, then you may need to review only what you have marked. However, if your reading system includes taking notes in a notebook or making study guides, then you need to review those also.

Controlling the Outcome

The outcome of reading is comprehension. To control the outcome, learn to *monitor,* or check, your comprehension. Recognize when you are comprehending well and when your comprehension fails. At the first sign of a loss in comprehension, try to determine the problem. Are you stuck on an unfamiliar word? Have you lost sight of the main idea? Do you lack necessary background knowledge? Are the explanations too difficult or complex for you to follow?

At first monitoring your comprehension may be difficult because you may mistakenly think you understand what you are reading. For example, you may read a chapter, study it, think you know the information, but fail a test that covers it. With enough practice and an appropriate strategy, monitoring your comprehension should become easier. Try these suggestions.

- **Read one section at a time.** If a section is very long, break it down into smaller parts. (It is easier to process small chunks of information than large ones.) Start with a guide question formulated from the title or a heading. At the end of the section or "chunk," see if you can answer your question. If not, reconsider your guide question and reread the section.

- **Make connections among ideas.** As you finish each section, take a moment to figure out how it relates to the section before it and anticipate what will follow. Consider why the information is important or how you can use it. Place a question mark in the margin beside anything you do not understand. This will remind you to ask about it in class.

- **Reconstruct the information in your own words.** Test your comprehension by trying to restate the writer's ideas in your own words. If you cannot, you probably have not understood the material. Summarize ideas as you go, either in the margin or at the end of a section. After reading and marking a chapter, meet with a study partner to review it. Take turns explaining to each other what seems important in each section. You may be able to fill in the gaps in each other's knowledge.

Exercise 1.3   Does your reading comprehension need improvement? Take this informal survey to decide. Check the statements that apply to you.

1. When I am reading, I often encounter unfamiliar words.   _____

2. Much of what I read in my textbooks is new or unfamiliar to me.   _____

3. When I am reading, everything seems to make sense, but then I have trouble remembering what I've read.   _____

4. I sometimes "wake up" in the middle of a page not knowing what I've read.   _____

5. I have a hard time putting what the writer said into my
   own words.   _____

A check beside statement 1 may mean that your vocabulary needs improving. Keep a dictionary handy when you read, or use your textbook's glossary. See Chapter 2 for vocabulary-building strategies. A check beside statement 2 may mean you lack sufficient background on the topic. To build background, read introductory sections or paragraphs, review previous chapters, or refer to another source containing the same information at a more basic level.

A check beside statement 3 may indicate that you are not reading actively. Try the strategies covered on page 13 of this chapter. A check beside statement 4 may indicate a need to improve concentration. A check beside statement 5 may indicate that the material is highly difficult or complex. To cope with this, make notes, find a study partner and try to think through difficult ideas together, try to restructure the information in your own words, or seek help from your instructor or a tutor.

Exercise 1.4   Now practice monitoring your comprehension. Read the following textbook excerpt, then complete the items that follow it.

Margaret Mahler's Object Relations Approach Margaret Mahler   1
(Mahler et al., 1975) conducted systematic observational studies of
normal infants and their mothers guided by a psychodynamic perspec-
tive. Based on these observations, Mahler proposed that an infant
goes through four phases in developing a sense of psychological self.

During the **autistic phase** (birth to two months), the infant expe-   2
riences a sleeplike psychological state that allows a transition from the
protected world of his mother's uterus to the demands of the world in
which he now lives. During the second or **symbiotic phase** (two to
six months), the child begins to develop a "dim awareness of the
need-satisfying object." Here *object* refers to an emotionally charged
mental representation or image of the mother (or other primary care-
taker) as a satisfier of his needs.

Mahler's third or **separation-individuation phase** (six to 24   3
months) involves three subphases. During the *hatching* subphase (six
to 10 months), the infant learns to recognize and respond differently
to her parents versus other people. In the *practicing* subphase (10 to
16 months), toddler and mother learn to separate and disengage

while still feeling safe and comfortable. In the *rapprochement* sub-phase (16 to 24 months), major growth in the child's physical and cognitive capabilities allow the child to experiment more fully with alternating between going off on her own and returning for "refueling" to the safe home base of her mother.

In Mahler's fourth and final phase, the **object constancy phase**   4 (24 to 36+ months), the child becomes capable of maintaining a reliable, emotionally stable mental image (object) of the mother as a source of both gratification and frustration. The child's increasingly stable sense of the "object" is associated with a more stable and complex sense of individuality.

1. How would you rate your overall comprehension of this excerpt: good, fair, or poor? Why?

_____

_____

2. Where in the excerpt did you feel that you were comprehending well? (Identify by sentence and paragraph.) Describe how you felt at that point in the reading.

_____

_____

3. Where in the excerpt did you have difficulty comprehending? (Identify by sentence and paragraph.) Describe how you felt at that point in the reading.

_____

_____

4. When did you feel the need to use a strategy such as note taking or underlining to strengthen comprehension? (Identify by sentence and paragraph.)

_____

_____

5. To test your comprehension further, answer the following questions.

   a. What are Mahler's four stages in the development of psychological self?

   _____

   _____

   b. What are the substages of the *separation-individuation phase?*

   _____

   _____

   c. During which stage does the infant experience "a sleeplike psychological state"?

   _____

   _____

   d. Mahler's theory is called the *object relations approach.* Who or what is the object? What relationship does the theory describe?

   _____

   _____

THE WRITING PROCESS AND OUTCOME

When asked how they write, many students answer, "I just start writing and see what develops." When asked to describe their writing problems, many students respond in one of the following ways:

"I have trouble getting started."

"I choose a topic but then can't think of anything to say."

"I have ideas but don't know how to organize them."

"My grammar skills need improvement."

"I'm a bad speller."

If you find yourself agreeing with any of these comments, you may not be writing as successfully as you could. The outcome of writing is a well-organized, well-developed paragraph, essay, or other piece of writing. To improve your writing, you need to understand the process so that you can control the outcome.

Understanding the Process

Why is it usually not a good idea to "start writing and see what develops?" Without a plan or a purpose, nothing significant may develop. Although writing is a highly individual process, and writers have many ways to go about it, most experienced writers agree that planning saves time. If you plan before you write, you are more likely to get the results you want.

Exercise 1.5   Do your writing skills need improvement? Your responses to the following items may help you decide.

1. Put a check beside each of the following writing activities that are difficult for you:

_____ Choosing a topic

_____ Thinking of what to write

_____ Introducing my topic

_____ Deciding on a main idea

_____ Supporting or explaining my main idea

_____ Organizing my ideas

_____ Writing my conclusion

_____ Choosing the right words

_____ Using grammar correctly

_____ Spelling correctly

2. How much time do you spend on a writing assignment?

_____

3. How far ahead do you begin writing before an assignment is due?

_____

4. When you finish writing, do you usually feel positive or negative about the result?

_____

5. What are your strengths and weaknesses as a writer?

_____

_____

Like reading, writing is an *active* process that requires your full concentration and involvement. The three steps of the writing process illustrated in Figure 1.1 on page 8 are the key to active writing and may be the solution to any writing difficulties you identified in Exercise 1.5. Review Figure 1.1 now before reading the next section.

Step 1: Before writing you need to *prewrite,* or plan. Begin by choosing a topic. At this stage of the process, you are checking your background—what you know and do not know about your topic. To aid your thinking, jot down any ideas about your topic that may be useful in your writing. If you have trouble getting started, *choose a prewriting strategy. Clustering* is one strategy that can help you generate ideas about your topic. Figure 1.4 illustrates an idea cluster for the topic "A Behavior I Wish People Would Change."

Brainstorming and *questioning* are two more strategies that can help you get started. To brainstorm a topic, jot down whatever words and phrases come to mind until you have at least twenty items. Later you can decide which ideas you can use, which ones to omit, and how to organize those that remain. If you have trouble making a list, perhaps you have chosen a topic for which you have little background knowledge or experience. Choose another topic and start again.

The journalist's six questions are good ones to ask about your topic:

FIGURE 1.4

Idea Cluster for "A Behavior I Wish People Would Change"

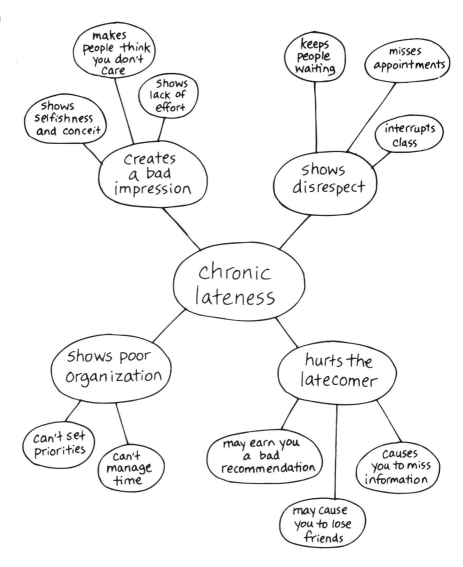

who, what, where, when, why, and *how?* For example, in writing about a car accident you might ask: Who was involved? What happened? Where did it happen? Why did it happen? How did it happen? Asking and answering these questions can help you think through your topic and gather evidence about it.

Exercise 1.6   To practice prewriting, choose one of the topics below or make up your own topic. Use clustering, brainstorming, or the journalist's questions to generate ideas for a possible paragraph or essay.

A place I would like to visit

Qualities I look for in a friend

How to prepare for a test

My favorite holiday

A movie I would recommend

A habit people should break

As a result of your prewriting activities, you should be able to *write with a purpose.* Thinking about your topic will help you discover a central idea and purpose, determine your audience, and make some preliminary decisions about tone and organization. These choices are summarized on the inside front cover of *Reading and Writing with Confidence* and are explained further in Chapter 9.

Step 2: During writing you will begin putting your ideas together. *Drafting* and *organizing* are the major activities at this stage of the process. The word *draft* can be used as a verb meaning *to write* or a noun meaning *a copy.* Your first draft is a rough copy. It represents your first effort at putting your ideas together. You may go through several drafts before you produce your final draft, a corrected copy that represents your best effort. Your first draft will probably contain a main idea, some support, and the beginning of an organizational plan. As you write, your choices include whether to stick with the topic and main idea you have chosen, how much and what kind of support you need, and how to organize your ideas logically. These choices are explained in Chapters 4, 6, and 7–10. Following is a first draft developed from the idea cluster in Figure 1.4. This draft is sketchy, and the instructor's marginal notes suggest ways to develop the ideas in future drafts.

Introduction needed to establish purpose and background for central idea

First Draft of
A Behavior I Wish People Would Change

Chronic lateness is a behavior I wish people would change because it not only hurts others but it also hurts themselves.

Provide evidence to show "what" his attitude is and "how" it shows disrespect.

Jim has never arrived anywhere on time in his life. He is late for work, late for class, late for dates, late for appointments. Jim's attitude is a good example of how a person's chronic lateness shows disrespect and a lack of consideration.

Again, explain "what" the impression is.

Without realizing it, Jim is creating a bad impression with his boss and coworkers. However, he may need a recommendation someday, so he should take the job more seriously.

Jim's lateness hurts him in other ways, too. To be late to class sends a message to the instructor that <u>a student lacks organization</u>. Also, Jim does not date a woman for very long. She is just not going to keep seeing a guy who does not respect her enough to arrive on time. His friends do not even want to <u>invite him places where time is a factor</u>.

Add an example

Add an example

Can you expand conclusion? What might result from a change in behavior?

Most people who are chronically late are like Jim. They either do not realize the effect their behavior has on others or the ways lateness can hurt them. If they did, maybe they would make more of an effort to arrive on time.

Step 3: After writing comes rewriting. Rewriting involves two steps: *revising* and *editing*. Each time you *revise* a draft, you are rewriting it to make it better. Your choices at this stage include whether to add content, improve organization, or refine your style. Whether to add, take out, or rearrange sentences and paragraphs are other choices you can make. Revision, therefore, is an ongoing process that starts the minute you begin to make changes in your first draft.

Editing is also part of the rewriting process. When you edit, you read your draft carefully to find and correct errors in grammar, spelling, and punctuation before writing your final draft. You also make an effort to tighten and trim your essay by eliminating unnecessary words and phrases. *Proofreading* is one last editing check before handing in your essay. Proofreading is a close reading to find any previously missed errors and to make sure that your essay is neat and legible. For a list of common errors and how to correct them see the *Appendix*, pages 295–300. Following is a revised and edited draft of "A Behavior I Wish People Would Change."

Revised Draft of
A Behavior I Wish People Would Change

Being late once in a while is excusable, but the chronically late are late 1
for everything, all the time. They are rude and inconsiderate of others'
feelings. What they do not seem to realize is that their lateness creates a bad impression, making them appear disrespectful and disorganized. Chronic lateness is a behavior I wish people would change
because it not only hurts others but it also hurts the latecomers.

Jim has never arrived anywhere on time in his life. He is late for 2
work, late for class, late for dates, late for appointments. As far as he
is concerned, no one at work has complained, so why should he
knock himself out to get there on time? As for his professors and the
students in his classes, "They can start without me." He probably
thinks his dates are so grateful for the opportunity to go out with him
that they are willing to wait for hours for him to appear. As for appointments, well, everyone knows that dentists, doctors, and barbers
overschedule. If he arrived on time, they would make him wait! Jim's
attitude is a good example of how chronic lateness shows disrespect
and a lack of consideration for others.

Without realizing it, Jim is creating a bad impression. His boss and 3
coworkers can assume that Jim's job is not very important to him. For
example, they may assume that the job is just something Jim has to
do for the money while he is in school, so he does not put any more
effort into it than necessary. But he may need a recommendation
from these people someday, and he should take this job as seriously
as any other.

Jim's lateness hurts him in other ways. Being chronically late to class 4
sends a message to the instructor that Jim is disorganized and unable
to manage time effectively. Students who do arrive on time are annoyed when he walks in late, interrupting a lecture by noisily getting
into his seat and shuffling papers. Jim does not date a woman for very
long. To hear him tell it, he is the one who ends the relationship, but I
don't believe it. A woman is just not going to keep seeing someone
who does not respect her enough to be on time. Even Jim's friends
have stopped inviting him places where time is a factor. They do not
want to miss the beginning of a concert or a movie because Jim is late.

Most people who are chronically late are like Jim. They either do 5
not realize the effect their behavior has on others or the ways lateness
can hurt them. If they did, maybe they would make more of an effort
to arrive on time. Perhaps our lives would be improved as well. For example, we could get through a movie without latecomers tripping
over us, spilling popcorn in our laps, and whispering loudly to their
friends who had arrived on time, "What did I miss?"

No one can tell you what is the best way to write an essay, but as you prewrite, draft, and organize, and rewrite essay after essay, you will develop a process that works for you. What is important is that you make a point and support it, that you organize your ideas logically and state them clearly, and that you spend enough time revising and editing so that your essay represents your best achievement.

Exercise 1.7   Think about the last time you wrote a paper as an assignment for one of your courses. List the stages you went through. Compare your stages with the three stages of the writing process explained on pages 21–23. What conclusions can you draw? What do you need to spend more time doing? Less time?

Controlling the Outcome

The outcome of writing is a finished product that represents your best effort, whether it be a single paragraph or a multiparagraph essay. To control the outcome, you need to review the difference between a paragraph and an essay and understand how to connect paragraphs to develop an essay.

A *paragraph* is a unified group of sentences written on a single topic. The sentences taken together support one main idea, which is often stated in a *topic sentence*. An *essay* is a unified group of paragraphs written on a single topic. The paragraphs taken together support one central idea, which is often stated in a *thesis statement*.

In an essay, the central idea, or thesis, is supported with details. The way the details are organized is the essay's *direction of development*. The most usual direction of development is to start with an introductory or body paragraph that either begins with or leads up to a thesis statement. Continue with body paragraphs that provide details to support or explain the thesis. End with a concluding paragraph that completes the essay.

Writers develop their essays in different ways. Some essays have little or no introduction. Others have a lengthy introduction. Some writers do not state the thesis until the end. As a beginning writer you will probably want to follow the more usual direction of development illustrated in Figure 1.5. This plan is easy for both you and your readers to follow.

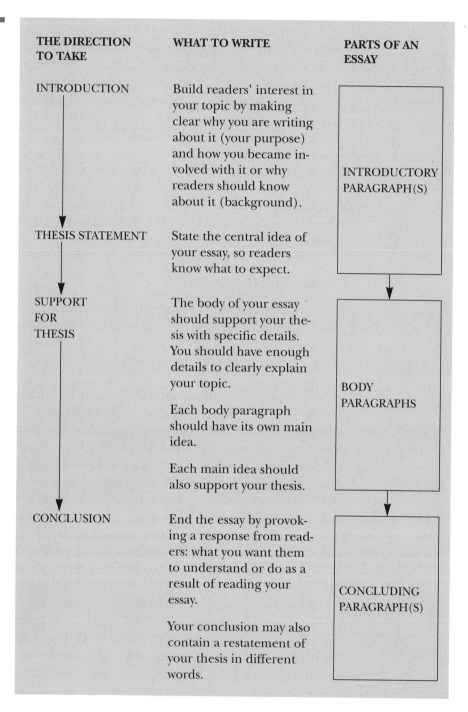

FIGURE 1.5

An Essay's Direction of Development

THE DIRECTION TO TAKE	WHAT TO WRITE	PARTS OF AN ESSAY
INTRODUCTION	Build readers' interest in your topic by making clear why you are writing about it (your purpose) and how you became involved with it or why readers should know about it (background).	INTRODUCTORY PARAGRAPH(S)
THESIS STATEMENT	State the central idea of your essay, so readers know what to expect.	
SUPPORT FOR THESIS	The body of your essay should support your thesis with specific details. You should have enough details to clearly explain your topic. Each body paragraph should have its own main idea. Each main idea should also support your thesis.	BODY PARAGRAPHS
CONCLUSION	End the essay by provoking a response from readers: what you want them to understand or do as a result of reading your essay. Your conclusion may also contain a restatement of your thesis in different words.	CONCLUDING PARAGRAPH(S)

Exercise 1.8   Can you follow the direction of development in Mike Pride's essay on pages 3–5? To find out, answer the following questions.

1. List the number(s) of the paragraph(s) that make(s) up the introduction.

   _____

2. List the number(s) of the paragraph(s) that make(s) up the body.

   _____

3. List the number(s) of the paragraph(s) that make(s) up the conclusion.

   _____

4. In which paragraph is the thesis stated?

   _____

5. Does Pride conclude with a restatement of the thesis, provoke a response from readers, or both? Explain your answer.

   _____

THINKING ABOUT PROCESS

To improve the way you read and write, keep three key ideas in mind.

1. Reading and writing are *recursive* processes because their steps can be repeated or done out of order.

2. Reading and writing are most effective when they are *active* processes. Reading systems such as SQ3R and writing strategies such as brainstorming and clustering help you to read and write actively.

3. What you do *before, during,* and *after* reading or writing positively influences the outcome.

HOW READING AND WRITING CONNECT

Readers and writers are engaged in a two-way communication process. A writer has something to share: ideas or information. A reader has something to gain: knowledge, information, or pleasure—perhaps all three. A writer's choices determine how the topic is presented. A reader's comprehension depends on how well he or she understands the writer's choices. Writing is a multifaceted process. Reading is a highly individual experience. What connects reading and writing are the choices common to both. Vocabulary, which is covered in Chapter 2, is one of these choices. Chapters 3–10 focus on five essential others:

1. Main idea

2. Details

3. Organization

4. Purpose, audience, tone

5. Inferences and conclusions

These choices are the basics of effective writing and the keys to successful reading comprehension. The rest of this section provides a brief overview of the choices. The inside front cover of your book summarizes them on a chart for quick reference. Take a minute to review the chart now.

Main Idea

The *main idea* is also called the *central idea* or the *thesis*. It is the one idea that all the other ideas in a paragraph or longer piece of writing support. Suppose you say to a friend, "I read a good article in the newspaper this morning," and your friend asks, "What was it about?" You say, "The Hale-Bopp comet." Your friend asks, "That's interesting, but what did the author *say* about it?" Your friend wants to know the author's main idea. Imagine you have written a paper, and your English instructor comments, "Your paper rambles. What is your point?" This comment means that your paper needs a main idea to pull your other ideas together.

A single paragraph has a main idea. A longer piece of writing made up of several paragraphs has a central idea that unites the paragraphs. To find the main idea in a paragraph, look for one sentence that states both the topic and what the author says about the topic. This sentence is called the *topic sentence*. To find the central idea of a multiparagraph essay or article, look for one sentence that states both the topic and what the author says about the topic. This sentence is called the *thesis statement*. What if a paragraph has no topic sentence? What if an essay has no thesis statement? In either case, the main or central idea is *implied* or suggested. When no main idea is stated, you have to figure it out by carefully reading the details and by trying to decide which one idea they support.

As a writer, you cannot write paragraph after paragraph with no clear topic in mind and no point to make. Each paragraph must either have a topic sentence or clearly implied main idea. Your whole essay must have a thesis statement or clearly implied central idea. Chapter 3 explains how to find main ideas in your reading, and Chapter 4 explains how to state main ideas in your writing. For an example of a main idea, read again the first sentence of paragraph 3 in the essay on pages 3–5. This sentence is the topic sentence. The author's topic is Christa McAuliffe. What the author says about her is that she made Concord proud.

For an example of a thesis statement, read again the last sentence of paragraph 2. The author's point is that the people of Concord were like a family. When Christa died, the whole town struggled to understand what losing her had meant. The rest of the essay and especially the last sentence of paragraph 12 provide the answer.

Details

Details, also called *evidence*, are the secondary ideas that support the main idea. Details include facts, opinions, reasons, and examples that help explain or clarify the main idea. When Mike Pride says, "Christa made Concord proud," he does not leave you to figure out what he means. He provides details in the form of examples that support his main idea. Following is an outline of paragraph 3 of Mike Pride's essay.

Christa made Concord proud. (main idea)

She was the best we had to offer. (example)

She spoke out for her profession. (example)

She was robust and confident. (example)

She was a volunteer. (example)

She was a role model. (example)

As you can see, these details help you understand the author's point and why he thinks the way he does.

As a reader, you must look for the details that support the author's main idea. As a writer, you must provide enough details to support your main idea so that readers will understand why you think the way you do. Chapter 5 explains how to find details in your reading, and Chapter 6 explains types of details and how to use them in your writing.

Organization

You know the difference between someone who is well organized and someone who is not. For example, an organized person's closet has a place for everything. He or she knows exactly where to look for something stored in the closet. An unorganized person's closet is a mess. He or she has difficulty finding anything in the closet.

Similarly, organized writing is like the well-arranged closet. The author has a plan. Main ideas, details, and conclusion have their places. You have no trouble following the ideas and finding the information you need. Unorganized writing, like the haphazardly arranged closet, has no clear pattern and may be difficult to follow. Either something is missing or some things do not belong. Organization does not come naturally; it is a skill you have to learn. *Coherence, unity,* and *pattern* are the principles of organization that you need to look for in reading and plan for in your writing. When your details support your main idea, your paragraph or essay has *coherence.* When your paragraph or essay does not stray from the topic, it has *unity.* When your details are arranged logically, for example by comparison and contrast or by cause and effect, your paragraph or essay has an *organizational pattern.* Chapter 7 explains how recognizing and following the author's principles of organization can improve your reading comprehension, and Chapter 8 explains how you can use these principles of organization to improve your writing.

Purpose, Audience, Tone

Although purpose, audience, and tone are actually three choices, they are so interdependent that you can think of them as the facets of one decision-making process. An author's *purpose* is his or her reason for writing. An author's *audience* consists of his or her readers, real or imagined. An author's *tone* is the mood, feeling, or tone of voice that comes through in his or her choice of words. As a reader, determining the author's purpose, audience, and tone will give you an insight into the writing that will enhance your comprehension. As a writer, you must have a purpose, know what audience you are writing for and what they expect or need, and select a tone that is appropriate.

In "There Had Been a Death in the Family," Mike Pride's purpose is to honor the memory of Christa McAuliffe. Because Pride is a journalist and because the essay appeared in *Newsweek,* you can assume that his audience is the general population.

Pride's tone is *reverent* (respectful) and *solemn* (serious and dignified). The respectfulness of his tone is evident in his praise for McAuliffe's accomplishments and for her community spirit. The seriousness and dignity of his tone are reflected in his choice of words. He calls Christa's death a "tragedy." He refers to her journey into space as an "odyssey" recalling Homer's classic poem *The Odyssey* about Ulysses, a hero of Greek mythology. He compares Christa's death to the assassination of a U.S. president, John F. Kennedy. Solemn words such as "tears have flowed," "swollen eyes and stricken looks," "the green and fertile days of midsummer," "the cold heart of winter," and especially the last sentence of paragraph 12 help convey Pride's tone. See Chapter 9 for a more detailed explanation of purpose, audience, and tone.

Inferences and Conclusions

In reading, two levels of meaning are often at work: what the author *says* and what the author *means*. To understand what an author says, you must read the words and be able to define them. To understand what an author means, you must read between the lines to uncover the author's message and its significance for you. In writing, the same two levels apply. As a writer, you must make sure that what you say will enable readers to interpret what you mean accurately. Although many students read and write well enough on the first level of meaning, they may have difficulty at the second level making inferences and drawing conclusions.

A *conclusion* may be the result of an act or process. It may also be a judgement or decision you arrive at after carefully considering a set of facts or opinions. An *inference* is the act of reasoning itself that leads you to draw a conclusion or to make a judgement or decision. The following conversation is a brief example of how we make inferences and draw conclusions.

Student A: Do you want to get together to study for tomorrow's math test?

Student B: I don't need to study.

Student A: Why not?

Student B: I've made nothing but A's on the homework, so I already know the material.

Student B infers from her homework grades that she already knows the material. Based on this inference, Student B concludes that she does not need to study.

Just as you must make inferences from the details an author provides, your readers will make inferences from the details you provide. Just as an author's organizational pattern leads you to a desired conclusion, your organizational pattern should lead your readers to the conclusion you desire. For a more detailed explanation of inferences and conclusions in reading and writing, see Chapter 10.

Exercise 1.9   Try this discovery exercise to find out what you have learned so far about the five choices for readers and writers. Read the following essay and answer the questions based on it.

Remembering Grandma

We always thought my grandmother liked to save things, but when she died a few years ago and we were going through her belongings, we found out what a pack rat she was. Grandma saved every birthday and Christmas card she ever got. We found them in her cedar chest, still inside the envelopes they came in, stacked and tied with pink and blue ribbons. She saved receipts, paper bags, coat hangers, tissue paper, and string, anything she might use again someday. We found dozens of sheets of colorful wrapping paper on her closet shelf along with empty boxes, sorted according to size, that had held presents.   1

We found most of the presents too, unused. Nightgowns in every color, enough stockings to last a working woman a year, blouses folded neatly with the tags still on them. It wasn't that Grandma had not liked the gifts but that she hated to put on anything new when her old clothes still had wear in them.   2

We found a drawer full of pencil stubs, dog-eared decks of play-   3 ing cards, and a shoe box full of matchbooks, though Grandma had never smoked. Broken toys, worn-out kitchen appliances, ropes of frayed extension cords, and unmatched drinking glasses of every imaginable size and color were more of the useless items she saved and stacked on shelves in the attic.

4

Browsing through those attic shelves was like being in a department store for the ghosts of our pasts. There was the doll with its little sailor hat that each of us had played with on summer visits, then forgotten until now. Like all pack rats, Grandma saved the used, the useless, and the never-used.

1. What is the author's thesis? (Start at the beginning and look for one sentence that states the main idea of the whole essay.)

_____

_____

2. The details provide examples of things Grandma saved. List one example each of something *used, unused,* and *useless.*

_____

_____

_____

3. How is the essay organized? Check one of the following.

_____ Cause and effect (why Grandma saved things)

_____ Narration (an important event in Grandma's life)

_____ Process (Grandma's method for saving things)

_____ Classification (the types of things Grandma saved)

4. What are the author's purpose, audience, and tone?

   a. What is the author's purpose? Check one of the following:

_____ To entertain readers with an interesting story

_____ To inform readers about the proper way to store items

_____ To persuade readers that they should be pack rats

b. Who is the intended audience? Check one of the following:

_____ Members of the general population

_____ Pack rats

_____ Students only

c. What is the author's tone? Check one of the following:

_____ Mocking (making fun of)

_____ Nostalgic (looking to the past with longing)

_____ Sentimental (overly sensitive or emotional)

5. Based on the last sentence of paragraph 2, what inference can you make about Grandma? Check one of the following. Then explain your choice on the last two lines.

_____ Grandma's clothes were out of style.

_____ Grandma was a thrifty woman.

_____ Grandma did not like new clothes.

_____

_____

THINKING IT OVER

Test your recall of this chapter's concepts by completing the following statements. If you cannot complete a statement, look back through the chapter to find the answer.

1. The reading and writing processes can be broken down into steps that tell you what to do _____, _____, and _____ reading or writing.

2. The outcome of the reading process is _____. The outcome of the writing process is a finished product: a _____ , _____, or _____.

3. _____ is a classic reading system that helps you read actively.

4. Three prewriting strategies that can help you generate ideas are _____, _____, and _____.

5. The _____ _____ is the one idea that all the other ideas in a paragraph or longer piece of writing support.

6. _____ are secondary ideas that include facts, opinions, reasons, and examples.

7. Coherence, unity, and pattern are principles of _____ you should recognize in reading and apply in writing.

8. Readers and writers must also make decisions about purpose, _____, and _____.

9. To read or write at the second level of meaning, you must be able to make _____ and draw _____.

10. Choose one of the Thinking First questions at the beginning of the chapter to answer on the following lines.

_____

_____

_____

TOPICS FOR WRITING

Choose one of the topics below or make up your own topic. Write an essay in which you apply what you have learned so far about writing. If you have trouble getting started try clustering, brainstorming, or questioning. If you have trouble planning your essay, review the writer's choices listed on the inside front cover and Figure 1.5.

Something you read that excited you or made you angry

An important issue being discussed in the news

Something you have learned that you think everyone should know

Something you believe and why

Something you have recently found out about yourself

Why you are attending college

Why you admire a certain person

Checklist for Revision

As you revise and edit your essay, check for the following:

1. Does your essay introduce the topic?

2. Does your essay contain a clear statement of your main idea (thesis statement)?

3. Have you supported your point with enough details?

4. Does your essay have a conclusion?

5. Have you found and corrected your errors?

REFLECTIONS ON READING AND WRITING

This section of the chapter asks you to reflect on, or think about, something you read in the chapter and what it has added either to the information stored in your memory or to your developing self-awareness as a reader or writer.

For your first reflection, focus on either your reading or writing process. Describe the process. Explain exactly how you complete a reading or writing assignment. What can you do to improve the process? Which of the strategies explained in this chapter are you currently using? Which ones are you willing to try?

Write your reflections on paper. You may even want to keep a journal of your reflections so that you can track your progress in reading and writing.

Chapter 2

Building Vocabulary for Reading and Writing

THINKING FIRST

- *What must I know about an author's choice of words?*
- *How can I improve my own choice of words?*
- *What can I do to develop my vocabulary?*

Words are the foundation of the communication process. When people make agreements, they "come to terms." Those who argue "have words" with each other. A person who wants your trust says, "I give you my word." In a dispute with someone you reply, "My word is as good as yours." Those whose feelings are impossible to describe may use the phrase "words cannot express," or they may say their feelings go "beyond words." Generally, we praise people who are able to say much in few words, but we ridicule those who are "wordy."

Words have started and ended wars; they have been the downfall of some people, but they have earned others a place in history. Marie Antoinette said, "Let them eat cake." Patrick Henry said, "Give me liberty or give me death." General MacArthur said, "I shall return." John F.

Kennedy said, "Ask not what your country can do for you; ask what you can do for your country." Martin Luther King, Jr., said, "I have a dream." Words include and words exclude. When you join an organization, become a member of a profession, or take a job with a company, you learn the vocabulary of that group. These special terms can create a bond among group members, but they can also make others feel like outsiders.

Words have the power to convey an overall impression about you to those with whom you interact: your peers, family, instructors, coworkers, future employers. What you say, how you say it, and the words you choose reflect you, your personality, and your level of knowledge. Are you satisfied with your vocabulary? Do you feel that, most of the time, you understand what you read in your textbooks and what you hear in lectures? Do you ever find yourself groping for words when asked to write?

A good vocabulary and reliable strategies for learning new words are your keys to improved reading comprehension and increased confidence in your ability to communicate in writing. This chapter explains how to develop your vocabulary so that you can make sense of an author's choices and make better word choices of your own.

BACKGROUND CHECK

Before reading the following essay, check your knowledge and assumptions about the Hispanic influence on American culture and language.

1. If English is your native language, what Spanish words and phrases do you hear or use in everyday conversation? If Spanish is your native language, what Spanish words and phrases have you noticed native speakers of English using in everyday conversation?

2. Give examples of Spanish words or phrases used in American advertising, television, movies, or popular music.

3. Estimate the percentage of people living in the United States today who speak Spanish as their native language.

4. Based on your survey of the title, author information, and first two paragraphs, what do you expect to follow?

5. What else do you know or think about the topic?

Spanglish Spoken Here

Janice Castro
(with Dan Cook and Cristina Garcia)

Many Spanish words and expressions have become part of our every-day vocabulary. In this article, the authors discuss how American English has been influenced by the Spanish-speaking people who have settled in the United States. Castro, Cook, and Garcia write for Time *magazine.*

VOCABULARY CHECK

bemused (1)	confused
patter (3)	meaningless talk, chatter
phenomena (5)	unusual occurrences
brisk (5)	quick, energetic
languorous (5)	dreamy, lazy
hybrids (6)	of mixed origin
gaffes (10)	mistakes

In Manhattan a first-grader greets her visiting grandparents, happily exclaiming, "Come here, *sientate!*" Her bemused grandfather, who does not speak Spanish, nevertheless knows she is asking him to sit down. A Miami personnel officer understands what a job applicant means when he says, "Quiero un part time." Nor do drivers miss a beat reading a billboard alongside a Los Angeles street advertising CERVEZA—SIX-PACK!   1

This free-form blend of Spanish and English, known as Spanglish, is common linguistic currency wherever concentrations of Hispanic Americans are found in the U.S. In Los Angeles, where 55% of the city's 3 million inhabitants speak Spanish, Spanglish is as much a part of daily life as sunglasses. Unlike the broken-English efforts of earlier immigrants from Europe, Asia and other regions, Spanglish has become a widely accepted conversational mode used casually—even playfully—by Spanish-speaking immigrants and native-born Americans alike.   2

Consisting of one part Hispanicized English, one part American-   3
ized Spanish and more than a little fractured syntax, Spanglish is a bit
like a Robin Williams comedy routine: a crackling line of cross-cultural
patter straight from the melting pot. Often it enters Anglo homes and
families through the children who pick it up at school or at play with
their young Hispanic contemporaries. In other cases, it comes from
watching TV; many an Anglo child watching Sesame Street has
learned *uno dos tres* almost as quickly as one two three.

Spanglish takes a variety of forms, from the Southern California   4
Anglos who bid farewell with the utterly silly "*hasta la* bye bye" to
the Cuban-American drivers in Miami who *parquean* their *carros.*
Some Spanglish sentences are mostly Spanish, with a quick detour for
an English word or two. A Latino friend may cut short a conversation
by glancing at his watch and excusing himself with the explanation
that he must "*ir al* supermarket."

Many of the English words transplanted in this way are simply   5
handier than their Spanish counterparts. No matter how distasteful
the subject, for example, it is still easier to say "income tax" than *im-
puesto sobre la renta.* At the same time, many Spanish-speaking immigrants have adopted such terms as VCR, microwave and
dishwasher for what they view as largely American phenomena. Still
other English words convey a cultural context that is not implicit in the
Spanish. A friend who invites you to *lonche* most likely has in mind
the brisk American custom of "doing lunch" rather than the lan-
guorous afternoon break traditionally implied by *almuerzo.*

Mainstream Americans exposed to similar hybrids of German,   6
Chinese or Hindi might be mystified. But even Anglos who speak little
or no Spanish are somewhat familiar with Spanglish. Living among
them, for one thing, are 19 million Hispanics. In addition, more American high school and university students sign up for Spanish than for
any other foreign language.

Only in the past ten years, though, has Spanglish begun to turn   7
into a national slang. Its popularity has grown with the explosive increases in U.S. immigration from Latin American countries. English has
increasingly collided with Spanish in retail stores, offices and class-
rooms, in pop music and on street corners. Anglos whose ancestors
picked up such Spanish words as *rancho, bronco, tornado,* and *in-
communicado,* for instance, now freely use such Spanish words as
gracias, bueno, amigo, and *por favor.*

Among Latinos, Spanglish conversations often flow easily from   8
Spanish into several sentences of English and back.

Spanglish is a sort of code for Latinos: the speakers know Span-   9
ish, but their hybrid language reflects the American culture in which
they live. Many lean to shorter, clipped phrases in place of the longer,

more graceful expressions their parents used. Says Leonel de la Cuesta, an assistant professor of modern languages at Florida International University in Miami: "In the U.S., time is money, and that is showing up in Spanglish as an economy of language." Conversational examples: *taipiar* (type) and *winshi-wiper* (windshield wiper) replace *escribir a maquina* and *limpiaparabrisas*.

Major advertisers, eager to tap the estimated $134 billion in spending power wielded by Spanish-speaking Americans, have ventured into Spanglish to promote their products. In some cases, attempts to sprinkle Spanish through commercials have produced embarrassing gaffes. A Braniff airlines ad that sought to tell Spanish-speaking audiences they could settle back *en* (in) luxuriant *cuero* (leather) seats, for example, inadvertently said they could fly without clothes (*encuero*). A fractured translation of the Miller Lite slogan told readers the beer was "Filling, and less delicious." Similar blunders are often made by Anglos trying to impress Spanish-speaking pals. But if Latinos are amused by mangled Spanglish, they also recognize these goofs as a sort of friendly acceptance. As they might put it, *no problema.*

10

THINKING CRITICALLY

Main Idea

1. What is the authors' thesis, or central idea, in "Spanglish Spoken Here"? Hint: look for the thesis statement near the beginning of the essay.

Details

2. According to the authors, what is *Spanglish?* Give several examples from the essay.

3. The authors give several reasons to explain the popularity of Spanglish. What are the reasons?

Organization

4. Which paragraphs make up the essay's introduction, body, and conclusion?

Purpose, Audience, Tone

5. What is the authors' tone? How do you think they feel about Spanglish, and how do they want their audience to feel? For example, are they angry, amused, or uninterested? Back up your answer with evidence from the essay.

Inferences and Conclusions

6. What additional Spanglish words or phrases can you think of that are not mentioned in the essay? Of those that are mentioned, which ones are familiar to you?

Making Connections

According to the authors, the use of Spanglish may help to bring people of different cultures together. What else can people do to bridge the gap between cultures?

USING CONTEXT CLUES

When you read, do you occasionally stumble on a word you do not know? If you do, then you are not alone. Most people encounter unfamiliar words while reading. How you deal with this problem can either hinder or help your comprehension. Information that is new or unfamiliar requires slow and careful reading. An essential part of this process is taking time to look up or figure out the meanings of unfamiliar words.

When you write, do you avoid using a certain word because you are unsure of its meaning or spelling and do not want to take the time to look it up? How you deal with this problem can influence the outcome of your writing either negatively or positively. An essential part of the writing process is taking time to choose and use words carefully.

Using context clues is a useful strategy for readers and writers. As a reader, you can use context clues to help you determine word meanings. As a writer, you can provide context clues in your own writing as an aid to your readers.

The *context* of a word or term is the sentence or paragraph in which it appears. Many times the surrounding words, or context, provide clues to the meaning of a word or term. Suppose you read this sentence in your psychology text.

> Asthma, in some cases, is a *psychosomatic illness,* a physical disorder either caused or aggravated by emotional processes.

What is a psychosomatic illness? The context tells you that it is *a physical disorder either caused or aggravated by emotional processes.* Furthermore, if you make a conscious effort to learn this meaning, then every time you read about illnesses that are psychosomatic in origin, you may remember that they are the results of emotional processes rather than physical disorders. Using the context can help you accomplish two goals: figuring out the meaning of unfamiliar words and adding new words to your vocabulary.

Not only does the context provide clues to a word's meaning, but it provides specific kinds of clues. Figure 2.1 lists four types of context clues, an explanation of each, and an example sentence. In the examples, the part of the sentence that provides the clue is either underlined or explained in parentheses.

The Definition Clue

Sometimes the context in which an unfamiliar word or term appears contains a definition either in the form of a synonym or a longer explanation. A *synonym* is a word that means the same or about the same thing as another word. In the following example, the word in bold type is defined by a synonym.

> Jane **commiserated,** or sympathized, with a friend who had lost her pet.

In this example, *sympathized* is a more familiar word that means the same or about the same thing as *commiserated.* In the next example, the word in bold type is defined by a longer explanation.

> The **hypotenuse** of a right triangle is the sum of the squares of the other two sides.

FIGURE 2.1

Four Types of Context Clues

CLUE	EXPLANATION	EXAMPLE
1. DEFINITION	A definition follows the word.	*Phototropism* refers to the growth of plants toward or away from light.
2. EXAMPLE	Illustrations or examples clarify the word's meaning.	The committee *festooned* the church pews for the wedding by draping them with ribbons and flowers.
3. CONTRAST	The word's opposite, or antonym, appears in the sentence.	Although some students are *elated* when they receive grades, some are saddened.
4. INFERENCE	You must apply logic and experience to the information supplied by the context.	A *versatile* actor is one who can do drama as well as comedy. (*Versatile* means having the ability to do more than one thing well.)

In this example, *the sum of the squares of the other two sides* explains what is meant by the word *hypotenuse.* This definition requires more than one word because it describes a complex concept.

It may be that writers choose synonyms to define words when they believe that you are familiar enough with the synonym to not need a longer explanation. Or, as is the case with *hypotenuse,* it may be because the word has no synonym. Whatever the case, to use the definition clue successfully, you need to be able to spot both synonyms and longer explanations.

Exercise 2.1

In each sentence, use the context to help you define the word in bold type. Look for either a synonym or a longer explanation. Then underline the definition.

1. To **harass** someone means to annoy him or her repeatedly.

2. A **zygote** is a cell formed by the union of a mature sperm and egg.

3. Winona **meandered,** or wandered, down the path through the garden.

4. Some people who refuse to learn how to use computers have **technophobia,** or the fear of technology.

5. **Cognition,** the study of how people think and learn, is a field that attracts many psychology majors.

Certain clue words or phrases can alert you that a definition follows: *Refers to, is defined as, means,* and *is* are some familiar ones. In the following examples, the words defined are in bold type, clue words or phrases are in italics, and the definitions that follow clue words are underlined.

Photosynthesis *is defined* as the process by which plants use light to break down nutrients extracted from the soil.

The **grip** *is* that part of a golf club that you grasp with both hands when preparing to take a swing. **Grip** also *refers to* how you position your hands.

To **procrastinate** *means* to put off doing something you should do now.

Punctuation, too, may serve as a clue by separating a word from its definition. *Commas, parentheses,* and *dashes* are the forms of punctuation commonly used in this way. In the following examples, the words defined are in bold type and their definitions are underlined. Notice the punctuation that sets off each definition.

Partitions, or screens, divide the room into several smaller offices.

A row of **luminarias** (lanterns) on each side lit the walkway from the street to the front door.

Photosynthesis—the process by which plants use light to break down nutrients extracted from the soil—is an important biological concept.

Exercise 2.2 In each sentence, use the context to help you define the word in bold type. Look for clue words and punctuation clues. Then underline the definition.

1. **Cubism** refers to a type of art based on the use of geometric forms.

2. This book is made of **recycled** (reclaimed or reused) paper.

3. Museums are the **repositories**—storehouses—of art and antiquities.

4. Rainfall is necessary to refill the **aquifers,** the underground rivers and streams, from which we get our drinking water.

5. A fence that **encroaches** on neighboring land trespasses on that property.

The Example Clue

Writers often use examples to clarify the meaning of unfamiliar words and terms. Examples are vivid illustrations or explanations that define either by creating familiar images in your mind or by recalling familiar objects, ideas, or situations. In the following sentence, look for the examples that clarify the term in bold type.

> **Film genres** such as the western, the musical, the gangster film, and the horror film have been the subject of extensive study and much critical commentary.

The western, the musical, the gangster film, and the horror film are examples of film genres. Therefore, a *genre* must be a type—in this case a type of film. *Genre* may be a useful word to add to your vocabulary. If you take any literature courses, you will find that this word also describes types of literature—for example, the novel, poem, short story, and play are four literary genres.

Certain clue phrases can alert you that an example follows: *for example, for instance, to illustrate,* and *such as* are some familiar ones. In the next four examples, the words defined are in bold type, clue words or phrases are in italics, and the definitions are explained following each example.

According to psychologists, humans have **physiological needs,** *such as* those for safety, hunger, and sex, that are necessary to sustain life.

In this sentence the phrase *necessary to sustain life* and the examples of safety, hunger, and sex make clear that the physiological needs are also the biological needs that make it possible for humans to stay alive.

The "terrible twos" are so called because children at that age are often **intractable;** *for example,* they have a will of their own and may refuse to obey.

In this sentence, the examples "a will of their own" and "refuse to obey" may help you conclude that intractable children are stubborn children.

To illustrate how **tawdry** were the dresses sold in the store, Lula pointed out their cheap fabrics, uneven seams and hemlines, and tasteless styles.

In this sentence, you can tell from the examples that *tawdry* means "cheap" and "tasteless."

Benadryl and Seldane, *for instance,* are only two of the many **pharmaceuticals** now sold over the counter that used to be available only by prescription.

In this sentence, the examples *Benadryl* and *Seldane* may help you define pharmaceuticals if you are familiar with these two popular drugs for the relief of allergies. If these are not familiar examples, then the word *prescription* may be a clue that pharmaceuticals are drugs or medications.

Exercise 2.3   In each sentence, look for the clue phrases and examples that can help you define the word in bold type. Then write the definition on the line following each sentence. The first one is done for you.

1. To get along with your roommate, do your share of the **chores,** for example, cooking, cleaning, doing laundry, and taking out the garbage.

   tasks or things to do around the house
   _____

2. Headaches, minor coughs and colds, and muscular aches and pains illustrate a few of the common **ailments** that are usually not serious unless they persist.

   _____

3. It is easy to gain a reputation as a **malcontent** if you have traits such as a negative attitude and a tendency to find fault with everything.

   _____

4. The **legumes,** peas and beans for example, have an outer shell called a *pod.*

   _____

5. The fabric in this blouse is made of a combination of **fibers** such as rayon, cotton, and linen.

   _____

The Contrast Clue

Sometimes the context in which an unfamiliar word or term appears contains an *antonym* that helps you define the word. An antonym is a word that means the opposite of another word. *Hot* and *cold* are antonyms, as are *rough* and *smooth.* In the following example, the word in bold type is defined by an antonym.

> Though the corporation's testimony seemed unbelievable, its attorneys hoped the jury would find it **credible.**

What did the attorneys hope? They hoped that the jury would *believe* the testimony. They hoped that the jury would believe the opposite of what the testimony seemed. The testimony seemed unbelievable, but the attorneys hoped it would be credible. Therefore, if something is credible, it is believable. Now read the next sentence.

> Although Maria is a very outgoing person, her best friend, Cristina, is an **introvert.**

Maria is being contrasted with Cristina. Maria is outgoing, so Cristina must be the opposite. Cristina is probably quiet and withdrawn. So an *introvert* must be "a person who is quiet and withdrawn," someone who is not outgoing. Notice, too, that this example and the jury example both begin with words that show contrast: *though* and *although.* These words are additional contrast clues. Other contrast clues include *yet, but, however, on the contrary, conversely,* and *on the other hand.*

Exercise 2.4   In each sentence, look for any clue words and phrases or antonyms that can help you define the word in bold type. Then write the definition on the line following each sentence. The first one is done for you.

1. The temperature in this part of the country is never **static;** on the contrary, it changes almost daily.

   still, unchanging
   _____

2. Drinking water should be clear, but the water coming out of this faucet looks **murky.**

   _____

3. Some people who have reached positions of **affluence** have worked their way up from backgrounds of poverty.

   _____

4. I consider myself an **optimist,** but I still don't expect to have everything I want.

   _____

5. Although we first thought that the painting was a forgery, it turned
   out to be **authentic.**

The Inference Clue

You may have noticed that as you were doing exercises 2.3 and 2.4, the
example and contrast clues alone for some of the words were not
enough to help you figure out the definitions. You had to apply prior
knowledge and experience to the information that is given in order to
infer, or guess, the meaning.

An *inference* is an informed guess based on what you already know
and the information that is available. If you are making inferences
about the definitions of words or terms, you can test those inferences
by verifying them with a dictionary.

The inference clue, therefore, is often a clue *you* bring to your reading by asking yourself, "What information is provided, and how does it
fit with my experience?" Now read the next sentence and the explanation that follows it.

Some carry a rabbit's foot, but my **talisman** is a four-leaf clover.

Even if you do not know what a *talisman* is, your experience probably
tells you that some people believe that a rabbit's foot or four-leaf clover
will bring them luck. Therefore, a talisman must be a good-luck charm.

Obviously you need some prior knowledge about a subject to make
inferences about new information. If you know nothing about good-
luck charms, carrying a rabbit's foot, or looking for four-leaf clovers,
then the context in the example cannot help you. Instead, you must
rely on your dictionary to define the word.

Making inferences is a critical skill for both readers and writers. As
a reader, you must make inferences to interpret an author's meaning.
As a writer, you must be aware that your readers will make inferences
about your meaning based on the details you provide. Making inferences is explained at length in Chapter 10.

Exercise 2.5   You can do this exercise either on your own or with a partner. In the following sentences make inferences to define the words in bold type. Use the information given in the sentence, your prior knowledge, and your reasoning powers to figure out the definition. Write your definition and an explanation of how you arrived at the definition on the lines provided. The first one is done for you.

1. The living room was **commodious** enough to contain two large sofas, a grand piano, and several other pieces of furniture.

   large and roomy

   The room would have to be big enough to hold so much furniture.

2. When Horace fell out of the tree, he landed on his right leg and fractured the **tibia** in two places.

   _____

   _____

3. Some professors resort to calling on students because it is often difficult to **elicit** answers from volunteers.

   _____

   _____

4. The outdoor wedding turned into a **fiasco** when heavy rains and wind interrupted the reception.

   _____

   _____

5. The bookstore manager was **irate** when the student demanded a full refund for a book that was not only dirty but filled with notes.

   _____

   _____

THINKING ABOUT PROCESS

The skills you use as a reader to determine the meanings of words in context you can also apply as a writer to your own choice of words.

1. If you want to define a word for your readers, build into your sentence one of the four types of context clues: definition, example, contrast, or inference.

2. If you want to provide a punctuation clue for readers, use commas, parentheses, or dashes to set off a word from its definition.

3. As additional context clues for readers, introduce your definitions with signal words such as *for example* (to illustrate an idea) and *however* (to show contrast).

USING THE DICTIONARY EFFICIENTLY

If you learn how to use context clues effectively, you may need to use your dictionary only as a last resort or to verify your understanding of a word's meaning. To improve your use of the dictionary, make sure you know how to read each entry. A *dictionary entry* consists of a word and its definitions. An entry contains five common parts.

1. The Word Divided into Syllables Words are broken down into syllables for ease of pronunciation—for example,

pe·des·tri·an

2. Pronunciation The bottom of each page of the dictionary has a pronunciation guide. Within each entry, the pronunciation of each syllable is indicated by a mark above the vowel or by a special symbol. Accent marks show which syllables to emphasize. The full pronunciation for a word appears in parentheses beside it:

pe·des·tri·an (pə-dĕs'-trē-ən)

FIGURE 2.2

**Pronunciation
Symbols for
Vowels**

Symbol	Example
ă	acrobat
ā	display
â	bare
ä	farther
ĕ	met
ē	flee
ĭ	sit
ī	ripe
î	weird
ŏ	rot
ō	hoe
oi	poise
ou	pout
ŏŏ	cook
ōō	boot
ŭ	but
ûr	purge

The upside-down *e* indicates a special vowel sound similar to the sound of the a in *about* and the *e* in *item.* Every dictionary contains a pronunciation key in its introductory pages. Figure 2.2 shows common pronunciation symbols for the vowels (*a, e, i, o,* and *u*) and example words to show how they sound.

3. Part of Speech The part of speech follows each word and is indicated by an abbreviation—for example, *n.* for *noun, v.* for *verb, adj.* for *adjective.* When more than one definition is given, a part of speech indicator appears before each definition. This can be very useful if you are writing a paper and you need to check whether you have used the correct form of a word.

4. *Definitions* Most words have more than one definition; each one is numbered. Don't make the mistake of looking up a word, reading the first definition, and believing you have found the appropriate meaning. The first definition may not fit the context in which your word appears. For example, read the following sentence:

> It is strange how an experience can seem unique or unusual to some people and merely **pedestrian** to others.

Now read the American Heritage College Dictionary's entry for *pedestrian*.

> **pe·des·tri·an** (pə-dĕs′tre-ən) *n.* One who travels on foot; a walker. —*adj.* **1.** Of, relating to, or made for pedestrians. **2.** Going or performed on foot. **3.** Undistinguished; ordinary: *pedestrian prose.* [< Lat. *pedester, pedestr-*, going on foot < *pedes*, a pedestrian < *pēs, ped-*, foot. See ped-*.] —**pe·des′tri·an·ism** *n.*

You can see that definition 3 best fits the meaning intended in the sentence.

Some entries show the meanings of words or terms as used in particular disciplines. The following example shows a dictionary entry for the word *phase*, which has several meanings. If you were checking this entry for the meaning of *phase* as used in your chemistry class, the definition you would need is the one preceded by the word *chemistry* and the number 6. The entry shows that three other disciplines use *phase* as a term. Can you find them?

> **phase** (fāz) *n. Abbr.* **ph. 1.** A distinct stage of development; *"The American occupation of Japan fell into three successive phases"* (Edwin O. Reischauer). **2.** A temporary manner, attitude or pattern of behavior: *just a passing phase.* **3.** An aspect: a part: *every phase of the operation.* **4.** *Astronomy.* One of the cyclically recurring apparent forms of the moon or a planet. **5.** *Physics.* **a.** A particular stage in a periodic process or phenomenon. **b.** The fraction of a complete cycle elapsed as measured from a specified reference point and often expressed as an angle. **6.** *Chemistry.* **a.** Any of the forms or states, solid, liquid, gas, or plasma, in which matter can exist, depending on temperature and pressure. **b.** A discrete homogeneous part of a material system that is me-

> chanically separable from the rest, as is ice from water. **7.** *Bi-ology.* A characteristic form, appearance, or stage of development that occurs in a cycle or that distinguishes some individuals of a group: *the white color phase of a weasel; the swarming phase of locusts.* —**phase** *tr. v.* **phased, phas·ing, phas·es. 1.** To plan or carry out systematically by phases. **2.** To set or regulate so as to be synchronized. —*phasal verbs,* **phase in.** To introduce one stage at a time. **phase out.** To bring or come to an end, one stage at a time. —*idioms,* **in phase.** In a correlated or synchronized way. **out of phase.** In an unsynchronized or uncorrelated way [Back-formation from New Latin *phasēs,* phases of the moon, from Greek, pl. of *phasis,* appearance, from *phainein,* to show. **See bhā-**[1] in Appendix.] —**pha´sic** (fā´zĭk) *adj.*

*5. **Etymology*** A dictionary entry also contains the word's origin in square brackets. Look again at the entry for *pedestrian.* The explanation that follows the abbreviation *Lat.* in brackets tells you that *pedestrian* comes from a Latin root meaning "foot."

In some dictionaries, a list of synonyms (words similar in meaning) may be included in an entry. Some dictionaries even include a sample sentence to show how a word is used.

You need a desk dictionary in your study area—in addition to any paperback version that you take to class. A desk dictionary contains more complete entries for each word. As a reader, you need to look up any unfamiliar words for which you have no context clues. As a writer, you may need to verify the meanings of some of your word choices.

Exercise 2.6   Read the following excerpt from a chemistry textbook. Then answer the questions that follow it.

MIXTURES   Most of the materials around us are mixtures. A **mixture** is a *material that can be separated by physical means into two or more substances.* Unlike a pure compound, a mixture has variable composition. When you dissolve sodium chloride in water, you obtain a mixture; its composition depends on the relative amount of sodium chloride dissolved. You can separate the mixture by the physical process of distillation.   [1]

Mixtures are classified into two types. A **heterogeneous mixture** is a *mixture that consists of physically distinct parts, each with different properties.* Figure 1.15 shows a heterogeneous mixture of potassium dichromate and iron filings. Another example is salt and sugar that have been stirred together. If you were to look closely, you would see the separate crystals of sugar and salt. A **homogeneous**   [2]

mixture (also known as a **solution**) is *a mixture that is uniform in its properties throughout given samples.* When sodium chloride is dissolved in water, you obtain a homogeneous mixture, or solution. Air is a gaseous solution, principally of two elementary substances, nitrogen and oxygen, which are physically mixed but not chemically combined.

A **phase** is *one of several different homogeneous materials present in the portion of matter under study.* A heterogeneous mixture composed of salt and sugar is said to be composed of two different phases; one of the phases is salt, the other is sugar. Similarly, several ice cubes in water is said to be composed of two phases; one phase is ice, the other is liquid water. Ice floating in a solution of sodium chloride in water also consists of two phases, ice and the liquid solution. Note that a phase may be either a pure substance in a particular state or a solution in a particular state (solid, liquid, or gaseous). Also, the portion of matter under consideration can consist of several phases of the same substance or several phases of different substances.

3

1. List two terms that are glossed (*glossed* means followed by brief definitions).

2. Which terms in the excerpt do you think a chemistry instructor would expect you to learn and remember?

3. In this sentence from the first paragraph, what does the word *distillation* mean? "You can separate the mixture by the physical process of distillation." Were you able to determine the meaning from context, or did you have to use the dictionary?

4. Read the definition of *phase* in the third paragraph. To which definition in the dictionary excerpt on page 55 does this one correspond: 6a or 6b? How can you tell?

_____

_____

5. Find three words in the excerpt that begin with the prefix *com-*. What does this prefix mean?

_____

_____

STUDY TIP: *Keep a list of frequently looked up words and definitions. Review your list often so that you add these words to your permanent vocabulary.*

UNDERSTANDING DENOTATION AND CONNOTATION

Readers and writers need to understand the difference between a word's *denotation* and its *connotation*. The dictionary definition is a word's *denotation*. The emotional associations that a word evokes are its *connotations*. For example, *thin, slender, slim, skinny,* and *emaciated* all have the same denotation: weight that falls below the average. However, each of these words has different connotations. *Skinny* connotes unattractiveness; *emaciated* connotes malnourished; and *thin, slim,* and *slender* usually connote degrees of attractiveness. However, people may disagree over what a word connotes. Some people might say that fashion models are skinny, whereas others would call them slender. Your choice of one of these words to describe a fashion model would depend upon whether you think that the size and body type of a typical model is attractive.

Connotations also can change over time. For example, *awesome,* an adjective that denotes mixed feelings of wonder, reverence, and dread, was once reserved for use in a spiritual context. The word still has this connotation in the following two sentences:

As Greta listened to the *awesome* strains of Beethoven's Ninth Symphony, her eyes filled with tears.

Some people say that while standing before El Greco's *awesome* painting *The Crucifixion,* they can feel the presence of God.

Recently *awesome* has developed a new usage as a slang term and therefore new connotations, as in the following two sentences:

Mikey whipped out the plastic minicar from the cereal box and said, "Wow, this is *awesome!"*

Jennifer said to Angela, "Wear your red leather miniskirt to the party; it looks *awesome* on you."

Used as slang, *awesome* still carries connotations of wonder, but the wonder is more generalized to cover anything that might be called "great" or "terrific."

Understanding the difference between denotation and connotation can help you select the words that will most effectively communicate your ideas.

Exercise 2.7   Each of the word groups in the following exercise contains three words that have approximately the same *denotation* but different *connotations.* For each word group, write their *denotative* and *connotative* meanings and rate them as positive, negative, or neutral. The first one is done as an example.

1. Worn out, used, preowned

   Denotation: The terms all mean "not new."

   Connotation: Worn-out suggests "unusable" and is the negative term. "Used" means "not new" though there may be some use left. "Used" is the neutral term, and "preowned" is the positive term. It suggests that

an item had a prior owner but is neither used up
nor worn out.

Positive	Neutral	Negative
preowned	used	worn-out

2. obese, large, plump

3. persistent, stubborn, unyielding

4. synthetic, fake, artificial

5. act, stunt, trick

6. stroll, swagger, walk

7. to boss, to control, to manage

8. disrobe, strip, undress

9. cheap, bargain-priced, inexpensive

10. crippled, differently abled, handicapped

11. show, expose, display

Exercise 2.8   Because of their connotations, the six underlined words in the following paragraph do not match the tone of the rest of the paragraph. First
determine why each of the six words is inappropriate, then replace
each one with a word that has an appropriate connotation.

Three friends meet once a week to play poker. Although they only
play for pennies, the game can get very intense with heated arguments on all sides. Before they know it, one is accusing the other of
cheating. To solve these problems so they can all relax and have an
enjoyable game, they have come up with some new rules. First of all,
they have to wear ski masks so that the expressions on their <u>mugs</u> will
not reveal the cards they are <u>hugging</u>. Second, they have to <u>keep</u> their
<u>mitts</u> above the table at all times. In addition, they play at a glass-
topped table to prevent anyone from sneaking a hand underneath to

<u>pluck</u> a hidden card. Also, they always play with a new pack of cards so that no one can mark the cards ahead of time or <u>cram</u> extras into the deck. The friends find their game amusing and think they are wonderfully creative to have come up with a way to play it and avoid getting <u>peeved</u>.

 ## THINKING IT OVER

Test your recall of this chapter's concepts by completing the following statements. If you cannot complete a statement, look back through the chapter to find the answer.

1. Four types of context clues are _____, _____, _____, and _____.

2. Synonyms and terms such as *refers to* and *means* are _____ context clues.

3. Explanations that create images in your mind and phrases such as *for example* and *to illustrate* are _____ context clues.

4. Antonyms, punctuation clues, and words such as *although* and *however* are _____ context clues.

5. When you use your experience and prior knowledge to help you define a word, you are using _____ context clues.

6. The five parts of a dictionary entry are _____, _____, _____, _____, and _____.

7. Some dictionary entries also show the meaning of a word as used in a particular _____.

8. A word's dictionary definition is its _____.

9. A word's suggested meaning is its _____.

10. Choose one of the Thinking First questions at the beginning of the chapter to answer on the following lines.

_____

_____

_____

TOPICS FOR WRITING

Write an essay about an event that has special significance for you. Remember to choose words carefully to describe your event. Following are some suggestions.

Your first date

A time you received a gift you really wanted

An event that taught you a lesson

An accident, illness, or hardship you overcame

An event that cost you a relationship

An incident that strengthened a relationship

An event that has been widely publicized

An event that involves someone you admire or care about

Checklist for Revision

1. Does your essay introduce the topic?

2. Does your essay contain a clear statement of main idea (thesis statement)?

3. Have you supported your thesis with enough evidence?

4. Does your essay have a conclusion?

5. Are you satisfied with your word choices?

6. Have you found and corrected your errors?

REFLECTIONS ON READING AND WRITING

Think about your experiences with reading textbooks, listening to lectures, watching the news on television, reading about current events, or writing on various topics. In which of these situations do you feel most confident about your vocabulary? Least confident? In which of these situations do you think having a good vocabulary can be most helpful and why? How do you plan to develop your vocabulary?

Chapter 3

Reading for Main Ideas

THINKING FIRST

- *How can I recognize main ideas?*
- *Where will I find a main idea stated?*
- *How will finding the main idea help me?*

One of your most important tasks as a reader is to get the writer's point. The point is the *main idea*—the writer's message to you, the reader. Main ideas take many forms. For example, a main idea may state an important concept or a strongly held opinion. Paragraphs have a main idea. Entire essays and articles have a main idea, which is also called the *central idea,* or *thesis.* A textbook chapter has a main idea, as does each section and paragraph within a chapter. *Main idea, central idea,* and *thesis* are similar terms.

Whatever you read—an essay or article from a periodical, a pamphlet on display at your doctor's office, a section from a page in your college catalog, or a textbook chapter for one of your courses—you must be able to find the main idea. Sometimes the main idea is clearly stated, sometimes not. In either case, you have to read carefully and use some analytical reasoning to find the main idea.

Main ideas can help guide your reading because they often tell you what to expect. If you know the main idea of a paragraph, or any piece of writing, you may be able to predict what comes next. Having expectations and formulating questions as you read makes you an active reader, keeps your attention focused, and improves your comprehension. This chapter explains how to find stated and implied main ideas in paragraphs and longer reading selections.

BACKGROUND CHECK

Before reading the following essay, check your knowledge and assumptions about people who have physical or other disabilities.

1. What are some of the problems you think a physically disabled child might encounter at school?

2. Some people make fun of others' disabilities. What reasons can you think of for this behavior?

3. What can parents and teachers do to increase children's sensitivity toward disabled people?

4. Based on your survey of the title, author information, and first two paragraphs, what do you expect to follow?

5. What else do you know or think about the topic?

It's OK to Be Different

Angie Erickson

Angie Erickson attends high school in Plymouth, Minnesota. She wrote this essay, which appeared in Newsweek, *when she was in the ninth grade. Erickson challenges readers to consider what life is like for the child who is made fun of because of a disability. Erickson also explains how she overcame the insensitivity of others to become the strong and capable person that she is today.*

VOCABULARY CHECK

Pictionary (5)	a game played by adults and children
insecurity (8)	lack of self-confidence
presume (11)	take for granted

Why me, I often ask myself. Why did I have to be the one? Why did I   1
get picked to be different? Why are people mean to me and are always treating me differently? These are the kinds of questions that I
used to ask myself. It took more than 10 years for me to find answers
and to realize that I'm not *more* different than anyone else.

I was born on June 29, 1978. Along with me came my twin sister,   2
Stephanie. She was born with no birth defects, but I was born with
cerebral palsy. For me, CP made it so I shake a little; when my sister
began to walk, I couldn't. The doctors knew it was a minor case of
cerebral palsy. But they didn't know if I'd ever walk straight or do
things that other kids my age could do.

At first my disability did not bother me, because when you're a   3
toddler, you do things that are really easy. When it took me a little
longer to play yard games, because I couldn't run that well, my
friends just thought I was slow. My disability was noticed when other
children were learning how to write and I couldn't. Kids I thought
were my friends started to stay away from me because they said I was
different. Classmates began commenting on my speech. They said I
talked really weird. Every time someone was mean to me, I would
start to cry and I would always blame myself for being different.

People thought I was stupid because it was hard for me to write   4
my own name. So when I was the only one in the class to use a typewriter, I began to feel I was different. It got worse when the third
graders moved on to fourth grade and I had to stay behind. I got held
back because the teachers thought I'd be unable to type fast enough
to keep up. Kids told me that was a lie and the reason I got held back
was because I was a retard. It really hurt to be teased by those I
thought were my friends.

After putting up with everyone making fun of me and me crying   5
about it, I started sticking up for myself when I was 10, in fourth
grade. I realized if I wanted them to stop, I would have to be the person who made them stop. I finally found out who my real friends
were, and I tried to ignore the ones who were mean. Instead of constantly thinking about the things I couldn't do, I tried to think about
the things I *could* do, and it helped others, and myself, understand

who I really was. When there was something I couldn't do, such as play Pictionary, I sat and I watched or I would go find something else to do. A few people still called me names and made fun of me, but after a while, when they saw they didn't get a reaction, they quit, because it wasn't fun anymore. What they didn't know was that it did still hurt me. It hurt me a lot more than they could ever imagine.

When I was 12, my family moved. I kept this fairy tale in my head that, at my next school, no one would be mean to me or would see that I had a disability. I'd always wished I could be someone other than myself. I found out the hard way that I wasn't going to change, that I'd never be able to write and run with no problems. When kids in my new school found out that I couldn't write and my talking and walking were out of the ordinary, they started making fun of me. They never took time to know me. 6

Everything went back to the way it was before. I went back to blaming myself and thinking that, since I was different, I'd never fit in. I would cry all the time, because it was so hard for me to make friends again. I didn't know whether I should trust anyone—I thought that if people knew that I had a disability they would not like me anymore. It took me a long time to understand that I had to return to not caring about what other people say. 7

People make fun of others because of insecurity. They have to show off to feel better about themselves. When a person made fun of me everyone thought it was just a big joke. After a while I just started laughing along with them or walking away. It really made some kids mad that they weren't getting any reaction out of me. Yeah, it still hurt a lot. I wanted to break down and start crying right then and there, but I knew I didn't want them to get their pleasure out of my hurt feelings. I couldn't cry. 8

I still get really frustrated when I can't do certain things, and I probably always will. I thought I should give people a better chance to get to know me, but I knew that I would probably get hurt. I never thought that anyone would want to be friends with somebody who had cerebral palsy. At times I have trouble dealing with kids making fun of me, but these are people who need help figuring out things in life and need to be treated better themselves. Maybe then they'll treat others the same. They look disappointed when I walk away or laugh when they try to make fun of me. Perhaps they're hurting more than I am. 9

It took a lot of willpower on my part and a lot of love from family and friends to get where I am today. I learned that no one was to blame for my disability. I realize that I can do things and I can do them very well. Some things I can't do, like taking my own notes in class or running in a race, but I will have to live with that. At 16, I believe I've learned more than many people will learn in their whole lives. I have 10 worked out that some people are just mean because they're afraid of being nice. They try to prove to themselves and others that they are cool, but, sooner or later, they're going to wish they hadn't said some of those hurtful things. A lot of people will go through life being mean to those with disabilities because they don't know how to act or what to say to them—they feel awkward with someone who's different.

Parents need to teach their children that it's all right to be different and it's all right to be friends with those who are. Some think that the disabled should be treated like little kids for the rest of their lives. They presume we don't need love and friends, but our needs are the same as every other human being's.   11

There are times when I wish I hadn't been born with cerebral palsy, but crying about it isn't going to do me any good. I can only live once, so I want to live the best I can. I am glad I learned who I am and what I am capable of doing. I am happy with who I am. Nobody else could be the Angela Marie Erickson who is writing this. I could never be, or ever want to be, anyone else.   12

THINKING CRITICALLY

Main Idea

1. What is Erickson's thesis or central idea? Hint: Look for a sentence near the end of the essay that states the author's point—what the whole essay is about.

Details

2. Erickson lists several reasons why children made fun of her. What are the reasons?

3. What was one effective way Erickson found to cope with those who made fun of her because of her disability?

Organization

4. Erickson organizes her essay by relating a series of events that happened to her at different stages of her life. To follow the events, explain what happened to her as a toddler, as a third grader, at age 10, age 12, and age 16.

Purpose, Audience, Tone

5. What is Erickson's purpose? What attitudes or behaviors does she want readers to change?

Inferences and Conclusions

6. Using evidence from the essay, explain why you think Erickson might agree or disagree with the following statement:

   Disabled children should be isolated in special classes away from other children.

Making Connections

What do you think a teacher or parent can or should do to discourage children from making fun of disabled classmates? How do you help children understand that "it's OK to be different," as Erickson says? Write about a method that you think might work.

GENERAL AND SPECIFIC IDEAS

One key to recognizing main ideas is to know the difference between *general* and *specific* ideas. *General* ideas are broad. *Specific* ideas are narrow and limited. A general idea is broad enough that it can be broken down into more narrow but related ideas. "Bread," for example, is a general idea. "Rye," "wheat," and "pumpernickel" are specific ideas because they each express one kind, or type, of bread. Can you find the most general idea in the following list?

1. My mother-in-law likes cranberry bread for breakfast.

2. Aunt Sarah has a wonderful recipe for blueberry muffins.

3. Homemade biscuits are a special favorite of mine.

4. Everyone in my family loves to make and eat bread.

5. My ten-year-old sister is learning to make cornbread.

The fourth idea is the most general one. This idea is broad enough to include all members of the family and all kinds of bread, whereas the other ideas are limited to only one family member and one kind of bread.

Exercise 3.1   Following are several groups of specific ideas. On the line above each group, write the general idea. The first one is done for you.

1. *stringed instruments*

violin
viola
cello
harp

2. _____

basketball
baseball
football
soccer

3. _____

newspaper
magazine
journal
quarterly

4. _____

daisy
snapdragon
lily
camellia

5. _____

senator
representative
governor
judge

6. _____

Barbara Bush
Hillary Clinton
Betty Ford
Nancy Reagan

Exercise 3.2   Now list your own specific ideas on the lines beneath the general ideas. The first one is done for you.

1. action heroes

Batman

Superman

Wonder Woman

Spider Woman

2. ground transportation

_____

_____

_____

_____

3. singing groups   4. sports equipment

_____   _____

_____   _____

_____   _____

_____   _____

5. horror movies   6. capital cities

_____   _____

_____   _____

_____   _____

_____   _____

To find the main idea of a paragraph, look for the most general statement. The following list of sentences could be the sentences of a paragraph. Try to determine which is the main idea.

1. Algebra I is a general education requirement for all students who want to graduate.

2. Students who are seeking an A. S. or A. A. degree must take Freshman Composition.

3. At my college, everyone must take certain courses.

4. Introduction to the Humanities is another course that all students must take.

The first statement provides an example of a course a student must take, as do the second and fourth statements. But the third one is a general one about "certain courses" college students must take. This is the main idea, and the other statements offer specific examples to support it. Now try another example. Which statement is the main idea?

1. Seeing Eye dogs enable blind people to lead more normal lives.

2. Dogs need humans, but humans may need the services of dogs even more.

3. Dogs are excellent companions for people who are depressed because of age or illness.

4. In many parts of the world, farmers depend on dogs to herd sheep or cattle.

The second statement is the main idea. It is a general statement that people need dogs. Statements 1, 3, and 4 each provide a specific reason why people need dogs: Dogs help the blind lead normal lives, they are companions for the old and the ill, and they help farmers herd cattle and sheep.

Exercise 3.3   Underline the main idea in each group of sentences. Hint: Look for the most general sentence.

1a. Grant was a man who would not give up a fight.

 b. He wanted, above all, to keep the nation together.

 c. Ulysses S. Grant was an effective general.

 d. Grant was daring and resourceful in battle.

2a. The first Dracula was Max Shreck, whose ratlike appearance horrified silent screen audiences.

 b. Bela Lugosi, the most famous Dracula, played the count as a more human yet sinister being.

 c. Frank Langella, one of the screen's more recent Draculas, played the role with sensitivity and sensuality.

 d. The vampire, Count Dracula, has been interpreted differently by each actor who has played him.

3a. The sticker price may be only a fraction of the price you pay to own a car.

 b. The costs of maintenance and repairs vary with the make and model of car you buy.

   c. Gas mileage is another factor that may increase your cost of operating a car.

   d. Insurance premiums are an added cost and are higher for some makes of cars than for others.

4a. Maggots, denizens of your garbage can, speed up the process of decay.

   b. Spiders, insects, and other creepy creatures help us in ways we may not realize.

   c. Dragonflies engage in population control because they eat mosquitoes by the thousands.

   d. Florida's large brown house spider is nice to have around because roaches are its favorite dish.

5a. Bass fishing, whether for food, recreation, or tournament prizes, is a popular sport among men and women.

   b. Water skiing and jet skiing satisfy a young person's need for speed and for keeping cool.

   c. Lakes are a source of recreation for all, providing many opportunities for engaging in water sports.

   d. Swimming and boating are favorite weekend activities for families and for people of all ages.

MAIN IDEAS IN PARAGRAPHS

Every paragraph has a main idea. Sometimes the main idea is clearly stated in one sentence called the *topic sentence*. Often the main idea is implied. An *implied* main idea is an unstated main idea, one that is suggested by the details in the paragraph. Comprehension depends on your being able to find the author's main idea whether it is stated or implied.

The Stated Main Idea

To find the main idea of a paragraph, ask yourself three questions. Your answers may lead you to the topic sentence.

1. What is the author's topic?

2. What is the author's opinion about the topic?

3. Does the paragraph have a sentence that states both the topic and the author's opinion?

If your answer to question 3 is *yes,* then you may have found the topic sentence.

Exercise 3.4   Each of the following sentences could be a topic sentence of a paragraph. Each one states a topic and an author's opinion about the topic. In each sentence, underline and label the topic and author's opinion. The first one is done as an example.

1. The bat is an animal that many people fear without reason.

2. A fashion coordinator must have a strong sense of color and style.

3. Spending holidays away from home has some advantages.

4. One way to improve grades is to avoid procrastination.

5. The time you spend waiting in lines can be used in several ways.

6. A course in public speaking can be a career asset.

A topic sentence can be anywhere in a paragraph, at the beginning, the end, or somewhere in between. Most often, however, the first sentence is the topic sentence. Figure 3.1 reviews the characteristics of a topic sentence.

Exercise 3.5   Using the three questions at the top of this page and Figure 3.1 as references, read each paragraph and underline the topic sentence.

FIGURE 3.1

Characteristics of a Topic Sentence

It is a general statement.

It states the author's topic.

It states the author's opinion about the topic.

It can be anywhere in the paragraph, but is often the first sentence.

1. The advantages of flight undoubtedly played a large role in the success of the Class Insecta. Insects were the first creatures on earth capable of flight, which allowed them to more easily escape their enemies, to cover more territory in search of food, water, or mates, and to colonize new areas. They could cross large bodies of water, which were insurmountable barriers to most nonflying terrestrial animals.

   From *The Practical Entomologist,* Rick Imes, Quarto Publishing, 1992.

2. *Memory* is based in the central nervous system—in the billions of cells in the brain. It depends on biochemical and electrical processes in the molecular structures of nerve tissue. Memory is an essential part of basic human communication. Without understanding its role in the communication process, we would find it difficult to comprehend the process, effects, and limitations of mass communication.

   From *Understanding Mass Communications,* 5th ed., Melvin L. DeFleur and Everette E. Dennis, Houghton Mifflin Co., 1994.

3. These cars were not the staid models of the 1940s. Detroit built sleeker, bigger, gaudier, and more expensive machines than ever before. The public adored two- and three-tone models, tail fins,

wrap-around windshields, power steering, automatic transmissions, and air conditioning. This emphasis on power gadgets and sex appeal helped to spur automania as a cultural force. Auto tourism became a major form of family leisure. Nat King Cole's hit song "Get Your Kicks on Route 66" reflected the increasingly common cross-country family trips to national parks and new amusement complexes such as Disneyland. Motel chains proliferated. So did other spinoff industries such as fast-food outlets and drive-in theaters.

From *Present Tense,* Michael Schaller, Virginia Scharff, and Robert D. Schulzinger, Houghton Mifflin Co., 1992.

4. Sharpening your listening techniques will help you get more out of lectures. Focus on the speaker. Watch for gestures he or she may use to emphasize a point. Listen for clue words that alert you to a sequence of ideas such as *first, second, next, another.* Listen for examples that illustrate a point. Listen, too, for sound clues. The speaker may raise or lower the voice for emphasis. Pay particular attention to anything the speaker writes on a chalkboard or displays on an overhead transparency. Finally, take notes that are well organized and thorough. Leave space between major points so you can write in examples or add to your notes later on. The speaker may jump around in the lecture, returning to a previous point to add another example. If you have left some space between points, it will be easy to squeeze in the speaker's afterthoughts.

5. Three robberies that have been reported in the Oak Hill subdivision during the past week have angered residents. A drug dealer was ar-

rested for soliciting business in the playground of a nearby middle school. A few isolated instances of vandalism have occurred, mostly to automobiles. One resident reported a cracked windshield; two others reported that gasoline had been siphoned from their gas tanks. The brick fence that surrounds the subdivision has been attacked by spray-paint-can-wielding teens from another neighborhood across town. As a result of these and other disturbances, the residents of Oak Hill have decided to establish a neighborhood crime watch in their area.

The Implied Main Idea

Suppose you cannot find a topic sentence in a paragraph. Then the main idea may be implied. To find the main idea, you must look for clues in every sentence. Finally, when you think you know what the main idea is, try to state it in your own words. Ask yourself two questions. Your answers may lead you to the main idea when no topic sentence exists.

1. What general idea do the details in every sentence seem to support?

2. How can I express this idea in a sentence of my own?

Read the following list of details. As you read them, try to determine what main idea they all seem to support.

First of all, my alarm did not go off.

Then I had to fix breakfast for my children.

Also I had to stop for gas on the way to work.

When I arrived, the parking lot was full.

It took me another 20 minutes to find a place to park.

These details seem to imply that the author is having trouble getting to work on time. The details all seem to state reasons why this person is late. What main idea can you think of that could be supported by these details? The following statement is one possibility:

Several things happened this morning that caused me to be late.

Details consist of facts, reasons, examples, and other bits of information. Details provide the clues that can help you determine a paragraph's main idea.

> **STUDY TIP:**   *Watch for transitional words and phrases such as* **for example, in addition, first, next, another,** *and* **because.** *These can alert you to important details. Making inference from these details can lead you to the main idea.*

Exercise 3.6   Reach each list of details and try to determine what main idea they support. Write the main idea on the line beneath the list of details.

  1a. Drink plenty of fluids.

   b. Take aspirin to reduce fever.

   c. Get enough bed rest.

   d. See a doctor if symptoms persist.

   _____

  2a. Recite from your lecture notes.

   b. Review textbook chapters.

   c. Try to anticipate test questions.

   d. Learn from mistakes on previous tests.

   _____

  3a. For one thing, she respects my opinions.

   b. Also, I can depend on her to keep my secrets.

   c. She is supportive of my decisions.

   d. Most important, her values are the same as mine.

   _____

4a. Cost is an important consideration.

 b. Gas mileage is a big factor.

 c. The reputation of the service department has to be good.

 d. The style and design of the car mean a lot to me.

_____

5a. Good employees should be dependable.

 b. They must also be self-motivated.

 c. Employees who can work well with others are valuable.

 d. They need to be skilled at what they do.

_____

If you were successful with this exercise, you should be able to infer the main idea of a paragraph that does not have a topic sentence. Try to think of this type of paragraph as a list of details that have been arranged in a paragraph format. Your job is to determine the main idea that all the details support.

The following paragraph is from N. Scott Momaday's book *The Names, A Memoir* (The University of Arizona Press, 1976), in which he explores his Native American roots. Read the paragraph and determine its main idea. Then read the explanation following the passage to verify your conclusion.

Dusk was falling at five o'clock, when the dancing came to an end, and on the way home alone I bought a Navajo dog. I bargained for a while with the thin, wary man whose dog it was, and we settled on a price of five dollars. It was a yellow, honest-to-goodness, great-hearted dog, and the man gave me a bit of rope with which to pull it home. The dog was not large, but neither was it small. It was one of those unremarkable creatures that one sees in every corner of the world. If there were only thirty-nine dogs in Creation, this one would be the fourth, or the thirteenth, or the twenty-first, the archetype, the common denominator of all its kind. It was full of resistance, and yet it was ready to return in full measure my deep, abiding love. I could see that. It needed only, I reasoned, to make a small adjustment in its style of life, to shift the focus of its vitality from one frame of reference to another, in order to be perfectly at home with me. Even as it was nearly strangled on the way, it wagged its bushy tail happily all the while. That night I tied the dog up in the garage, where there was a warm, clean pallet, wholesome food, and fresh water, and I bolted the door. And the next morning the dog was gone, as in my heart of hearts I knew it would be, I believe. I had read such a future in its eyes. It had gnawed the rope in two and squeezed through a vent in the door, an opening much too small for it, as I had thought. But, sure enough, where there is a will there is a way, and the Navajo dog was possessed of one indomitable will. I was crushed at the time, but strangely reconciled, too, as if I had perceived some truth beyond billboards. The dog had done what it had to do, had behaved exactly as it must, had been true to itself and to the sun and moon. It knew its place in the order of things, and its place was away out there in the tracks of a wagon, going home. In the mind's eye I could see it at that very moment, miles away, plodding the familiar shadows, its tail drooping a little after the harrowing night, but wagging, in its dog's mind contemplating the wonderful ways of mankind.

Momaday's topic is the Navajo dog. Some of the details describe the dog, tell you how the author got it, what he expected of it, and what he did with the dog after he got home. Additional details tell you how the dog reacted. From these details you can infer that Momaday misjudged the dog. He thought that he could turn the dog into a companion by loving it and taking care of it. He tied the dog in the garage and bolted the door, indicating that he was afraid the dog might run away because it was not yet used to its new home. Also, when he discovered that the dog was gone, the author says he somehow knew this would happen.

Other details suggest that Momaday is making a point about dogs in general, and that the Navajo dog is but one example. He calls the dog "the archetype, the common denominator of all its kind." In other words, the Navajo dog is like other dogs, but in what way? Near the end of the paragraph, the author answers this question. He says that the dog "behaved exactly as it must" and "knew its place." The author's comment seems to be that a dog's place is not at the end of a rope but running free. Also, the "gnawed" rope and the dog having "squeezed" out of an opening that had seemed too small suggest that he struggled to gain his freedom. A possible main idea statement that combines the author's topic and comment is, *A Navajo dog, like any other, must be true to its nature and will struggle to get free.*

Exercise 3.7   None of the following paragraphs has a topic sentence, but each has a main idea. Read each paragraph using the details to help you infer the main idea. Then write the main idea on the line beneath the paragraph. Your main idea should be a general statement that accounts for the details in the paragraph. The first one is done as an example.

1. **Savanna** is grassland with scattered individual trees. Extensive savanna covers wide tropical and subtropical areas of central South America, central and southern Africa, and parts of Australia. There are generally three distinct seasons in these regions: cool and dry, hot and dry, and warm and wet, in that sequence. Some savanna soils are quite fertile, but most are porous, resulting in the rapid drainage of water. Porous soils have only a thin layer of the rich, partially decomposed organic matter called humus.

   From *Biology*, 3d ed., Neil A. Campbell, Benjamin/Cummings Publishing Co., 1993.

   Implied main idea:

   A savanna has several characteristics.

   _____

2. During a typical meditation session, breathing, heart rate, muscle tension, blood pressure, and oxygen decrease (Shapiro & Gilber, 1978; Wallace & Benson, 1972). Most forms of meditation also produce a considerable amount of alpha-wave activity, the brainwave pattern commonly found in a relaxed, eyes-closed, waking state. . . . Meditators often report significant reductions in stress-related problems such as general anxiety, high blood pressure, and insomnia (Carrington, 1986; Eppley, Abrams, & Shear, 1989; Smith, 1975). More generally, meditators' scores on personality tests indicate

increases in general mental health, self-esteem, and social openness (Alexander, Rainforth, & Gelderloos, 1991; Shapiro & Gilber, 1978). Exactly how meditation produces its effects is unclear. Many of its effects can also be achieved by biofeedback, hypnosis, and just relaxing (Holmes, 1984).

From *Psychology,* 3d ed., Douglas A. Bernstein et al., Houghton Mifflin Co., 1994.

Implied main idea:

_____

_____

3. Classified advertisements in many school newspapers advertise "Term papers for sale on any topic," "Just send $5 for a sample list of topics," "Guaranteed satisfaction." We all know that it is unethical to submit another person's written work for a class assignment as one's own. The fraud here is the quality of term papers purchased. You would not believe the poor quality of the products sold by most of these firms. They are almost a joke. A sophomore who is barely passing high school could throw together most of the papers with just a couple hours of research. Still, there are a few consumers who insist on spending their money on such products.

From *Consumer Economic Issues in America,* E. Thomas Garman, Houghton Mifflin Co., 1991.

Implied main idea:

_____

_____

4. The three major networks are, of course, ABC (American Broadcasting Corporation), CBS (Columbia Broadcasting System), and NBC (National Broadcasting Corporation). All three have been in business for decades. Much newer are the Fox network and CNN (Cable News Network). The Fox system is owned by Rupert Murdoch, whose holdings also include a newspaper empire. . . . CNN is a specialized operation that delivers programming to cable systems. In addition, there are regional systems formed of local stations that band together and share programming and promote advertising. The noncommercial Public Broadcasting System (PBS) is also a network overseas. Ostensibly for members of the armed forces, AFRTS (Armed Forces Radio and Television Service), as it is called, reaches into seventy countries and is seen not only by people in the armed forces, but also by millions of U.S. and foreign civilians.

From *Understanding Mass Communications*, 5th ed., Melvin L. DeFleur and Everette E. Dennis, Houghton Mifflin Co., 1994.

Implied main idea:

_____

_____

5. Did you know that some pills and powders sold in health food stores can make you high? These natural drugs are made from herbs, are relatively cheap, and they are legal. Marketed as food supplements, they promise to boost energy, control weight, soothe nerves, or produce euphoria. But are these seeming benefits worth the risks? As some chronic users have found, it takes a lot of product to get the

desired effect, and certain herbs can be harmful when taken in large doses. Ephedra, for example, has been known to cause serious illness and even death. The FDA is worried, and many health professionals are calling for government regulation of herbal products. Implied main idea:

_____

_____

CENTRAL IDEAS IN LONGER PASSAGES

Longer passages are made up of paragraphs. To read a passage with understanding, you must be able to follow the author's ideas from one paragraph to another. Just as the sentences of a paragraph all support one main idea, the paragraphs of a longer passage all support one central idea. Sometimes the central idea is clearly stated in one sentence called the *thesis statement*. Often the central idea is implied. An *implied thesis*, or central idea, is suggested by the details throughout the passage. Comprehension depends on your being able to find the author's thesis and follow its development.

The Stated Central Idea

The thesis statement of a longer passage is similar to the topic sentence of a paragraph in two ways. First, just as the topic sentence states the main idea of a whole paragraph, the thesis statement tells you the central idea of an entire passage. Second, the thesis statement, like the topic sentence, is a general statement supported by specific details.

To find the thesis statement of a longer passage, start at the beginning. Look for a general statement that seems to express what the whole passage is about. The title of the passage is often a clue to the writer's central idea. Erickson's essay title, "It's OK to Be Different," is reflected in her thesis statement in which she says, "Parents need to teach their children that it's all right to be different and it's all right to be friends with those who are." Every paragraph in Erickson's essay relates in some way to her thesis by explaining either what it was like for

Erickson to be different, how other children treated her because she was different, or how she learned to cope with the way she was treated and to take pride in those things she was able to do well.

Similarly, the title of a textbook chapter, or even a major heading near the beginning, may be a clue to the chapter's thesis. Consider the following excerpt from the chapter "Introduction to Human Relations" in *Effective Human Relations in Organizations*, 5th ed., by Barry L. Reece and Rhonda Brandt, Houghton Mifflin Co., 1993. The excerpt is annotated to show how the thesis relates to the rest of the excerpt.

Hallmark Cards Inc. has been described as the General Motors of emotion. Each day this midwestern company produces the millions of greeting cards that help sustain relationships in a society where people are less likely to write letters and are too busy to call. The leaders at Hallmark know that sentimental verses, funny birthday greetings, and intimate anniversary messages cannot be created in a negative or divisive work environment. To keep the atmosphere cheery, the company employs a "Creative Paradox." This is the official title given to Gordon MacKenzie, who roams the halls of Hallmark making sure people do not take themselves too seriously. His goal is to build greater understanding between highly creative employees (writers and sketch artists) and employees who work in management, accounting, marketing, and distribution. He sometimes conducts New Age workshops that prompt self-examination and new ways of thinking. *[At Hallmark, the atmosphere is positive. Employee relations are good.]*

The emphasis on relationships at Hallmark is not an isolated case. Organizations throughout the United States are discovering and rediscovering the benefits to be achieved from improving the quality of work life. A growing number of organizations, from hospitals to hotels, are giving greater attention to the human side of enterprise. Most of the organizations that survive and prosper over a long period of time maintain a balance between concern for production and concern for people. *[Most companies emphasize employee relations.]*

THE NATURE, PURPOSE, AND IMPORTANCE OF HUMAN RELATIONS

Many of America's best-managed organizations are not simply being "nice to people"; they are genuinely helping employees come alive through their work. Managers have learned that the goals of worker and workplace need not conflict. This chapter focuses on the nature of human relations, its development, and its importance to the achievement of individual and organizational paths.

What are "human relations?" Why important?

Thesis: This is what the chapter is about.

Human Relations Defined

The term **human relations** in its broadest sense covers all types of interactions among people—their conflicts, cooperative efforts, and group relationships. It is the study of *why* our beliefs, attitudes, and behaviors sometimes cause interpersonal conflict in our personal lives and in work-related situations. The study of human relations emphasizes the analysis of human behavior, prevention strategies, and resolution of behavioral problems. . . .

definition

Why human relations are important.

The passage begins with a brief story, or *anecdote,* about Hallmark Cards Inc., a company that understands the importance of human relations and that works hard to provide a positive, cooperative working atmosphere for its employees. Following this introduction, the first chapter heading, "The Nature, Purpose, and Importance of Human Relations," serves two purposes: It signals the first major division, or section, of the chapter, and it provides a strong clue to the writers' thesis—what the whole chapter is about. Notice how the thesis statement repeats three terms from the chapter heading: *nature, importance,* and *human relations.*

Following the thesis statement is the first subheading "Human Relations Defined," which lets you know that a definition follows. The writers want to make sure you know what *they* mean by human relations before you read any further. By defining a key term that is essential to your understanding of the thesis statement and of the chapter as a whole, the writers make clear what they want you to focus on as you read.

As a college student, you are required to read many kinds of materials. In most books and in journal and magazine articles, writers may not signal the organization of their ideas in the same way as do the writers of textbooks. How are you to get the point if the title does not provide a clue to the main idea and there are no headings and sub-headings to guide you? One helpful strategy is to read the first and last paragraph. The first paragraph may introduce the topic and state the thesis. The last paragraph may restate the thesis or summarize major supporting details. If reading the first and last paragraphs does not help, you may have to read further to get the point. Remember that the thesis statement may appear anywhere in the passage, and sometimes there is no thesis statement.

The Implied Central Idea

When a writer's thesis is implied, you will not be able to find it clearly stated anywhere in the passage. Instead, you must determine the thesis based on your reading of the whole passage and your understanding of the main ideas and details of each paragraph. If, after reading a passage, you are not certain of the writer's central idea and you cannot find a stated thesis, try to determine the implied central idea. Begin by asking yourself three questions:

1. What is the whole passage about?

2. What general idea do the details throughout the passage seem to support?

3. How can I express this idea in a sentence of my own?

Your answers should lead you to the implied thesis. Asking yourself questions, using titles and headings as clues, and paying attention to the details are additional strategies you can use to find implied central ideas of longer passages. Titles sometimes provide strong clues to the topic covered, and they may give you insight into the central idea. Headings are helpful in three ways. First, they are clues to the important ideas covered in the sections that follow. Second, they help you anticipate or predict what is to come. Third, you can use headings to guide your reading by turning them into questions and looking for the answers. For example, the heading "Human Relations Defined" from the excerpt on pages 85–86, can be restated as the question, "How do the authors define *human relations?*" As you read, you should look for the definition.

Exercise 3.8   The following excerpt is from "Careers and Other Key Factors that Affect Income," Chapter 2 of *Personal Finance,* 4th ed., by E. Thomas Garman and Raymond E. Forgue (Houghton Mifflin Co., 1994). Look the excerpt over and answer questions 1–4, then read the excerpt and answer questions 5–11. Paragraphs are numbered for your convenience.

Before You Read

1. According to the first, or major, heading what is this excerpt about?

   _____

2. What background do you bring to this excerpt—what thoughts do you have about career planning?

   _____

   _____

   _____

3. Based on the information provided in paragraph 1, what in your own words seems to be the implied thesis, or central idea, of this whole excerpt?

   _____

   _____

4. Turn the major heading and the two subheadings into questions to guide your reading.

   Heading   Your question

   _____   _____

   Subheadings   Your questions

   _____   _____

   _____   _____

Career Planning, Phase One—
Getting to Know Yourself

The career planning sequence is as follows: First, discover what you   1
want out of life; second, decide on a career that is likely to permit
you to lead such a satisfying life; and third, seek a job or series of jobs
that serve as the means by which you achieve your career and life
goals. If you are going to take charge of choosing your career, you
must begin by examining your values, beliefs, and attitudes, which
will help you analyze your work values, work style, and lifestyle.
Then you can begin to assess your interests, abilities, and skills more
carefully.

Discover Your Values

A systematic approach to the job hunt and a career change involves   2
knowing what skills you enjoy using, determining where you want to
use those skills, and finding the person who has the power to hire
you. Prerequisite to the job search is understanding yourself. Knowing
yourself better will enable you to select a career path that suits your
interests, abilities, and skills. In today's world, you must accept respon-
sibility for who you are and where you are going, as well as how you
are going to get there. To be successful, your career must be considered a high-priority, do-it-yourself project.

As we contemplate major choices in life, we need to be aware of   3
what is important to us personally. We need to be aware of our values, attitudes, and beliefs that influence such choices. Many are con-
sciously held concerns, while others are unconscious. **Values** are the
principles, standards, or qualities considered worthwhile or desirable
that provide a basis for goals, thereby giving continuity to decisions.
Values provide a base for decisions about how to live because they
serve as guides to future action and as standards or criteria by which
our actions can be directed. Attitudes and beliefs that qualify as values are prized, publicly affirmed, chosen from alternatives, and acted
on repeatedly and consistently. Values are not right or wrong, or true
or false—they are profound preferences.

Values, Beliefs, and Attitudes

As people go through life, their fundamental values change little. For   4
example, an accountant working for the Internal Revenue Service (IRS)
might personally value honesty. Note, though, that attitudes and beliefs
are frequently changed or modified by the experiences we undergo. A
belief is the mental acceptance of or conviction about the truth or

actuality of some statement or some thing based on what one implicitly considers adequate grounds. An **attitude** is a persistent, learned predisposition to behave in a consistent way toward a given object or set of objects not necessarily as they are, but as they are conceived to be. An IRS accountant, after a number of years on the job, might come to believe that most people are anything but honest. That accountant could maintain an attitude that causes him or her to suspect dishonesty when conducting audits of income tax returns. Attitudes are often reflected as evaluative beliefs by which we express our likes and dislikes. Together, our values, attitudes, and beliefs help us make sense of the world, and they determine how we think, feel, and act.

Most of us are unclear about or not even aware of what our values actually are. However, the better we understand our values, the better we can plan our lives to be consistent with them. By developing a greater awareness of your own values, you can become more aware of the unseen forces that guide you and, at the same time, you can make conscious decisions about alternative directions you want to pursue.   5

Following are some values: family, friends, helping others, religious commitment, security, honesty, pleasure, good health, material possessions, financial achievement, and a satisfying career. Some examples of confusion and conflict centering on values include family versus friends, love versus sex, religious beliefs versus actions, and work versus leisure. Conflicts such as these constantly require us to make choices, and the choices can be difficult unless we know what is most important to us. Of course, many decisions are based on value judgments determined in the past, thus allowing us to conserve time, energy, and often money.   6

When you make important decisions, you might be wise to think carefully to clarify your values before taking action. You should realize, too, that when used as guidelines for action, your values, attitudes, and beliefs tell you what to do. . . .   7

After reading, answer the following questions:

5. According to the details in paragraph 2, what do you first have to know before you can begin planning your career?

_____

6. According to the details in paragraph 3, what is a *value?*

_____

7. Why are values important? (paragraphs 3, 5, and 7)

_____

_____

8. What is a *belief*? (paragraph 4)

_____

9. What is an *attitude*? (paragraph 4)

_____

10. Do beliefs change over time? Do attitudes? Explain.

_____

_____

11. Based on your answers to questions 5–10 about the details in this excerpt, what do you now think is the implied thesis of the passage? Is it the same as you thought when you answered question 3?

_____

_____

THINKING ABOUT PROCESS

The steps for finding implied main ideas in paragraphs or longer passages are essentially the same, but for some longer passages you may have two additional clues: the title and headings.

1. After reading the paragraph or passage, ask yourself, "What is the author's topic? What is the author's opinion about the topic?"

2. Pay attention to *all* the details and make inferences from them. Whether you are trying to find the main idea of a paragraph or the central idea of a longer passage, you want to know what general idea all the details seem to support.

3. Come up with your own statement of the main or central idea.

THINKING IT OVER

Test your recall of the chapter's concepts by completing the following statements. If you cannot complete a statement, look back through the chapter to find the answer.

1. Two other terms that mean *main idea* are _____ and _____.

2. Main ideas guide your reading because _____ _____.

3. Ideas can be general or _____.

4. Within a paragraph, the main idea is the most _____ idea.

5. Details that support the main idea are _____ ideas.

6. The main idea of a paragraph is often stated in a _____ _____.

7. The central idea of a longer passage is often stated in a _____ _____.

8. When a main or central idea is not stated, it is _____.

9. To find unstated main ideas, you must make inferences from the _____.

10. Choose one of the Thinking First questions at the beginning of the chapter to answer on the following lines.

_____

_____

_____

TOPICS FOR WRITING

To practice your writing skills, try one of the following suggestions.

1. Can you relate to Angie Erickson's experience? As a child, were you made fun of because you were different? Write an essay in which you explain what happened and how you coped with the situation.

2. Examine an essay that has been returned to you. Do your paragraphs have topic sentences? Does your whole essay have a central idea? Rewrite your essay to improve your topic sentences and central idea statement.

3. Write a paragraph or essay using one of the topics from the list at the end of Chapter 2. Choose a topic you have not yet used.

Checklist for Revision

1. Does your essay introduce the topic?

2. Does your essay contain a clear statement of main idea (thesis statement)?

3. Do your paragraphs have topic sentences?

4. Have you supported your thesis with enough evidence?

5. Does your essay have a conclusion?

6. Are you satisfied with your word choices?

7. Have you found and corrected your errors?

REFLECTIONS ON READING AND WRITING

Think about your reading. Also think about the courses you are taking this term and the reading demands of each. Do you find some subjects harder than others? Is one of your textbooks more difficult to read or to stay interested in than your others? What do you think accounts for the difference? What can you do to overcome the problem?

Chapter 4

Writing Your Main Idea

THINKING FIRST

- *How do I write a topic sentence for a paragraph?*
- *How do I write a thesis statement for an essay?*
- *How do a topic sentence and a thesis statement compare?*

Remember that when you read, you are the writer's audience, and you expect certain things. You want to know what the writer's topic is, what the writer thinks about the topic, and why or how the writer came to think that way. To understand what the writer thinks about the topic, you must find the main idea. To understand why or how the writer thinks a certain way, you must examine the details that support or explain the main idea.

Remember, also, that when you write, your readers are the audience and they expect the same things from you that you expect from other writers. You can meet those expectations by having clearly stated main ideas in your paragraphs and essays and by supporting your main ideas with details.

Getting started is often the biggest problem for writers. Some begin by selecting a topic and writing a brainstorming list as explained in Chapter 1. The details on the list may suggest a main idea. Other writers begin with a main idea in mind. They may brainstorm to discover the details that will best support it. How you begin is your choice. What is most important in writing is that you make a point and support the point.

This chapter explains how to write main ideas: topic sentences for paragraphs and a thesis statement for an essay. Because talking about main ideas without also mentioning details is difficult, this chapter mentions them. Details in reading and writing are discussed at length in Chapters 5 and 6.

BACKGROUND CHECK

Before reading the following essay, check your knowledge and assumptions about what it means to be excluded from a team.

1. What is your opinion about the value of school sports?

2. Those who do not make a team are "cut" from the team. Sometimes, the names of those who are cut are posted on a list for all to see. What is the effect of such lists?

3. Are both boys and girls victims of cut lists? What examples can you give?

4. Based on your survey of the title, author information, and first two paragraphs, what do you expect to follow?

5. What else do you know or think about the topic?

Cut

Bob Greene

Bob Greene is a columnist for the Chicago Tribune *and the author of many books. In the following essay Greene discusses the effects of trying out for a sports team and being rejected.*

VOCABULARY CHECK

vividly (1)	clearly and distinctly
descending (3)	from higher to lower, most to least
curious (6)	strangely interesting
inordinately (6)	unreasonably
relatively (8)	in comparison
articulate (12)	to express clearly
perceptions (13)	understanding arrived at through the senses
stoic (18)	unemotional
clutched (22)	became tense
fantasize (32)	imagine, dream

I remember vividly the last time I cried. I was twelve years old, in the   1
seventh grade, and I had tried out for the junior high school basketball team. I walked into the gymnasium; there was a piece of paper
tacked to the bulletin board.

It was a cut list. The seventh-grade coach had put it up on the   2
board. The boys whose names were on the list were still on the team;
they were welcome to keep on coming to practices. The boys whose
names were not on the list had been cut; their presence was no
longer desired. My name was not on the list.

I had not known the cut was coming that day. I stood and I   3
stared at the list. The coach had not composed it with a great deal of
subtlety; the names of the very best athletes were at the top of the
sheet of paper, and the other members of the squad were listed in
what appeared to be a descending order of talent. I kept looking at
the bottom of the list, hoping against hope that my name would
miraculously appear if I looked hard enough.

I held myself together as I walked out of the gym and out of the   4
school, but when I got home I began to sob. I couldn't stop. For the
first time in my life, I had been told officially that I wasn't good
enough. Athletics meant everything to boys that age; if you were on
the team, even as a substitute, it put you in the desirable group. If you
weren't on the team, you might as well not be alive.

I had tried desperately in practice, but the coach never seemed to   5
notice. It didn't matter how hard I was willing to work; he didn't want

me there. I knew that when I went to school the next morning I
would have to face the boys who had not been cut—the boys whose
names were on the list, who were still on the team, who had been
judged worthy while I had been judged unworthy.

All these years later, I remember it as if I were still standing right   6
there in the gym. And a curious thing has happened; in traveling
around the country, I have found that an inordinately large proportion
of successful men share that same memory—the memory of being cut
from a sports team as a boy.

I don't know how the mind works in matters like this; I don't know   7
what went on in my head following that day when I was cut. But I
know that my ambition has been enormous ever since then; I know
that for all of my life since that day, I have done more work than I had
to be doing, taken more assignments than I had to be taking, put in
more hours than I had to be spending. I don't know if all of that came
from a determination never to allow myself to be cut again—never to
allow someone to tell me that I'm not good enough again—but I know
it's there. And apparently it's there in a lot of other men too.

Bob Graham, thirty-six, is a partner with the Jenner & Block law firm   8
in Chicago. "When I was sixteen, baseball was my whole life," he said.
"I had gone to a relatively small high school, and I had been on the
team. But then my family moved, and I was going to a much bigger
high school. All during the winter months I told everyone that I was a
ball-player. When spring came, of course I went out for the team.

"The cut list went up. I did not make the team. Reading that cut   9
list is one of the clearest things I have in my memory. I wanted not to
believe it, but there it was.

"I went home and told my father about it. He suggested that   10
maybe I should talk to the coach. So I did. I pleaded to be put back on
the team. He said there was nothing he could do; he said he didn't
have enough room.

"I know for a fact that it altered my perception of myself. My   11
view of myself was knocked down; my self-esteem was lowered. I felt
so embarrassed; my whole life up to that point had revolved around
sports, and particularly around playing baseball. That was the group I
wanted to be in—the guys on the baseball team. And I was told that I
wasn't good enough to be one of them.

"I know now that it changed me. I found out, even though I   12
couldn't articulate it at the time, that there would be times in my life
when certain people would be in a position to say 'You're not good
enough' to me. I did not want that to happen ever again.

"It seems obvious to me now that being cut was what started me   13
in determining that my success would always be based on my own

abilities, and not on someone else's perceptions. Since then I've always been something of an overachiever; when I came to the law firm I was very aggressive in trying to run my own cases right away, to be the lead lawyer in the cases with which I was involved. I made partner at thirty-one; I never wanted to be left behind.

"Looking back, maybe it shouldn't have been that important. It   14
was only baseball. You pass that by. Here I am. That coach is probably still there, still a high school baseball coach, still cutting boys off the baseball team every year. I wonder how many hundreds of boys he's cut in his life?"

Maurice McGrath is senior vice-president of Genstar Mortgage Corpo-   15
ration, a mortgage banking firm in Glendale, California. "I'm forty-seven years old, and I was fourteen when it happened to me, and I still feel something when I think about it," he said.

"I was in the eighth grade. I went to St. Philip's School in   16
Pasadena. I went out for the baseball team, and one day at practice the coach came over to me. He was an Occidental College student who had been hired as the eighth-grade coach.

"He said, 'You're no good.' Those were his words. I asked him   17
why he was saying that. He said, 'You can't hit the ball. I don't want you here.' I didn't know what to do, so I went over and sat off to the side, watching the others practice. The coach said I should leave the practice field. He said that I wasn't on the team, and that I didn't belong there anymore.

"I was outwardly stoic about it. I didn't want anyone to see how I   18
felt. I didn't want to show that it hurt. But oh, did it hurt. All my friends played baseball after school every day. My best friend was the pitcher on the team. After I got whittled down by the coach, I would hear the other boys talking in class about what they were going to do at practice after school. I knew that I'd just have to go home.

"I guess you make your mind up never to allow yourself to be   19
hurt like that again. In some way I must have been saying to myself, 'I'll play the game better.' Not the sports game, but anything I tried. I must have been saying, 'If I have to, I'll sit on the bench, but I'll be part of the team.'

"I try to make my own kids believe that, too. I try to tell them   20
that they should show that they're a little bit better than the rest. I tell them to think of themselves as better. Who cares what anyone else thinks? You know, I can almost hear that coach saying the words, 'You're no good.'"

Author Malcolm MacPherson *(The Blood of His Servants),* forty, lives in   21
New York. "It happened to me in the ninth grade, at the Yalesville

School in Yalesville, Connecticut," he said. "Both of my parents had just been killed in a car crash, and as you can imagine, it was a very difficult time in my life. I went out for the baseball team, and I did pretty well in practice.

"But in the first game I clutched. I was playing second base; the batter hit a popup, and I moved back to catch it. I can see it now. I felt dizzy as I looked up at the ball. It was like I was moving in slow motion, but the ball was going at regular speed. I couldn't get out of the way of my own feet. The ball dropped to the ground. I didn't catch it. 22

"The next day at practice, the coach read off the lineup. I wasn't on it. I was off the squad. 23

"I remember what I did: I walked. It was a cold spring afternoon, and the ground was wet, and I just walked. I was living with an aunt and uncle, and I didn't want to go home. I just wanted to walk forever. 24

"It drove my opinion of myself right into a tunnel. Right into a cave. And when I came out of that cave, something inside of me wanted to make sure in one manner or another that I would never again be told I wasn't good enough. 25

"I will confess that my ambition, to this day, is out of control. It's like a fire. I think the fire would have pretty much stayed in control if I hadn't been cut from that team. But that got it going. You don't slice ambition two ways; it's either there or it isn't. Those of us who went through something like that always know that we have to catch the ball. We'd rather die than have the ball fall at our feet. 26

"Once that fire is started in us, it never gets extinguished, until we die or have heart attacks or something. Sometimes I wonder about the home-run hitters; the guys who never even had to worry about being cut. They may have gotten the applause and the attention back then, but I wonder if they ever got the fire. I doubt it. I think maybe you have to get kicked in the teeth to get the fire started. 27

"You can tell the effect of something like that by examining the trail you've left in your life, and tracing it backward. It's almost like being a junkie with a need for success. You get attention and applause and you like it, but you never quite trust it. Because you know that back then you were good enough if only they would have given you a chance. You don't trust what you achieve, because you're afraid that someone will take it away from you. You know that it can happen; it already did. 28

"So you try to show people how good you are. Maybe you don't go out and become Dan Rather; maybe you just end up owning the Pontiac dealership in your town. But it's your dealership, and you're the top man, and every day you're showing people that you're good enough." 29

*   *   *

Dan Rather, fifty-two, is anchor of the *CBS Evening News.* "When I   30
was thirteen, I had rheumatic fever," he said. "I became extremely
skinny and extremely weak, but I still went out for the seventh-grade
baseball team at Alexander Hamilton Junior High School in Houston.

"The school was small enough that there was no cut as such; you   31
were supposed to figure out that you weren't good enough, and quit.
Game after game I sat at the end of the bench, hoping that maybe
this was the time I would get in. The coach never even looked at me; I
might as well have been invisible.

"I told my mother about it. Her advice was not to quit. So I went   32
to practice every day, and I tried to do well so that the coach would
be impressed. He never even knew I was there. At home in my room I
would fantasize that there was a big game, and the three guys in
front of me would all get hurt, and the coach would turn to me and
put me in, and I would make the winning hit. But then there'd be another game, and the late innings would come, and if we were way
ahead I'd keep hoping that this was the game when the coach would
put me in. He never did.

"When you're that age, you're looking for someone to tell you   33
you're okay. Your sense of self-esteem is just being formed. And what
that experience that baseball season did was make me think that perhaps I wasn't okay.

"In the last game of the season something terrible happened. It   34
was the last of the ninth inning, there were two outs, and there were
two strikes on the batter. And the coach turned to me and told me to
go out to right field.

"It was a totally humiliating thing for him to do. For him to put   35
me in for one pitch, the last pitch of the season, in front of all the
other guys on the team . . . I stood out there for that one pitch, and I
just wanted to sink into the ground and disappear. Looking back on
it, it was an extremely unkind thing for him to have done. That was
nearly forty years ago, and I don't know why the memory should be
so vivid now; I've never known if the coach was purposely making fun
of me—and if he was, why a grown man would do that to a thirteen-
year-old boy.

"I'm not a psychologist. I don't know if a man can point to one   36
event in his life and say that that's the thing that made him the way
he is. But when you're that age, and you're searching for your own
identity, and all you want is to be told that you're all right . . . I wish I
understood it better, but I know the feeling is still there."

THINKING CRITICALLY

Main Idea

1. What is Bob Greene's thesis, and where is it stated?

Details

2. What was Greene's experience of being cut, and how did he feel about it at the time?

3. How has the experience affected Greene in later life?

Organization

4. To organize his essay, Greene provides examples of men who, like him, recall being cut from a sports team and how the experience changed them. Briefly explain who these men are and what happened to them.

Purpose, Audience, Tone

5. Who is Greene's audience? What does he expect his audience to know in order to get his point?

Inferences and Conclusions

6. Do you know of women who have had experiences similar to those Greene describes? Give an example.

Making Connections

Based on your reading of the essay, do you think Greene would agree or disagree with the statement, "sports build character"? Do you agree with the statement? Why or why not?

WRITING A TOPIC SENTENCE

As explained in Chapter 3, the main idea of a paragraph is often stated in a topic sentence, which tells you what the writer's topic and opinion about the topic are. These two parts of the topic sentence are sometimes called the *topic* and the *focus*. To write a topic sentence, ask yourself two questions to help you determine a topic and focus.

1. What is my topic?

2. What is my opinion about the topic?

In addition to having a topic and focus, a good topic sentence is neither too general nor too specific. It is general enough to tell your readers what the whole paragraph is about, but it is specific enough to focus on a single idea, thought, or opinion that you can explain. Read the next three example sentences.

1. Everyone recognizes that crime is a problem.

2. My parents' home was burglarized two months ago.

3. Burglar-proofing your home is easy if you follow these steps to discourage robbers.

The first sentence is too general to be a topic sentence for two reasons. First of all, *crime* is too broad a topic for a single paragraph. What does the writer want to say about crime? What kind of crime does the writer want to discuss and why? Does the writer plan to offer a solution to the problem of crime? Second, the writer says that everyone knows crime is a problem, but what does the writer think and why? None of this is clear because the sentence lacks a focus.

The second sentence is too specific to be a topic sentence because it simply states a fact that need not be explained further. Also, it is not clear what this writer's topic is. Perhaps the writer wants to write a paragraph about the burglary of his or her parents' home. It could be that the real topic is home burglaries in general and that they are on the rise. The second sentence may be an introductory sentence that the writer plans to follow with a topic sentence that does make clear what the topic and focus are.

The third sentence is neither too general nor too specific. It would make a good topic sentence because the topic, *burglar-proofing your home,* and the focus, *it is easy if you follow these steps,* are clear. The sentence also tells us what details to anticipate: the steps to follow and an explanation of each one.

Exercise 4.1   In each of the following topic sentences, underline the *topic* once and the *focus* (writer's opinion) twice. Be prepared to explain your choices.

1. Fast-food junkies can break the habit by following three simple steps.

2. Those who are against the building of a new city hall can think of better ways to spend the money it will cost.

3. The macaw has several features that make it a desirable pet.

4. Cereal commercials are aimed at two main groups: children who like sweets and adults who are interested in fiber and nutrition.

5. The annual meeting of the Experimental Aircraft Association provides activities that the whole family can enjoy.

Exercise 4.2   Choose three topics from the following list and write a topic sentence for each. Make sure your sentence states your topic and focus and is neither too general nor too specific.

    Clothing styles   Low-calorie foods

    Apartment living   Athletes' salaries

    Cellular phones   Stress reduction

Exercise 4.3   As explained in Chapter 3, some of the paragraphs you read have topic sentences while in others the main idea is implied. To find an implied main idea, you must make inferences from the details. Read the following paragraph and answer the questions to infer the main idea. Then write a topic sentence for the paragraph.

The first thing to go wrong was that all the parking spaces were taken, so I had to park on the grass and hope that I would not get a ticket. When I got to the admissions office, the line was already all the way out the door. By the time it was my turn to register, all but one of the courses I needed were filled, so I had to go back to my adviser and make out a whole new schedule. Although I did finally get registered, I missed lunch. As I was leaving, I wondered what else could possibly go wrong.

1. What is the writer's topic?

2. What are the details that reveal the writer's topic?

3. What is the writer's focus? What do you think this writer thinks about the situation he or she is in?

4. What words or details help you infer the writer's focus?

5. Write a topic sentence for the paragraph. Make sure your sentence states the topic and focus.

_____

_____

As a beginning writer, you may find topic sentences very helpful. A good topic sentence controls your choice of details because each detail must support the topic sentence. As you gain experience, you may want to experiment with writing paragraphs that have implied main ideas. You can add variety to the paragraphs within an essay by stating some of your main ideas and implying others. At first, however, you should plan to write a topic sentence for every paragraph both as a guide for yourself and as a help for your readers.

WRITING A THESIS STATEMENT

Your *thesis* is the central idea of your essay. The *thesis statement* is usually one sentence in the introductory part of your essay that states your point. A good thesis statement clearly identifies your topic and sets limits that keep your ideas focused on the point you want to make. Everything you write, especially each main idea or topic sentence of every paragraph, should relate to your thesis. This section explains how to write a thesis statement.

Not just any sentence, or group of sentences, can be a *thesis* statement. As you think of ways to state your central idea, you need to be aware of the difference between simple statements and thesis statements. A simple statement is complete in itself and needs no further explanation. A thesis statement, however, contains both a *topic* and a *focus.* Your thesis statement should tell your readers not only what your topic is but what you think about it. Following are two statements: the first is a simple statement complete in itself. The second is a thesis statement.

1. Algebra is a required course at my college.

2. Students can improve their performance in algebra by applying ten strategies for success in math courses.

The first statement contains a topic only. All you can do is agree or disagree with the statement. The second statement contains both a topic and a focus. The topic is *performance in algebra* and the focus is that *students can improve their performance by applying ten strategies.* You can do a lot more with this statement than agree or disagree with it. You can ask yourself what the ten strategies are, how to apply them, and whether they will help you improve your performance in algebra.

In the following examples of thesis statements, the topic and focus are annotated for you.

Topic

Example 1:   Television commercials on Saturday morning cartoon shows [encourage the development of bad habits in children.]

Focus

Focus

Example 2:   [Parents should find a more beneficial activity to occupy their children on Saturday mornings than] watching cartoons on TV.

Topic

Focus

Example 3:   [A TV program that reflects the new permissiveness in childrearing] is *The Simpsons.*

Topic

Exercise 4.4   Read and think about each sentence below, then circle whether it is a thesis statement (TS) or a simple statement (SS). In the thesis statements you identify, draw a line under the writer's *topic* and bracket the writer's focus, as in the examples on page 105. Be able to explain your choices.

1. I have been working as a teller at First Union Bank on Center Street for the last fifteen years.   TS   SS

2. As a bank teller I have learned several effective ways to deal with difficult customers.   TS   SS

3. Some women work as volunteer firefighters.

   TS   SS

4. I like my job as a firefighter because it is both personally rewarding and socially responsible.   TS   SS

5. Armadillos should not be sold as pets because most people cannot provide the food, climate, and habitat these animals need.

   TS   SS

Exercise 4.5   Discuss the following simple statements with a partner. How could you rewrite them to make them into thesis statements? Report your conclusions to the whole class.

1. My dog is an expensive pet.

2. Most people get a driver's license when they are teenagers.

3. Many students have trouble concentrating.

5. An explosion occurred in the fitness center.

6. I do most of my studying in the library.

Understanding the Parts of the Thesis Statement

Although the thesis statement has two basic parts, *topic* and *focus,* the focus can be broken down further into *opinion, purpose,* and *parts.*

The *opinion* is what you think, believe, or know about the topic. The *purpose* is your reason for writing: what you want readers to know or understand. The *parts* suggest how you will analyze (break down) your topic and organize the supporting details. Suppose you believe that participating in a sport is beneficial in several ways. You have arrived at this opinion because you play tennis and it has become an important part of your life. You choose tennis as your topic because it has given you a great deal of pleasure, but you are having difficulty deciding what the focus is. Figure 4.1 lists five questions to ask that will help you think through your topic and come up with a focus to make an effective thesis statement. Answering the questions will help you limit your topic and identify the opinion, purpose, and parts of your focus.

Exercise 4.6   Choose two topics from the list below, or make up your own topics based on what interests you. Answer the five questions in Figure 4.1 on page 108 to limit each topic and break down your focus into opinion, purpose, and parts. Next, write a thesis statement for each of your two topics.

Sports	Recreational activities
College courses	Parties
Current fashions	Diets

Although writers may place the thesis statement anywhere in an essay, you will usually find it near the beginning of a short essay or near the end of an introduction to a longer one, as in Bob Greene's essay on pages 96–100. It is important for you as a beginning writer to state your thesis at the beginning of your essay for two reasons. First, your thesis lets your readers know what to expect. Secondly, just as the topic sentence of a paragraph limits and controls what you write in the rest of the paragraph, the thesis statement limits and controls what you write in the rest of your essay and helps you stay organized and on topic. In fact, topic sentences and thesis statements have several characteristics in common, as illustrated in Figure 4.2 on page 109.

Checking Thesis Statements for Completeness

If your thesis statement is missing a topic, opinion, purpose, or parts, you may run into one of several common problems. Read the example below:

1a.   We need to do something to solve the problem of crime in our cities.

This statement might work as an interest grabber in an introductory paragraph, but it is not a suitable thesis statement. Although it expresses a topic (crime in our cities) and an opinion (we need to do something) it lacks the *purpose* and *parts* that would limit the thesis and

---

FIGURE 4.1

**Writing
a Thesis
Statement:
Five
Questions**

QUESTION	ANSWER
1. What is the *general topic*?	Sports.
2. What is my *limited topic*?	The benefits of tennis.
3. What is my *opinion* about the limited topic?	Playing tennis is a sport I enjoy because of its benefits.
4. What is my *purpose* in writing about this topic?	To tell readers why I enjoy tennis so that they will have a better understanding of the benefits of playing this game.
5. How will I break down my topic into *parts* I can explain in two or more body paragraphs?	I will tell readers what the benefits of playing tennis are for me: social interaction, improved fitness, and challenge of the game.

To write a thesis statement that contains *topic, opinion, purpose,* and *parts* combine your answers to the five questions, and write a complete sentence like the ones below:

    Opinion   **Topic**   **Purpose**

I. I enjoy playing tennis because it gives me the benefits of [social interaction, improved fitness, and a challenging game.]

                               Parts

            Topic   **Purpose**

2. Attending a major league baseball game is better than watching one on television [because the crowd's excitement is contagious, the view of the field is unlimited, and it provides good entertainment for a date.]

                Purpose and parts are combined

FIGURE 4.2

Comparison of Topic Sentence and Thesis Statement

TOPIC SENTENCE	THESIS STATEMENT
Limits the topic covered in the paragraph	Limits the topic covered in the essay
States the main idea of the paragraph	States the central idea of the essay
Controls the selection of details to support the paragraph's main idea	Controls the selection of details to support the essay's thesis
Suggests how the writer has organized the paragraph	Suggests how the writer has organized the essay
Helps the writer maintain unity in the paragraph	Helps the writer maintain unity in the essay

clarify the writer's point. It is not clear *why* the writer chose the topic or *what* she wants to tell us about it. Also, "crime in our cities" covers a lot of ground. The writer should limit the topic to something more specific, such as "burglaries in our neighborhood." Below is a revision of example 1a that includes purpose and parts:

Purpose and opinion are combined: we started the program because we want to prevent burglaries.

Topic

1b.   To prevent burglaries in our neighborhood we have started a neighborhood watch program that includes a five-point plan for home protection.   **Parts**

The sentence in example 2a below is not a suitable thesis statement because it does not tell you what the writer thinks about the speed limit, what he thinks should be done about it, or why readers should be concerned. It lacks an *opinion, purpose,* and *parts.* Example 2b is a revision that includes the missing parts.

2a.   The 55-miles-per-hour speed limit is still the law in many parts of the United States. (unsuitable)

Purpose and parts are combined: why speed limit should be raised, how it causes problems

Topic

2b.   Although the 55-miles-per-hour speed limit has been raised on some interstate highways, it

Opinion   should be raised everywhere because it has created problems in traffic management and because it has not acted as a deterrent to speeding. (better)

The topic in example 3a is study skills, and the opinion is that study skills are important. The writer has broken the topic down into three parts: time management, goal setting, and note taking. But what is the writer's *purpose?* As a thesis statement, this sentence is unsuitable because readers cannot tell what the writer wants them to know or do about study skills. Example 3b provides the missing information.

3a. Time management, goal setting, and note taking are three important study skills. (unsuitable)

Parts

3b. Time management, goal setting, and note tak-
Topic ing are three important study skills college stu-   **Purpose**
dents can develop that may help them improve
their grades. (better)   **Opinion**

The writer of the sentence in example 4a has expressed two opinions about two topics in her thesis, so the statement is confusing. As a result, her purpose is unclear also. A thesis statement should cover only *one* topic. Examples 4b and 4c illustrate two ways to revise the statement.

4a. I disagree with those people who want to abolish college sports, and I also think college athletes should have to maintain good grades. (unsuitable)

                Opinion   **Topic**

Purpose and parts
are combined: why   4b. I disagree with those who want to abolish col-
she disagrees, how   lege sports because sports are a source of rev-
she breaks down   enue for the college, an extracurricular activity
topic   that appeals to most students, and an oppor-
                              tunity for athletic scholarships. (better)

                Topic   **Opinion**

Purpose and parts are   4c. College athletes should have to maintain good
combined: why ath-   grades because they should have to meet the
letes should keep good   same requirements as all students and because
grades; requirements   they should prepare themselves for careers
and careers are parts   outside the field of professional sports. (better)
that will be explained

Exercise 4.7   Check the thesis statements below for completeness, then rewrite them to add any missing parts.

1. Teenage alcohol abuse is on the rise.

2. People who run for office may have their private lives exposed in the media.

3. Many students are opting for careers in health care.

4. Even if I had the opportunity, I would not want to be sixteen years old again.

5. During President Clinton's first term, he was able to accomplish several of his goals within his first 100 days in office.

6. Right-to-work laws are in effect in several states.

THINKING ABOUT PROCESS

Which comes first, the main idea or the details? Remember that writing is a recursive process. The steps in the process and their sequence depend on the writer. We may speak of three basic steps—prewriting, drafting and organizing, rewriting—but this is for convenience only.

1. Some writers select a topic and immediately think of a main idea. These writers may start out with a working topic sentence or thesis statement that controls their selection of details. Later, they may revise the main idea.

2. Some writers select a topic but are not sure what they want to say about it. These writers may brainstorm their topic or generate an idea cluster that helps them discover a main idea. If these steps do not work, they may decide to change their topic. Once they have settled on a main idea, they may look at their lists or clusters again, selecting some details and rejecting others.

3. Writing, like reading, is an individual process. Although you can follow guidelines and use proven strategies that have worked for many readers and writers, in the end you must find the process that works for you.

INTRODUCING THE THESIS

Writing a good introduction to your essay is a way of building readers' interest and placing your thesis within a meaningful context. Your essay's introduction, therefore, is also the introduction to your thesis statement. Although many strategies exist for writing effective introductions, the five listed below may be especially helpful to you. Each strategy helps create a context for your thesis.

1. Supply *background information.*

2. Relate an *anecdote.*

3. Begin with a *quotation and explanation.*

4. Use interesting *facts and figures.*

5. Ask a revealing *question.*

Supply Background Information

Supplying background information creates a context for your thesis; it is like setting the scene of a play. Before you make your point in the thesis statement, lead up to it by identifying the situation, events, or issues that are relevant to your point. Suppose you are writing about why you think the 55-miles-per-hour speed limit should be raised in your community. You build a background for your discussion by reminding readers of why the speed limit was enacted into law in the first place: to conserve oil during the 1970s when the United States was in the middle of an energy crisis. Lowering the speed limit had the secondary effect of reducing the number of accidents resulting from speeding, so that was another good reason to keep the limit at 55 miles per hour. If your point is that the speed limit needs to be raised because the oil crisis is over and because traffic accidents resulting from speeding can be reduced in other ways, the background information you provide can help readers place your point in the proper context. The following excerpt from "I Married an Accountant" by Joe Queenan introduces a thesis by supplying background information. The thesis is underlined.

> At the mature age of 39, a somewhat immature 220-pound friend of   1
> mine took up ice hockey. Though he had never before strapped on ice
> skates and is far from fit, he has spent virtually every Sunday evening

for the past two summers barreling up and down the ice in a special hockey league for aging neophytes. He may be strange, but he is not boring.

2   Another person I know moved to Teheran in the late 1970s, met an Iranian woman, converted to Islam so he could marry her, and had to undergo a circumcision—all of this took place against the backdrop of massive civil unrest in Iran. He, too, may be strange, but he is not boring.

3   This is equally true of my wife, who for three years wrote video scripts for a man who had previously directed the Gothic soap opera *Dark Shadows*. Though the subject of her continuing-education scripts had few ghoulish elements, she can nevertheless claim to have worked closely with a colleague of Jonathan Frid, the famous TV vampire. It is an honor she will take to her grave. She, like the aging hockey player and the intrepid voyager to Iran, has led a rich, interesting life and has done exciting, unpredictable things. Like them, she is also an accountant.

4   Accountants have long been the targets of satirists and have been mercilessly lambasted by everyone from Monty Python to the rock group The Kinks. Personally, I hold no brief for accountants as a unit and would be loath to argue that they are, collectively or individually, electrifying fireballs. Yet nothing in my experience would lead me to the conclusion that accountants are quantifiably less interesting than people in other occupations.

5   Thus I have often wondered why these attacks on accountants continue at a time when numerous other professions would make equally suitable targets. . . .

Queenan's article takes a humorous look at the prevailing stereotype of accountants as boring. Queenan believes that many other professions would make suitable targets as "most boring job." To introduce his thesis, he provides background information in the form of three examples of accountants he knows who have led interesting lives. The rest of the article, contains examples of the professionals Queenan thinks are boring—for example: systems engineers, investment bankers, public relations consultants, and writers. Queenan's opinion is that accountants are no less interesting than anyone else. His implied purpose is to persuade readers through the use of humor that other professions are as boring, or even more so, than accounting. The phrase "numerous other professions" implies the parts of Queenan's thesis to be developed in the essay: examples of boring professions.

Relate an Anecdote

An *anecdote* is a brief story or narration of an event. Used as an introductory strategy, the anecdote can vividly establish a context for the point you make in your thesis. The first five paragraphs of Bob Greene's essay on pages 96–100 are an anecdote. By narrating the intense feelings surrounding his being cut from the high school basketball team, Greene establishes a context for his later thesis statement: that being "cut" early in life makes men more ambitious in later life.

In the following excerpt, Gregg Easterbrook uses an anecdote to begin his essay "Escape Valve." The thesis statement is underlined.

> A man and woman I know moved in together recently. It was, as such occasions are, a moment of sentiment and celebration. It was also a limited engagement. Before moving in, they had already set a fixed date when they would break up.
>
> They explained their reasons to one and all. In a year, the woman planned to change jobs and cities; the man did not plan to follow. An eventual split is unfortunate, they said, but also inevitable, so why not plan on it? Yet, far from being a sad twist of fate, my woman friend's scheduled departure, I fear, was a liberating force, making possible whatever short-term romance the couple will enjoy. Without the escape clause of a preset termination of their affair, they might never have lived together at all.
>
> This situation is not unique. More and more, people are ordering their lives along a principle I call the "automatic-out." <u>In love, friendship, work, and the community, people increasingly prefer arrangements that automatically end at some preset date.</u> . . .

The anecdote builds a context for Easterbrook's thesis statement by relating an incident that illustrates what he means by an "automatic-out"—a concept that may be new to many readers.

Begin with a Quotation and Explanation

Quotations from books, poems, articles, experts in a certain field, or interviews you have had with people who are involved in some way with your topic can add authority to your opinions. Using quotations shows readers that others have thought about your topic and formed opinions about it. If you begin with one or more quotations, you need to explain what they mean and how they relate to your thesis. The quotation may illustrate your point or back it up with an expert's opinion. The following excerpt is from the introduction to "Wagon Train Children," an essay by Elliot West. The thesis statement is underlined.

> The historian Francis Parkman, strolling around Independence, Mo., in 1846, remarked upon the "multitude of healthy children's faces . . . peeping out from under the covers of the wagons." Two decades later, a traveler wrote of husbands packing up "sunburned women and wild-looking children," along with shovels and flour barrels, in preparation for the journey West. In the gold fields of California in the 1850s, a chronicler met four sisters and sisters-in-law who had just crossed the Great Plains with 36 of their children. "They could," she wrote, "form quite a respectable village." 1
>
> In the great overland migration that lasted from 1841 until the start of the Civil War, more than a quarter of a million people pushed their way from the Missouri valley to the Pacific coast. Probably at least 35,000 of them were young girls and boys; except during the Gold Rush, at least every fifth person on the trails was a child. Yet in all we read today, these thousands of young emigrants are infrequently seen and almost never heard. 2
>
> The voices of many of them do survive, though. Some kept diaries along the way that have been preserved; many others wrote down their memories later. These records permit glimpses of a life that children of today might easily dream about—a child's life of adventure and purpose, of uncertainty and danger, albeit sometimes of sheer boredom. . . . 3

The rest of West's article explains some of the experiences recorded in the diaries and memoirs of pioneer children. His purpose is to reveal a point that historians have ignored even though plenty of evidence indicates that thousands of children traveled in wagon trains to the West. The quotations that introduce the thesis verify this point and therefore create a context for West's thesis.

Use Interesting Facts and Figures

Facts and figures such as dates, times, names of people, places, and statistics add interest and realism to your writing, and statistics can act as evidence to support your thesis. Suppose you are disturbed by the commercials on children's television programs that promote sugared cereals. To gather evidence, you count the number of times "sugar" or other words that refer to sweetness are mentioned in several commercials. You find that the number is surprisingly large, and you decide to use it in your introduction to establish a basis for your opinion that too much of this kind of advertising is directed at children.

Dates also provide historical context as in the excerpt from "Wagon Train Children." The dates mentioned in the essay's introduction, 1841 and 1846, establish the context of the westward migration of families that occurred during this period of the United States' history. Names of people and places can interest readers in your topic as illustrated in the following example in which the thesis statement is underlined.

> To the list of professional basketball players such as Magic Johnson, Michael Jordan, and Larry Bird who have become household words, we can now add another name: Shaquille O'Neal or "Shaq" for short. A few short years ago Shaq was yet another high school basketball player who had dreams of becoming an NBA player. But unlike the great majority of high school hopefuls, Shaq had the unbeatable talent of which sports fame and fortune are made. Shaq began his career with the Orlando Magic. He now plays for the Los Angeles Lakers. How Shaquille O'Neal was discovered, and how he became a nationally known player make an interesting story. . . .

People who follow sports will recognize the names of famous athletes that help provide a context for the thesis. Orlando, Florida, is a place many readers may recognize whether they follow sports or not. Shaquille O'Neal is the topic; the writer's opinion is that Shaq's rise to fame is an interesting story, and the writer plans to discuss how Shaq was discovered and how he became a nationally known player. The writer's purpose is to inform readers about Shaq, another household name in the world of professional basketball.

The following excerpt from "The Trouble with Television," an essay by Robert MacNeil, makes use of statistics to introduce the thesis, which is underlined.

> It is difficult to escape the influence of television. If you fit the statistical averages, by the age of 20 you will have been exposed to at least 20,000 hours of television. You can add 10,000 hours for each decade you have lived after the age of 20. The only things Americans do more than watch television are work and sleep.   1
>
>   Calculate for a moment what could be done with even a part of   2

those hours. Five thousand hours, I am told, are what a typical college undergraduate spends working on a bachelor's degree. In 10,000 hours you could have learned enough to become an astronomer or engineer. You could have learned several languages fluently. If it appealed to you, you could be reading Homer in the original Greek or Dostoyevsky in Russian. If it didn't, you could have walked around the world and written a book about it.

The trouble with television is that it discourages concentration. Almost anything interesting and rewarding in life requires some constructive, consistently applied effort. The dullest, the least gifted of us can achieve things that seem miraculous to those who never concentrate on anything. But television encourages us to apply no effort. It sells us instant gratification. It diverts us only to divert, to make the time pass without pain. . . .

3

Using facts and figures as an introductory strategy builds a context for MacNeil's thesis statement by establishing the pervasive influence of television. MacNeil's topic is television; his opinion is that there is *trouble* with television; he specifies the kind or *part* of trouble he will discuss as *discourages concentration*. Although MacNeil's purpose is not directly stated in his thesis, you can assume that he means to inform readers of the ways television discourages concentration. The rest of the essay explains how television's appeal to the short attention span has affected our language, the way we think, and our tolerance for effort.

Ask a Revealing Question

Beginning an essay with a question works best if the question you ask is new, surprising, or something readers may not have thought to ask. The question must also be a *revealing* one that clarifies what the essay is about. The following excerpt is from a section of the first chapter of *The Practical Entomologist* by Rick Imes. The thesis statement is underlined.

Just what are insects, anyway? Often, any small creature with more than four legs is indiscriminately labeled a "bug," but true bugs represent only one of many different groups of insects. What's more, many of these creepy, crawling critters are not insects at all, but may belong to one of several related but very different groups.

1

Insects, as it turns out, are characterized by several easily recog-   2
nized traits that set them apart from any other group of organisms.
Like other members of the Phylum Arthropoda (which, literally trans-
lated, means "jointed foot"), and unlike mammals, for example, insects possess an external skeleton, or *exoskeleton,* which encases
their internal organs, supporting them as our skeleton supports us
and protecting them as would a suit of armor on a medieval knight.
Unlike other arthropods, their body is divided into three distinct regions—the *head, thorax,* and *abdomen.* Insects are the only animals
that have three pairs of jointed legs, no more or less, and these six
legs are attached to the thorax, the middle region of the body. . . .

The first chapter of Imes's book is titled "The Basics of Entomol-
ogy," and in the excerpt above, his thesis, or point, is that several traits
determine which organisms can be classified as insects. The rest of the
excerpt following the thesis describes more of the traits. The question
that begins the thesis is a surprising one because most readers think
they know what an insect is. Furthermore, the question is central to the
development of Imes's chapter, which sets forth the basics of the study
of insects and their behavior.

Exercise 4.8   Identify which of the following introductory strategies the writers of the
next five passages use. In addition, underline the thesis statement in
each passage. Explain the reasons for your choices.

- Supply *background information.*
- Relate an *anecdote.*
- Begin with a *quotation and explanation.*
- Use interesting *facts and figures.*
- Ask a revealing *question.*

1. If you heard in a television commercial that half the dentists surveyed recommended SMILE toothpaste, you might want to try it.
   But if you were a wise consumer, you would realize that the other
   half didn't recommend the toothpaste, so maybe "half" isn't such a
   good number after all. You would also realize that although half of
   2,000 is 1,000 and that is a lot of dentists, half of two is just one dentist. In either case, however, 50 percent is still 50 percent, which

means that half the dentists surveyed would not recommend SMILE toothpaste. Untrained consumers have a way of hearing only the positive side of the messages in television commercials. You can become a wise consumer by learning to spot the seven common tricks that advertisers use to make you want to buy their products. . . .

2. Is high school football a luxury we cannot afford? A school district in our area is considering abolishing athletic events as a way to cut costs in this year of budget cutbacks and an uncertain economy. Uniforms cost money. So do coaches' salaries, equipment, concessions at football games, electricity for running the scoreboard and field lights, transportation to away games, and other related expenditures. The money saved from these could be used to buy science lab equipment, new books for the library, and computers, to name a few of our needs that the school board has been exploring. High school football is something most community members take for granted, and surely the students will be the losers if they do not have the experience of cheering their teams to victory. Perhaps if we can find other ways to cut costs, then football may be the luxury that we *can* afford. . . .

3. When the late president John F. Kennedy said, "Ask not what your country can do for you; ask what you can do for your country," he exhorted a nation of young people to get involved in the political process and to take an active role in the fashioning of their government. For the first time in the history of the United States, a president appealed to young people as adults, not children, and they rose in force to meet his challenge, joining the Peace Corps and the ranks of others in service to humankind. Kennedy was their man, and since his death there has been no other. If future presidents of the United States want to capture the youth vote, they will have to do several things to gain young people's respect and support. . . .

4. The story of the search for radium is a romantic and stirring one. Behind it is a woman who was passionately curious, daring in her convictions, and determined to work in an age hardly encouraging to professional aspirations among those of her sex. From a dilapidated shed, described by one German chemist at the time as a "cross between a stable and a potato-cellar," came a discovery that would throw light on the structure of the atom, open new doors in medicine, and save lives in future generations.

Marie Sklodowska came to Paris and the Sorbonne in 1891 as a reticent Polish woman of twenty-four. Taking a solitary room in the Latin Quarter, she began her studies in mathematics and physics. By 1897 she had two university degrees and a fellowship, as well as a husband and a newborn daughter. In the physicist Pierre Curie, Marie had found both an adviser and a lover, someone as serious as she, who shared her interests and became drawn into her quest. . . .

Excerpted from "How Did They Discover Radium?" in *How Did They Do That?* by Caroline Sutton.

Now read the next three paragraphs to see how you can introduce the same thesis three different ways. The thesis statement is underlined in each paragraph.

1. The headline "Dieters Gain Back More Weight than They Lost on Starvation Diet" introduced a newspaper article that appeared after several famous people who had lost as much as sixty pounds regained the weight. Now most of them are on another diet. Like many people, they are on a harmful gain-lose-regain cycle brought on by quick-loss diets that disrupt the metabolic process. Most doctors and nutritionists recommend that people lose no more than two pounds per week and that they eat balanced meals. To lose weight sensibly and without risking health, people should limit the number of calories they eat, continue to eat balanced meals, and do some form of aerobic exercise several times a week.

2. Only about 10 percent of the people who lose weight on highly advertised quick-weight-loss programs actually keep it off. The other 90 percent gain back all their weight and then some within about three to six months. Quick-loss programs fool the body into thinking it is starving. Metabolism slows down to adjust to the lowered caloric intake. When the dieter returns to normal eating habits, the metabolic rate stays low, so even fewer calories are burned than before the person went on the diet in the first place. As a result, he or she gains back the weight and has even more trouble losing it in the future. Diets do not work. A change in eating and exercise habits does. To lose weight sensibly and without risking health, people should limit the number of calories they eat, continue to eat balanced meals, and do some form of aerobic exercise several times a week.

3. The summer was just beginning, and Marina wanted to take off the weight she had put on during her first year of college. A year of

studying and partying had left her no time to fix and eat proper meals and even less time for exercise. Now she wanted to get in shape for a new bathing suit and weekends at the beach. She saw an ad in a magazine selling a new diet program that promised a loss of up to seven pounds in one week. The before-and-after pictures convinced her that in three weeks she could have the body she wanted. She started on the program, and in a little less than three weeks she had lost the weight. Marina was thrilled at first, but when the pounds started creeping back, she did not know what to do. Her doctor told her that quick-loss programs do not work because they disrupt the metabolic process. Most people who try these programs fail to keep the weight off. Marina learned the hard way that most activities that are worth the effort take time. She still wants to lose weight, but now she will follow her doctor's advice. To lose weight sensibly and without risking health, people should limit the number of calories they eat, continue to eat balanced meals, and do some form of aerobic exercise several times a week.

The first paragraph begins with a *quotation and explanation*. The second paragraph begins with a *figure*, and the third paragraph begins with an *anecdote*. All three paragraphs contain essentially the same information, and all introduce the same thesis. The choice of an introductory strategy depends upon your purpose and audience. In the preceding examples, the first two paragraphs might be more suitable for a general audience than the third one, which is aimed at college students.

How you begin your essay determines what the rest of your essay will be about. Without a well-thought-out introduction and clear thesis statement, you will have difficulty developing your ideas, and your readers will have difficulty following them. To avoid these problems write thesis statements that contain a *topic* and a *comment* that is broken down into *opinion, purpose,* and *parts*. In addition, use the five strategies explained in this chapter to introduce your thesis statements.

Exercise 4.9   Write introductory paragraphs for the two thesis statements you wrote in Exercise 4.6, or make up new thesis statements for this exercise. Use a different strategy in each paragraph to introduce your thesis.

THINKING IT OVER

Test your recall of this chapter's concepts by completing the following statements. If you cannot complete a statement, look back through the chapter to find the answer.

1. The _____ is what your paragraph is about.

2. The _____ is your opinion about the topic.

3. A topic sentence should be neither too _____ nor too _____.

4. A thesis statement has two parts: the _____ and the _____.

5. The _____ of a thesis statement can be further broken down into opinion, _____, and _____.

6. The _____ part of your focus explains what you think about the topic.

7. The _____ part of your focus explains why you chose the topic or what you want readers to know or understand about it.

8. The _____ part of your focus suggests how you will organize your essay.

9. Chapter 4 explains five ways to introduce your thesis. Two of them are _____ and _____.

10. Choose one of the Thinking First questions at the beginning of the chapter to answer on the following lines.

_____

_____

_____

TOPICS FOR WRITING

Choose an essay topic from the following list. Brainstorm your topic or use a prewriting strategy of your choice to generate ideas about your topic. During your drafting process, follow this chapter's suggestions for writing, introducing, and correcting your thesis statement. Make sure your body paragraphs have topic sentences that relate to your essay's thesis.

1. Write about a time you tried out for a sport or some other activity and did not make it.

2. Write about a sport that has harmful or beneficial effects on life in the United States.

3. Write about a time you accomplished something you wanted, such as making a team, getting a job, or competing in an event and winning. Explain how achieving success affected you.

4. Write an essay using one of the introductory paragraphs you wrote for Exercise 4.9.

5. Make up your own topic.

Checklist for Revision

As you revise and edit your essay, check for the following:

1. Is your thesis statement complete? Can you identify your topic, opinion, purpose, and parts?

2. Does your introductory paragraph establish a context for your thesis?

3. Have you introduced your thesis with one of the five strategies explained in this chapter?

4. Do your body paragraphs have topic sentences that are neither too general nor too specific? Do they have a focus?

5. Do your paragraphs contain enough details?

6. Have you found and corrected your errors?

REFLECTIONS ON READING AND WRITING

Reflect on your reading and writing experiences. Are you able to find main ideas in your reading? Are you able to write main ideas of your own? Which is easier for you and why? What have you learned about main ideas from this chapter that will help you in your reading and writing? What needs more explanation?

Chapter 5

Reading for Details

THINKING FIRST

- *What are supporting details?*
- *How do I identify them?*
- *Why are they important?*

*L*earning the difference between a main idea and a supporting detail is one of the most important things you can do to improve your reading comprehension. Without a clear understanding of the differences between main ideas and details, you are reading only words that may seem to have no relationship.

The main idea as explained in Chapter 4 is an author's overall point. All other ideas within a paragraph or longer passage *support,* or explain, the main idea. A main idea is a more general idea than the supporting details, which are more specific. Remember that the main idea tells you what an author's topic is and what he or she thinks, believes, or knows about it. The details explain how or why.

As a reader, you should not be willing to accept any opinion at face value. Instead you should seek the evidence behind it, think critically about it, and draw your own conclusion. As a writer, you can apply what you practice in reading to your writing. Just as you expect authors to support their main ideas with sufficient and convincing details, you should do the same for your readers.

This chapter explains three things you need to understand that will help you identify supporting details: types of details, levels of development, and *transitions,* which are certain words and phrases that signal idea relationships.

BACKGROUND CHECK

Before reading the following essay, check your knowledge and assumptions about waiting and how it affects you and others.

1. Estimate the number of times during a typical day that you find yourself waiting for someone or something.

2. In what situations does waiting annoy you the most?

3. In what situations is waiting unavoidable?

4. Based on the title, author information, and first two paragraphs, what do you expect the author to tell you?

5. What else do you know or think about the topic?

Wait Divisions

Tom Bodett

Like it or not, waiting is something we all have to do. In this essay from his book Small Comforts, *Tom Bodett writes about the ways we wait.*

VOCABULARY CHECK

apathy (2)	lack of interest or concern
lapse (2)	slip
render (5)	make, cause to happen
demise (6)	end
interludes (9)	intervening times
potent (10)	powerful

I read somewhere that we spend a full third of our lives waiting. I've also read where we spend a third of our lives sleeping, a third working, and a third at our leisure. Now either somebody's lying, or we're spending all our leisure time waiting to go to work or sleep. That can't be true or league softball and Winnebagos never would have caught on. 1

So where are we doing all of this waiting and what does it mean to an impatient society like ours? Could this unseen waiting be the source of all our problems? A shrinking economy? The staggering deficit? Declining mental health and moral apathy? Probably not, but let's take a look at some of the more classic "waits" anyway. 2

The purest form of waiting is what we'll call the *Watched-Pot Wait.* This type of wait is without a doubt the most annoying of all. Take filling up the kitchen sink. There is absolutely nothing you can do while this is going on but keep both eyes glued to the sink until it's full. If you try to cram in some extracurricular activity, you're asking for it. So you stand there, your hands on the faucets, and wait. A temporary suspension of duties. During these waits it's common for your eyes to lapse out of focus. The brain disengages from the body and wanders around the imagination in search of distraction. It finds none and springs back into action only when the water runs over the edge of the counter and onto your socks. 3

The phrase "a watched pot never boils" comes of this experience.   4
Pots don't care whether they are watched or not; the problem is that
nobody has ever seen a pot actually come to a boil. While they are
waiting, their brains turn off.

Other forms of the Watched-Pot Wait would include waiting for   5
your dryer to quit at the laundromat, waiting for your toast to pop
out of the toaster, or waiting for a decent idea to come to mind at
a typewriter. What they all have in common is that they render the
waiter helpless and mindless.

A cousin to the Watched-Pot Wait is the *Forced Wait*. Not for the   6
weak of will, this one requires a bit of discipline. The classic Forced
Wait is starting your car in the winter and letting it slowly idle up to
temperature before engaging the clutch. This is every bit as uninter-
esting as watching a pot, but with one big difference. You have a
choice. There is nothing keeping you from racing to work behind a
stone-cold engine save the thought of the early demise of several
thousand dollars' worth of equipment you haven't paid for yet.
Thoughts like that will help you get through a Forced Wait.

Properly preparing packaged soup mixes also requires a Forced   7
Wait. Directions are very specific on these mixes. "Bring three cups
water to boil, add mix, simmer three minutes, remove from heat, let
stand five minutes." I have my doubts that anyone has ever actually
done this. I'm fairly spineless when it comes to instant soups and usually just boil the bejeezus out of them until the noodles sink. Some
things just aren't worth a Forced Wait.

All in all Forced Waiting requires a lot of a thing called *patience,*   8
which is a virtue. Once we get into virtues I'm out of my element, and
can't expound on the virtues of virtue, or even lie about them. So let's
move on to some of the more far-reaching varieties of waiting.

The *Payday Wait* is certainly a leader in the long-term anticipation   9
field. The problems with waits that last more than a few minutes is
that you have to actually do other things in the meantime. Like go to
work. By far the most aggravating feature of the Payday Wait is that
even though you must keep functioning in the interludes, there is less
and less you are able to do as the big day draws near. For some of us
the last few days are best spent alone in a dark room for fear we'll
accidentally do something that costs money. With the Payday Wait
comes a certain amount of hope that we'll make it, and faith that
everything will be all right once we do.

With the introduction of faith and hope, I've ushered in the most   10
potent wait class of all, the *Lucky-Break Wait,* or the *Wait for One's
Ship to Come In.* This type of wait is unusual in that it is for the most
part voluntary. Unlike the Forced Wait, which is also voluntary, waiting
for your lucky break does not necessarily mean that it will happen.

Turning one's life into a waiting game of these proportions re- 11
quires gobs of the aforementioned faith and hope, and is strictly for
the optimists among us. For these people life is the thing that happens to them while they're waiting for something to happen to them.
On the surface it seems as ridiculous as following the directions on
soup mixes, but the Lucky-Break Wait performs an outstanding service
to those who take it upon themselves to do it. As long as one doesn't
come to rely on it, wishing for a few good things to happen never
hurt anybody.

In the end it is obvious that we certainly do spend a good deal of 12
our time waiting. The person who said we do it a third of the time
may have been going easy on us. It makes a guy wonder how anything at all gets done around here. But things do get done, people
grow old, and time boils on whether you watch it or not.

The next time you're standing at the sink waiting for it to fill while 13
cooking soup mix that you'll have to eat until payday or until a large
bag of cash falls out of the sky, don't despair. You're probably just as
busy as the next guy.

THINKING CRITICALLY

Main Idea

1. Write a sentence that best expresses the thesis, or central idea, of
   Tom Bodett's essay.

2. Which sentence is the topic sentence of paragraph 3?

Details

3. According to Bodett, how much time do we spend waiting?

4. What is the purest form of waiting? Which form of waiting requires discipline? Which requires a lot of patience?

Organization

5. The author's title "Wait Divisions" suggests that his primary
   means of organization is to divide the broad topic of *waiting* into
   several subclasses or categories. What are the categories? What is
   one example from each category?

Purpose, Audience, Tone

6. What is Bodett's tone? Is he serious or not? What specific words or phrases help you determine the tone?

Inferences and Conclusions

7. Into which of Bodett's categories would you place waiting for a traffic light to change?

8. Would Bodett agree with the saying, "time and tide for no man wait"? Why or why not? Use details from the essay to support your answer.

Making Connections

Think about Bodett's wait divisions. Which of them have you experienced? Can you think of another kind of waiting that Bodett does not explain? What kind of waiting is most annoying to you? What suggestions do you have for making wait time pass more quickly? Write a paragraph in which you answer one or more of these questions.

TYPES OF DETAILS

All day long, every day, you express opinions and make statements such as these:

"It looks like rain today."

"I think I'm going to do well on this test."

"I don't like Jones's class."

"I enjoy reading John Grisham's novels."

Think of these statements as main ideas. For each main idea you must have some evidence, or you would not be able to make the statement. Why does it look like rain? Probably the sky is cloudy. There may even be a light drizzle. The clouds and the drizzle are evidence; they are specific details that support your main idea. They explain *why* you think it looks like rain.

What could make you think that you will do well on a test? Did you study the night before? Does the test cover concepts with which you are familiar? Have you generally done well in the past? These reasons are the details that support your belief. Suppose your friend asks why you don't like Jones's class or why you enjoy reading Grisham's novels. Your friend is asking for details. Chances are you can come up with several details to support either point.

Whether in conversation or in reading, most of us are unwilling to accept others' ideas and opinions at face value. We want details, so we can better understand people's viewpoints and assess the accuracy of their claims. A writer who tries to meet readers' expectations chooses details that best support the main idea. Three common types of details writers use that you can learn to recognize are *facts, reasons,* and *examples.*

Facts

Facts include those things that can be proven true or false. They include statistics, names of people and places, dates of events, scientific and historical evidence, numbers and figures, amounts of money, testimony of experts and authorities, quotations from sources, and definitions. Anything that can be proven by direct observation is also considered a fact. For example, "Bees gather pollen from flowers to make honey" is a fact. We know that scientists have observed bees gathering pollen and have also determined how they make honey. We, too, can test this statement ourselves by going outside on any summer day and watching bees flit from flower to flower, their legs encrusted with yellow granules of pollen.

Suppose one of your state legislators is arguing for the appropriation of a large sum of money to be set aside for the building of a new road in your area. What facts would support the argument? The legislator might rely on a study done by traffic engineers showing an increase in traffic over the past few years. He or she might also gather statistics from the state Department of Motor Vehicles to show an increase in the number of accidents due to overcrowded conditions on existing highways.

Listed next are a main idea and the facts that support it.

Of the many birth-control methods that are available, some are more effective than others.

1. At a rate of 97 to 99 percent, oral contraceptives are the most effective.

2. The intrauterine device (IUD) is 94 to 98 percent effective.

3. Less effective are condoms at 90 percent, diaphragms at 80 to 90 percent, and the contraceptive cap at 80 to 90 percent.

4. Spermicidal creams, foams, and jellies used alone are only about 75 to 80 percent effective.

5. At a rate of 80 percent, natural family planning and *coitus interruptus* (withdrawal before ejaculation) are also among the least effective methods.

These details enable you to compare birth-control methods on the basis of their rates of effectiveness given as percents.

In the following paragraph, the main idea is bracketed, and the facts that support it are underlined.

Recently I saw in a catalog of gift items a book I wanted to buy. The book cost $24.95, and I decided that I would send for it as soon as I got my paycheck. Several days later, I saw the same book in a paperback version at my local bookstore for only $12.95, a savings of about 50 percent. What a lucky break for me. If I had not been worried about money, I would have ordered the catalog version at the higher price. It was just by chance that I happened to see the lower-priced one when I was in the bookstore looking for a magazine. [This incident reminded me to shop around before buying anything—I might find a better deal.]

The *facts* that help support the main idea in this paragraph are numbers: dollar amounts and a percentage.

Exercise 5.1   Read each paragraph. Bracket the main idea. Then underline the *facts* that help support it.

1. The labor market has become a place of churning dislocation caused by the heavy volume of mergers, buyouts, and business closings. These activities have been accompanied by thousands of layoffs

and the elimination of hundreds of product lines. Even those industries noted for job security have recently engaged in massive layoffs. A wave of consolidations in the nation's banking industry set the stage for more than 100,000 job losses in the early 1990s. Almost half the country's railroad jobs were lost during the past decade. The U.S. Postal Service plans to cut more than 80,000 career employees by the mid-1990s. During the past six years, the American Telephone and Telegraph Co. (AT&T) cut 92,000 workers through firings and early retirements. And such layoffs are likely to continue. As America attempts to cope with rapid technological change and new competition from multinational companies, there is every reason to believe we will see more, not less, volatility in the labor force. For large numbers of workers, interpersonal skills represent the critical "transferable skills" needed in an ever-changing labor market.

From *Effective Human Relations in Organizations*, 5th ed., Barry L. Reece and Rhonda Brandt, Houghton Mifflin Co., 1993.

2. A **molecular formula** is *a chemical formula that gives the exact number of different atoms of an element in a molecule.* The hydrogen peroxide molecule contains two hydrogen atoms and two oxygen atoms chemically bonded. Therefore, its molecular formula is H_2O_2. Other simple molecular substances are water, H_2O; ammonia, NH_3; carbon dioxide, CO_2; and ethanol (ethyl alcohol), C_2H_6O.

From *General Chemistry*, 4th ed., Darrell D. Ebbing, Houghton Mifflin Co., 1993.

3. The 1990 census revealed the persistence of the demographic, economic, and social trends that had taken shape in the 1960s and 1970s. The entire population stood at slightly under 250 million, a

gain of about 23 million in the decade. Americans continued to move to the Sunbelt states in the West and the South. . . . Immigration, mostly from the Third World, accounted for one-third of the population growth for the decade; older cities of the Northeast and Midwest lost population; and for the first time, [more than] 50 percent of Americans lived in the suburbs.

From *Present Tense*, Michael Schaller, Virginia Scharff, and Robert D. Schulzinger, Houghton Mifflin Co., 1992.

Reasons

Reasons are causes. Reasons explain why things happen, why you feel the way you do, why you act in certain ways. Where you have reasons, you may also have *results,* or *effects.* Effects are the consequences of actions. They are the results of behavior, the outcomes of events. If you say, "I believe the drinking age should be lowered," you probably have reasons to support your belief. Your reasons may or may not be based on a consideration of the results, or consequences, of lowering the drinking age. When writers support main ideas with reasons, they may use reasons alone or combined with effects.

Listed next are a main idea and the reasons that support it.

Being a veterinarian is a career I would enjoy.

1. I like animals.

2. Helping sick or wounded animals would give me a sense of accomplishment.

3. Working with others who share my interest in animals would be a rewarding experience.

4. I would be able to educate pet owners on how to care properly for their animals.

As you can see, the main idea expresses an opinion. The reasons listed explain *why* the writer holds that opinion.

In the following example paragraph, the main idea is bracketed and the reasons that help support the main idea are underlined.

[Neighborhood watch programs are good for everyone.] <u>One reason is that these programs unite neighbors in common goals</u>. Neighbors work together to protect each other. As a result, they develop a sense of community. <u>Another reason is that crime actually is reduced in neighborhoods where watch programs are in effect</u>. Posted signs act as a deterrent to criminals. Neighbors in these areas are more likely to report any suspicious persons or activities. <u>Finally, watch programs keep neighbors alert</u>. One thing burglers count on is the element of surprise. Neighbors in watch areas not only watch each other's property, but they watch out for themselves also.

Three reasons support the main idea. Each reason is followed by additional details that further explain it. Some of these additional details are results—outcomes of the neighborhood watch program.

Exercise 5.2   Read each paragraph. Bracket the main idea. Then underline the *reasons* that help support it.

1. Some schools are better than others and for several good reasons. They have high expectations. Many educators believe that students rise to the level of performance expected of them. A belief in student success, students' beliefs in themselves, and sound instructional methods are the keys to raising expectations and performance. Good schools have a sense of community. School spirit is encouraged and cultivated. Parents are involved. The school is the center of neighborhood activity. Size, too, may be a factor. The smaller the school the more likely it is that close relationships will develop among teachers and students, where teachers assume the role of mentors rather than authoritarians.

2. Hedgehogs are as prevalent in England as squirrels are in the United States. Brits call the hedgehog "the gardener's friend," and he is uniformly appreciated. Hedgehogs are small, about 6 to 8

inches long, and covered with prickly quills. When frightened, they roll themselves into a ball and quiver. Why is this odd little creature so beloved? He's quiet and he's harmless. He's cute. Another reason for his popularity may be his appetite for garden pests: beetles, wood lice, and slugs.

3. Have you ever wondered why you dream? Many theorists have searched for the reasons. Some believe that dreams help people process information necessary to their well-being and survival. Others, of whom Freud was one, believe that dreams function as windows into the unconscious, where our wishes and secret fears are stored. If, as some psychologists have proposed, dreams reflect our current mental state, they may be attempts to work out problems. When things are not going well for us, dreams set in the past may represent the desire to return to happier times. But it could be that dreams are simply the byproducts of sleep and have no significance of their own, making attempts to interpret them fruitless.

Examples

Examples are explanations that illustrate a point by describing it or clarifying it. Examples that describe create clear and vivid pictures in your mind. Examples that clarify help you interpret the meaning, or significance, of complex ideas.

   Because readers and writers view topics in different ways, examples are necessary to establish a common ground on which to base a discussion and make a point. In politics, what is a *conservative?* A *liberal?* These political points of view are based on shared values and attitudes. To explain conservatism, for example, one writer might spell out its characteristic values and attitudes. Another writer might provide as an example the name of a well-known or influential conservative. The reader could then infer from what he or she knows about that person's views the nature of conservatism.

Listed next are a main idea and the examples that support it.

A common theme in movies is that of an angel who is allowed a limited return to life to help those left behind or to complete unfinished business.

1. In *Heaven Can Wait,* a remake of *Here Comes Mr. Jordan,* a football player dies before his time and is sent back to earth to live out his life—in someone else's body.
2. In *Ghost,* a character played by Patrick Swayze is murdered but returns to avenge his death and comfort his wife.
3. In *The Preacher's Wife,* a remake of a Cary Grant film, Denzel Washington plays an angel sent to help a preacher and his wife save their church and their marriage.

These specific examples help clarify the main idea. Readers familiar with one or more of the films can recall vivid mental pictures to help them "see" what the writer means.

In the following paragraph, the main idea is bracketed and the examples that help support the main idea are underlined.

[Having lived most of my life in a warm climate, I had no idea how cold my first Maine winter would be.] It was so cold that the lock on my car door froze. To thaw it, I had to pour hot water on it and insert the key quickly before it froze again. Even my breath crystallized in the cold; I had tiny icicles in my nostrils. Cracking a window to get some fresh air let in a blast of cold that would chill the room in a few seconds. The most vivid example of the cold that I can recall is the tile floor in my bathroom. It felt like ice against my bare feet.

What seems cold to one person may not seem cold to another. Without examples, you cannot know what the writer of the preceding paragraph means by "cold." By using examples that appeal to your sense of touch, the writer lets you share his or her perception of a Maine winter.

Exercise 5.3   Read each paragraph. Bracket the main idea. Then underline the examples that help support it.

1. We characterize or identify a material by its various properties, which may be either physical or chemical. A **physical property** is *a characteristic that can be observed for a material without changing its chemical identity.* Examples are physical state (solid, liquid, or gas) and color. Measurable physical properties, such as mass and melting point (the temperature at which a material melts), are classified as either extensive or intensive. An *extensive property* is one whose magnitude depends on the amount of material. Mass and volume are examples. An *intensive property* is one whose magnitude is independent of the amount of material. Intensive properties are the characteristics used to identify a material. An example is the melting point.

   From *General Chemistry,* 4th ed., Darrell D. Ebbing, Houghton Mifflin Co., 1993.

2. Consumers have certain basic rights that guarantee them fair treatment in the marketplace. One of these rights is **choice.** Consumers are free to make their own decisions about what to buy because of competitive pricing and the availability of products and services. Consumers also have a right to **safety.** They should expect that when products are used as intended, they pose no hazards to life or health. **Information** is another consumer right. Consumers are entitled to protection from deceptive advertising and unfair sales tactics. Manufacturers and others must provide the facts that enable consumers to inform themselves about products and services. Consumers must have a **voice.** It is their right to express their interests, and government has an obligation to fairly consider consumers' needs. **Redress** is a right that ensures consumers have a remedy if

something goes wrong with a product or service and a procedure for expressing dissatisfaction. Finally, **consumer education** is the means by which consumers can learn ways to use the resources available to them to meet their needs more effectively.

Adapted from *Consumer Economic Issues in America,* E. Thomas Garman, Houghton Mifflin Co., 1991.

3. Despite the fact that most insects have no direct interaction with humans at all, some are unquestionably harmful. Mosquitoes can transmit such diseases as malaria, yellow fever, encephalitis, and elephantiasis. Fleas are the vectors of bubonic plague, typhus, and tapeworms. Houseflies have been implicated in the spread of tuberculosis, typhoid, cholera, amoebic dysentery, anthrax, and other illnesses. Human lice, though they are basically parasites that usually cause only discomfort, also may transmit typhus and relapsing fever. One of the best-known disease vectors is the tsetse fly, which transmits African sleeping sickness.

From *The Practical Entomologist,* Rick Imes, Quarto Publishing, 1992.

THINKING ABOUT PROCESS

Reading involves many skills applied simultaneously.

1. While you are reading, you are also thinking about the reading. You may be questioning the author, "What do you mean by this?" or you may be questioning yourself, "How does this relate to my experience?"

2. To find the main idea, you must also read and think about the details. The two depend on each other.

3. Concentration is essential to the reading process. If you have difficulty concentrating, your mind wanders and you forget what you
have read.

LEVELS OF DEVELOPMENT

Some details are more important than others; these details are called
major details. Other details, of lesser importance, are called *minor* details. Major and minor details together complete the evidence that supports a main idea.

Effective writing usually has at least three levels of development.
The main idea is the first, most general level. Major details, the second
level, support the main idea. Minor details, the third level, support major details. Thus minor details support the main idea also, but less directly than major details do. The map in Figure 5.1 illustrates the three
levels of development.

Reread the paragraph on page 135 about neighborhood watch programs. The underlined sentences are the major details that support the
main idea stated in the first sentence. Everything else, all the material
between the underlined sentences, consists of minor details. The map
in Figure 5.2 should help you visualize the paragraph's three levels of
development.

In a longer passage, such as a textbook chapter or section of a chapter, the same three levels of development are present. The main ideas
are supported by the major details, which are supported by the minor
details. Main ideas and details, taken together, support the thesis statement. Remember that the writer's *thesis* is the point, or central idea, of
the whole passage.

To analyze a long passage or make a study guide, illustrate the relationships among ideas either by constructing a map or diagram, such as
those in Figures 5.1 and 5.2, or by making a three-level outline. Figure
5.3 outlines the essay "Wait Divisions," providing a condensed version
of the ideas presented in the article. Notice that not everything mentioned in the article appears in the outline. For the most part, the author's words are *paraphrased,* or restated in different words, rather than
repeated exactly.

Outlines, like maps and other diagrams, have a purpose: to show
how ideas are related both sequentially and logically. If you intend to
use outlining as your means of taking notes from chapters and other
material, keep these guidelines in mind.

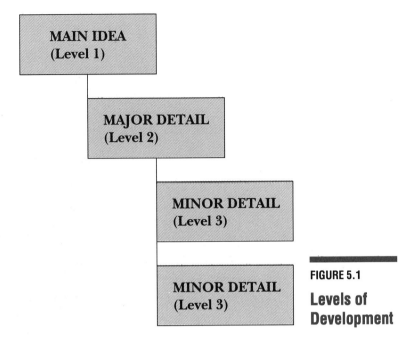

FIGURE 5.1

Levels of Development

- You do not have to include *everything* on your outline.

- Stick to essential information; include all main ideas but only those major and minor details needed to clarify the main idea.

- Do not copy information directly from the text into your notes. Paraphrase, or restate the information in your own words. It is much easier to remember your paraphrase than to try to recall the author's exact words.

Exercise 5.4 Practice distinguishing between major and minor details by either outlining or mapping the paragraph on page 144 to show its levels of development. Refer to Figures 5.1 and 5.2 as guides for mapping or to Figure 5.3 as a guide for outlining. When you are finished, compare your map or outline with a classmate's. Then revise as needed.

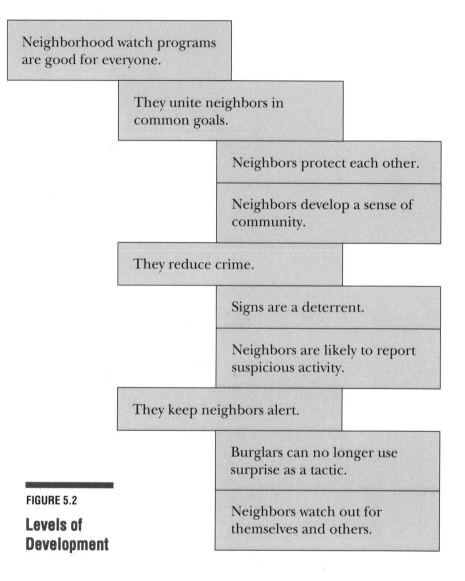

FIGURE 5.2

Levels of Development

FIGURE 5.3

Outline of "Wait Divisions"

Implied thesis: <u>Though you may not realize it, several classic types of waiting exist.</u>

  I. The Watched-Pot Wait
    A.   the most annoying kind
    B.   example: filling a sink
        1. nothing to do but wait
        2. eyes lose focus, brain disengages
    C.   more examples
        1. "a watched pot never boils"
        2. waiting for dryer
        3. waiting for toast
        4. waiting for an idea to come

 II. The Forced Wait
    A.   requires discipline and patience
    B.   difference from Watched-Pot Wait: you have a choice
    C.   two examples
        1. starting car in winter
        2. preparing packaged soup mixes

III. The Payday Wait
    A.   longer than others
    B.   must do something while waiting
        1. may run out of things to do
        2. must avoid spending money until payday
    C.   requires hope and faith

IV. The Lucky-Break Wait or Wait for One's Ship to Come In
    A.   most powerful kind
    B.   voluntary, unlike the others
    C.   for optimists—people who look on the bright side
    D.   disadvantages
        1. life happens while you wait
        2. breaks might not come

 V. Conclusion: Although we spend a lot of time waiting, things still get done.

Stress and the College Student

Many college students say that stress is one of their biggest problems. Where does this stress come from? Others' expectations are one source. Younger students feel pressured to perform well for parents who are paying the bills. Spouses, children, and coworkers may expect too much too soon from older students who need time to adjust to being "in school" again. Busy schedules are a cause of stress for most students, young and old. Few students have the luxury of having nothing to do but go to college. Most have jobs, many have families, all have outside interests and obligations that conflict with classes and studies. If you ask students what stresses them the most, many place grades high on the list of pressures they face. Keeping a scholarship requires good grades. Getting into a desired program, such as nursing, requires a certain grade point average. For some, unfortunately, grades are a measure of self-worth. These students place too high an emphasis on grades, and the result is unrelieved stress. Stress *is* a problem. To solve it, you have to first determine its cause.

STUDY TIP: *Taking good notes is largely a matter of distinguishing between essential and nonessential information. Listen for the same three levels of development in a lecture that you look for in reading. Take notes on main ideas and major details. Add whatever minor details are needed for clarification.*

TRANSITIONS

Sentences within paragraphs are related to each other. In fact, the relationships between sentences help you to follow a writer's ideas.

Transitions are the key to understanding how sentences are related. A *transition* is a word or a phrase that acts as a connector between ideas. Transitions help writers and readers move smoothly through the three levels of development: from main idea to major detail to minor detail. Following is the paragraph on neighborhood watch programs that you have seen before in this chapter. Notice now that the transitions are in **bold** type to call your attention to them.

> Neighborhood watch programs are good for everyone. **One reason** is that these programs unite neighbors in common goals. Neighbors work together to protect each other. As a result, they develop a sense of community. **Another reason** is that crime actually is reduced in neighborhoods where watch programs are in effect. Posted signs act as a deterrent to criminals. Neighbors in these areas are more likely to report any suspicious persons or activities. **Finally,** watch programs keep neighbors alert. One thing burglars count on is the element of surprise. Neighbors in watch areas not only watch each other's property, but they watch out for themselves also.

In this paragraph the main idea is supported by three reasons that explain why neighborhood watch programs are effective. To help you follow the development of ideas, each sentence that states a reason begins with a transition. "One reason" tells you that the first reason follows. "Another reason" tells you that a new reason is added. The word "finally" tells you two things: the discussion is drawing to an end, and you are about to get the last reason.

In the next example, paragraph 5 from "Wait Divisions," the transition in bold type helps you see the relationship between this paragraph and the two before it.

> **Other** forms of the Watched-Pot Wait would include waiting for your dryer to quit at the laundromat, waiting for your toast to pop out of the toaster, or waiting for a decent idea to come to mind at a typewriter. What they all have in common is that they render the waiter helpless and mindless.

The word *other* tells you that the writer is still on the topic of the Watched-Pot Wait, which he began discussing in paragraph 3. You have already read two examples of Watched-Pot Waits: waiting for the sink to fill and waiting for water to boil. The transition tells you that more examples follow.

So transitions not only help you trace ideas from sentence to sentence, they also help you see relationships between paragraphs. Figure 5.4 lists some common transitional words and phrases and the relationships they signal.

FIGURE 5.4

Transitions and the Relationships They Signal

ADDITION: One idea is added to an idea already mentioned.

also	one	next	finally
another	first	third	furthermore
in addition	second	last	moreover

CHRONOLOGY: Ideas are related by time and/or sequence.

first	before	now	until
next	after	later	immediately
then	during	soon	frequently

COMPARISON: Ideas are related by similarity.

as	like	equally
as if	similarly	in like manner
as well as	comparatively	

CONTRAST: Ideas are related by difference.

but	although	on the other hand	nevertheless
conversely	however	on the contrary	even though
despite	instead	in spite of	yet

ILLUSTRATION: One idea is given as an example of another.

for example	such as	exemplary
for instance	to illustrate	exemplify

CAUSE AND EFFECT: An idea is given as a reason or result.

as a result	if . . . then	so
because	one reason . . .	therefore
consequently	since	thus

Exercise 5.5

In each pair of sentences, underline any transitional word or phrase that you find. Then explain how the sentences are related. The first one is done as an example.

1. It is time for your annual teeth cleaning. You should <u>therefore</u> make an appointment with your dentist.

The sentences are related by cause and effect.

_____

2. I am going to wash my car this morning. After that, I will clean out the garage.

_____

_____

3. I usually do not like western movies. I did enjoy Clint Eastwood's *Unforgiven,* however.

_____

_____

4. The exam will consist of several types of questions. For example, there will be some multiple-choice items, some true-false questions, and an essay.

_____

_____

5. I enjoyed Sue Grafton's *A Is for Alibi.* I also enjoyed *G Is for Gumshoe* and *J Is for Judgment.*

_____

_____

6. "How is your research going?" he asked. "As well as can be expected," she answered.

_____

_____

7. One of Diane's children caught chicken pox. Then her youngest child came down with the disease.

_____

_____

8. First you should remove everything from the carton. Next find the instructions and make sure you have all the parts that should have been included.

_____

_____

9. Todd was exhausted from tossing a Frisbee for his dog, Max. Equally tired was the dog.

_____

_____

10. Marguerite likes violets. One reason is that they come in so many different colors.

_____

_____

Exercise 5.6   Following are three paragraphs from *Fundamentals of College Mathematics* by Sandra Pryor Clarkson and Barbara J. Barone (Houghton Mifflin Co., 1994). In each of the paragraphs, transitional words and phrases are underlined. On the lines beneath each paragraph, explain how sentences containing transitions are related to other sentences in the paragraph. Work on your own or with a partner.

1. Multiplication provides a quick way of calculating the result of adding the same number many times. <u>For example</u>, suppose you spend $3 a day on transportation. You can find how much you spend during the five-day work week with either *repeated addition* ($3 + $3 + $3 + $3 + $3 = $15) or *multiplication* (5 × $3 = $15).

_____

_____

2. Mathematics problems involving situations in the "real world" are usually presented as word problems. <u>Before</u> you can solve a word problem, you must understand the problem situation and what is being asked. <u>Then</u> you must decide which operation or operations to use on which numbers. <u>After</u> using an operation, you need to see if your answer makes sense in the problem situation.

_____

_____

3. In everyday language, the words *number* and *numeral* are often interchanged. Technically, <u>however</u>, a **number** specifies an amount; a **numeral** is a symbol, written with digits, that represents a number.

_____

_____

▶ THINKING IT OVER

Test your recall of this chapter's concepts by completing the following statements. If you cannot complete a statement, look back through the chapter to find the answer.

1. Knowing the difference between a _____ and a _____ is one of the most important things you can do to improve your reading.

2. Three types of details are _____, _____, and _____.

3. A *fact* is defined as _____.

4. Two kinds of facts are _____ and _____.

5. Reasons are _____, and where you find reasons you may also find _____.

6. Examples are explanations that illustrate a point by _____ it or _____ it.

7. Major details support _____.

8. Minor details support _____.

9. A _____ is a word or phrase that acts as a connector between ideas and suggests their relationship.

10. Choose one of the Thinking First questions at the beginning of the chapter to answer on the following lines:

_____

_____

TOPICS FOR WRITING

Choose one of the following topics and follow the directions.

1. Select a newspaper or magazine article that interests you. Read the article and write an essay about it. Your answers to the following questions will help you gather details to include in your essay.

   What is the source of the article?

   What is the article's title, and who is the author?

   What is the author's topic?

   What is the author's central idea or thesis, and is it stated or implied?

   What are the major details that support the thesis?

What have you learned from the article?

Do you agree or disagree with the author and why?

2. Carefully examine a returned essay or an essay in progress. Rewrite the essay to improve your thesis statement, topic sentences, and selection of details.

Checklist for Revision

As you revise and edit your essay, check for the following:

1. Have you clearly stated your thesis?

2. Have you introduced the thesis?

3. Do your body paragraphs have topic sentences?

4. Do your details include facts, reasons, and examples?

5. Can you identify three levels of development in your essay?

6. Have you used transitions between some sentences and paragraphs?

7. Have you found and corrected your errors?

REFLECTIONS ON READING AND WRITING

Many readers who chuckle at the humor in "Wait Divisions" also see some truth in it. Reflect on your reading of the essay. Were you able to find the main idea? Were you able to identify the supporting details? Which of Tom Bodett's examples seem especially funny or true in terms of your experience? Why?

Chapter 6

Writing Your Details

THINKING FIRST

- *What kinds of details should I choose?*
- *How should I arrange details in my paragraphs?*
- *How should I arrange details in my essays?*

Two college students are sitting outside the student center when an attractive member of the opposite sex walks by. The students exchange looks that clearly indicate what they are thinking, yet no word passes between them. Seeing the grade on a composition the professor has just returned, the writer says, "Yes!" Although no conversation ensues in which the student explains the work that went into the essay and the pleasure that comes from having the effort acknowledged, the other students in the class know how this writer feels and are hoping for similar results on their papers. In both cases, either a word or a look effectively communicates an idea that would probably take several sentences to write.

Writing is not like having a conversation. When people read your paragraphs and essays, they have only your written word to rely on. Therefore, you must provide readers with enough and the right kind of details. As explained in Chapter 5, the types of details and levels of development you look for in reading should also be present in your writing. This chapter explains how to choose and arrange details to support the main ideas of paragraphs and essays.

BACKGROUND CHECK

Before reading the following essay, check your knowledge and assumptions about clothes and shopping.

1. What specific items of clothing did you feel you *had* to have when you were a child?

2. Do you have now, or did you ever have, a favorite item of clothing, something that is uniquely "you" and that you feel you could not do without?

3. If you have children or younger brothers and sisters, would you say that shopping with them is usually a positive or negative experience? Why?

4. Based on your survey of the title, author information, and first two paragraphs, what do you expect to follow?

5. What else do you know or think about the topic?

Shopping with Children
Phyllis Theroux

Phyllis Theroux writes for popular magazines and newspapers, often about family relationships. This essay is from Night Lights, *a collection of her essays published in 1987.*

VOCABULARY CHECK

immaculate (3)	spotless, clean
adder (3)	a type of snake
extremists (3)	those whose beliefs are outside the norm for their group
heartfelt (8)	deeply or sincerely felt
eccentricities (8)	oddities, unusual behaviors
coerced (9)	forced or threatened
genuflect (11)	to kneel out of respect
retrieved (12)	to get back, regain
inventoried (12)	counted items or made a list of items
inadvertently (15)	unintentionally, not meaning to
sustained (15)	maintained, kept up
commodities (16)	useful things
cosmic (17)	universal, far reaching

1   Once upon a time there were three little children. By and large, dressing them was a joyful thing. At a moment's notice, their mother could turn the boys into baby Rothschilds, the girl into a shipping heiress, or even a Kennedy. In those early days of motherhood, I used to take a lot of photographs for the scrapbook. Now I flip through the scrapbook sometimes to remind myself that "those were the days."

2   The eldest son was the first to establish his individuality: sleeveless army jackets, kneecap bandannas and a pierced ear hidden under a lengthening style. Then the youngest son discovered dirt. He formed a

club, still active, called "The All Dirt Association." To qualify, one had to roll in the mud.

Fortunately, the little girl grows increasingly more tasteful and immaculate. She will get up at 5:30 A.M. to make sure she has enough time to wash and curl her hair so that it bounces properly on her shoulders when she goes off to school, and she screams as if bitten by an adder if a drop of spaghetti sauce lands on her Izod. The entire house is thrown into an uproar while she races for the Clorox bottle. This is a family of extremists, and nobody dresses for the kind of success I had in mind.

Time will tell what happens to these children. Who can say whether my son the dirt bomb will wind up sewing buttons on a seersucker sports jacket, or my daughter the Southamptonian will discover the joys of thrift-shop browsing. They are still evolving toward personal statements that are, at this writing, incomplete.

In the meantime, however, they must be dressed, which means taking them to stores where clothing for their growing bodies can be purchased. Shopping with children is exactly as awful as shopping with parents. But if the experience is to be survived there are certain rules all adults must follow. (If you are a child, you may not read any further. This is for your parents, who will deal with you very harshly if you read one more word!)

RULE I: Never shop with more than one child at a time. This rule is closely related to another rule—never raise more than one child at a time. If you understand the second rule, there is no need to elaborate upon the first.

RULE II: Dress very nicely yourself. After the age of nine, children do not like to be seen with their mothers in public. You are a blot upon their reputation, a shadow they want to shake. I, myself, always insisted that my mother walk ten paces behind me, take separate elevators and escalators and speak only when spoken to—which brings me to the next rule.

RULE III: Do not make any sudden gestures, loud noises or heartfelt exclamations such as "How adorable you look in that!" or "Twenty-nine ninety-five! Are you kidding? For a shirt?" Children are terribly embarrassed by our eccentricities, and it goes without saying that you must never buy their articles of "intimate apparel" in their presence. Children, until enough sleazy adults teach them that is old-fashioned, are very modest creatures. One time I ran out of the store and took the bus home by myself after my mother asked a salesclerk where the "underpants" counter was. Everyone in the store heard her. I had no choice.

RULE IV: Know your child's limits. If he can be coerced into a department store, coaxed into telling you that he wouldn't mind wearing this shirt or that pair of pants, don't insist that he go the whole distance—i.e., don't force him to try them on. Keep the sales slips; if something doesn't fit when he tries it on at home, return it. If he cannot be made to enter the store at all, say, "Fine. When you run out of clothes, wear your sister's." Children who won't go shopping at all save their parents a lot of time.

RULE V: Know your own limits. Do not be dragged to every sneaker store in the metropolitan area to find the exact shoes your child has in mind. Announce: "We're going to Sears—and Sears only—unless you want to wait for six more weeks, which is the next time I am free." Some children, with nothing but time and a passion to improve their image, will cheerfully go to three stores they know about and six more they don't, without blinking an eye.   10

RULE VI: Keep your hand on your checkbook. This is a very hard rule to follow if you are not strong-minded. Children can accuse you of ruining their lives because you do not genuflect before the entire line of Ocean Pacific sportswear, and girls have a way of filling you with guilt by telling you that every other girl in their confirmation class is going to be wearing Capezio sandals and if you want to make her look funny in front of the bishop she will never forgive you as long as she lives.   11

RULE VII: Keep on top of the laundry. Or, if you can't keep on top of the laundry, remember that the wardrobe your son or daughter wants is probably lying in the bottom of a hamper waiting to be retrieved. When packing a trunk for camp or school, insist that everything the child owns be washed (preferably by him or her), folded and ready to be inventoried before you go to the store to fill in the gaps. Your children will hate you for enforcing this rule, but remember that true love is strong.   12

RULE VIII: Avoid designer clothes. Shut your eyes to labels. Do not be intimidated by the "fact" that your daughter cannot go to the movies without swinging a Bermuda Bag, or that your son will not be able to concentrate in the library without Topsiders on his feet. Tell your children that the best thing about Gloria Vanderbilt is her bank account, fattened by socially insecure people which, thank God, they are not!   13

Having laid down the rules, it is important to refresh the adult's memory with "remembrances of things past." I have never met a child who did not remind me of how difficult it is to present a confident face to the world. Clothing is only the top blanket shielding them from the elements, and children need all the protective covering they can get.   14

As a child, I knew in an inarticulate way that I stood a better chance of surviving a windstorm in a circle of trees. My aim was to be the tree in the middle, identical and interchangeable with every other   15 sapling in the grove. How I dressed had everything to do with feeling socially acceptable and when I inadvertently slipped into an individualism I could not back up with sustained confidence, I would try to think what I could do to regain my place in the grove.

It seemed to me that social success depended on having at least 16 one of three commodities: a fabulous personality, fame, or a yellow Pandora sweater. These were the building blocks upon which one could stand.

A fabulous personality was beyond my power to sustain on a 17 daily basis. Fame. Like lightning, seemed to strike other people, none of whom I even knew. But a yellow Pandora sweater could be purchased at Macy's, if only my mother would understand its cosmic importance. Fortunately, she did.

For several days, or as long as it took for the sweater cuffs to lose 18 their elasticity, I faced the world feeling buttoned up, yellow and self-confident—almost as confident as Susan Figel, who had a whole drawerful of Pandora sweaters in different shades to match her moods.

Unfortunately, I remember that yellow Pandora sweater a little 19 too vividly. When I am shopping with my children, empathy continually blows me off course in the aisles. On the one hand, nobody wants her child to look funny in front of the bishop. On the other, it has yet to occur to my children that the bishop in full regalia looks pretty funny himself.

THINKING CRITICALLY

Main Idea

1. What is Phyllis Theroux's thesis, and how does she introduce it?

Details

2. How many children does Theroux have?

3. Theroux says that in her family nobody dresses for success. Describe how each child dresses.

Organization

4. In her essay, Theroux explains a process: how to shop with children. She organizes her ideas by providing readers with a list of rules to follow. Briefly summarize Theroux's rules.

Purpose, Audience, Tone

5. The tone of Theroux's essay is informal and conversational. What specific words and phrases give the essay its tone?

Inferences and Conclusions

6. Explain what Theroux means by this statement from paragraph 15: "My aim was to be the tree in the middle, identical and interchangeable with every other sapling in the grove."

7. Read the last sentence of Theroux's essay again. Why do you think she chose the word *regalia* instead of *costume* or *dress* to describe the bishop's clothes? Use your dictionary to find support for your answer.

Making Connections

You have probably heard the sayings, "Clothes make the man" and "It's what's on the inside that counts." What do you think these old sayings mean? Do you agree or disagree with either of them? Do you see any relation between one or both of the old sayings and Theroux's comments about shopping with children? Write an essay in which you answer these questions, or make up a new saying about the meaning of clothes and explain it.

SUPPORTING YOUR PARAGRAPH'S MAIN IDEA

As explained in Chapter 5, *facts, reasons,* and *examples* are three types of details that support main ideas. As a reader, your job is to find and follow the writer's details. As a writer, your job is to provide details for your readers to follow. Suppose you have chosen a topic for a paragraph, and you have a main idea in mind. Before you select your details, ask yourself two questions:

1. What kind of details will I choose?

2. How will they support my main idea?

Providing Facts

Remember that *a fact is anything that can be proven right or wrong through research, direct observation, or questioning.* Facts include statistics and other numerical data; information gathered through the senses of sight, hearing, smell, taste, and touch; and information collected from books, other printed sources, or from the testimony of experts. A fact is also anything we have observed so often that we commonly accept it as true, such as the laws of gravity or the process of photosynthesis. An opinion is more convincing if you support it with facts. Following are three topic sentences that state opinions with facts that support them:

Topic Sentences	Facts
Public officials have done a poor job of solving our city's traffic problems.	The city's main highway is operating at four times its intended capacity. Rush "hour" lasts from 6:45 A.M. to 8:30 A.M. and from 4:45 P.M. to 6:30 P.M.
	Traffic accidents, according to the highway patrol, have more than doubled in the past five years.
Julia Roberts is a versatile actress.	In *Pretty Woman* she plays a likable prostitute.
	In *Steel Magnolias* she plays an energetic young mother stricken with a fatal illness.
	In *Sleeping with the Enemy* she plays an abused wife.
	In *The Pelican Brief* she plays a serious law student.
This winter we lived through a terrible storm.	Two feet of snow fell during one evening.
	Winds along the coast raged at 60 miles per hour.
	Tides of 12 feet caused flooding in some areas. Several towns had to be evacuated.

Exercise 6.1   List three facts that could support each of the topic sentences below.

1. Each part of the newspaper offers a specific kind of information.

   a. _____

   b. _____

   c. _____

2. If you have the following symptoms, you are probably catching a cold.

   a. _____

   b. _____

   c. _____

3. To enter the career of my choice, I must have certain qualifications and skills.

   a. _____

   b. _____

   c. _____

Stating Reasons

Reasons help explain why something happens or why something is the way it is. Words and phrases such as *because, since, the causes are,* and *the purpose is* may help readers identify statements in your writing that contain reasons. Because there may be many different reasons to explain just about everything, you need to consider carefully your reasons for thinking the way you do about your topic. You also need to be aware of the reasons others may have for thinking differently. Following are three topic sentences with reasons that support them:

Topic Sentences	Reasons
Although I could have attended several colleges, I chose Valencia.	The campus is only three miles from my house.
	I can save money by living at home.
	The tuition is affordable.
	The atmosphere at Valencia is friendly and personal.
	The programs and services available are helping me plan my future.
To overcome math failure, you must first understand why so many students fail.	Math anxiety afflicts many students who have a "fear of failure."
	A fear of success can also affect student performance.
	Equating grades with self-esteem can lead to negative feelings that direct attention away from the task.
	Procrastination is the reason many students fall behind and never catch up.
So far, our community has remained safe even though we live near a high-crime area.	One reason is that the city has installed quartz halogen bulbs in the street lights to make it harder for criminals to hide.
	Police make regular neighborhood patrols.
	Also, we have a successful neighborhood watch program.
	Our school board approved a crime-prevention program for grades K–12 that has been in effect for several years.

Exercise 6.2   Make a list of your reasons for attending the college you have chosen, then write a topic sentence for a paragraph on your reasons for attending that college.

Giving Examples

An example is an illustration that clarifies a general statement such as a topic sentence. Examples usually appeal to one or more of the five senses of sight, hearing, taste, touch, and smell; and they help create clear and vivid pictures in your readers' minds. Examples are another type of detail you can use to support your main idea. You can use phrases such as *for example* and *to illustrate* to signal your readers that an example follows. An effective use of examples can create clear and vivid images for readers. Following are three topic sentences with examples that support them:

Topic Sentences	Examples
My car is unreliable.	Sometimes it will not start.
	The gas gauge gives incorrect readings.
	The oil light comes on even though I have just added oil.
	The tires will not stay balanced.
	This morning the brakes failed.
	For the last year my car has been in the shop at least once a month.
My grandmother's house is a collection of aromas, odors, and fragrances.	The aroma of chocolate chip cookies or a turkey baking in the oven fills the house.
	The fragrances of roses and gardenias come in through the windows when there is a breeze.
	The clean smells of wax, furniture polish, and freshly washed linens pervade the rooms.

Topic Sentences	Examples
	On clear, cool days when the wind is in the right direction, an unpleasant odor from the paper mill mingles with the fragrances in the house.
My job as a volunteer fire-fighter is a rewarding experience.	I have earned the respect of my male coworkers by proving that I am willing to work as hard as they do.
	I know I am making an important contribution to my community because of the commendations our department has received.
	I have felt the gratitude of the people I have helped to safety during a fire.
	I have developed new confidence in myself because I am doing a job that in the past women were not supposed to be able to do.

Exercise 6.3   List at least three specific examples you could use to support one of the three topic sentences below. Then write a topic sentence on a topic of your choice and three or more examples to support it.

1. My mornings are usually very hectic.

2. When looking for a part-time job, a person should consider several requirements.

3. My apartment is in a bad state of repair.

ARRANGING YOUR PARAGRAPH'S DETAILS

Whether you support a topic sentence with facts, reasons, examples, or some of each, be specific. Use the same three levels of development in your writing that you look for in your reading. As explained in Chapter

5, the main idea is the first level of development; major details are the second level; minor details are the third level.

Topic sentence:	**Level 1** My health club has become more of a social gathering place than a fitness center.
First major detail that supports the general statement:	**Level 2** For one thing, people come here to see and be seen.
Minor detail that supports the first major detail:	**Level 3** The men and women wear skimpy outfits that show off their bodies.
Minor detail that supports the first major detail:	**Level 3** The women wear makeup, and their hair is attractively styled as if they were going on dates.
Minor detail that supports the first major detail:	**Level 3** The men seek to impress the women by trying to outdo each other lifting weights.
Second major detail that supports the general statement:	**Level 2** Also, some people use the health club as a meeting place.
Minor detail that supports the second major detail:	**Level 3** Men and women join because they have heard it is a safe place to meet people.
Minor detail that supports the second major detail:	**Level 3** They can observe each other's behavior and get to know each other before going out.

The major details illustrate two ways in which the health club has become a social gathering place. People come there to see and be seen and to meet each other. The minor details provide specific examples of what people *do* to see and be seen, and *how* they use the club as a meeting place.

Exercise 6.4   Read the following paragraph, then complete the outline that follows it. The outline, which is partially filled in for you, illustrates the paragraph's three levels of development from main idea through major details to minor details and to the conclusion, which contains a restatement of the main idea.

> Getting a college education has not been easy for me. One thing that makes it difficult is that I am a working mother of two children who are still in school. I have to get up early to make their breakfast and see them off. Also, I try to arrange my schedule to be at home when they arrive. Helping them with their homework is important to me but leaves me less time to do my own studying. My job is another thing that makes it hard for me to get an education. I work as a receptionist in a doctor's office in the mornings from 8:00 until 11:30. If a class I need is scheduled at these times, then I have to postpone taking it until it is offered at a more convenient time. Because of my job, it will probably take me a long time to get my degree. Studying adds to these difficulties. It has been a while since I attended school, and my skills are a little rusty. Although getting a college education is difficult, the struggle is worth it not only for me but for the good example I am setting for my children.

Level 1
Topic sentence: Getting a college education has not been easy for me.

    Level 2
    I. One thing that makes it difficult . . .

        Level 3
        A. _____
        B. _____
        C. _____
        D. _____

    Level 2
    II. _____

Level 3

A. I work as a receptionist from 8:30 to 11:30.

B. I have to postpone taking classes offered at these times.

C. It will take a long time to get my degree.

Level 2

III. Studying adds to these difficulties.

Level 3

A. _____

B. _____

Level 1

Concluding sentence: Although getting a college education is difficult, the struggle is worth it not only for me but for the good example I am setting for my children.

THINKING ABOUT PROCESS

Two things to consider during your revision process are better selection of details and better arrangement of details. Try these steps.

1. Read over each paragraph to make sure that every detail in the paragraph supports the main idea.

2. Ask yourself, "Are my details *concrete?*" Concrete details are specific and descriptive. They appeal to your readers' five senses: sight, hearing, taste, smell, and touch. They create images, or pictures, in your readers' minds.

3. Check your paragraph for logical development. Do you have major details and minor details to support the main idea? Are the details arranged logically? What can you add, revise, or delete to improve your paragraph?

SUPPORTING YOUR ESSAY'S THESIS

Just as each detail in a paragraph supports the main idea, each paragraph within an essay supports the thesis. Remember that an essay's direction of development flows from the introduction, to the body, to the conclusion. The number of paragraphs in each part is up to you. Your choice of details determines where the divisions of your essay will fall.

One way to plan an essay is to choose a topic, come up with a preliminary thesis statement, and make an informal outline. Break down your thesis into several subpoints, or main ideas, each of which can be explained in a paragraph. Following are two examples of a thesis statement and informal outline.

EXAMPLE 1

A good weight-training program should concentrate on how to build and tone the muscles in four major parts of the body.

1. Chest muscles

2. Back muscles

3. Arm muscles

4. Leg muscles

From this outline, you could develop an essay that has at least four body paragraphs to support the thesis. During your drafting process, you would need to write a topic sentence and choose details for each body paragraph. In addition, you would need to write an introduction and a conclusion for your essay.

EXAMPLE 2

You can reduce stress by avoiding its common causes.

1. Taking on too many obligations is a common cause of stress.

2. Being a perfectionist is another common cause.

3. The most common cause of stress is poor time management.

From this outline, you could develop an essay that has at least three body paragraphs to support the thesis. Each body paragraph could begin with a topic sentence listed on the outline. During your drafting process, you could choose details to support these topic sentences. In addition, your essay would need an introduction and a conclusion.

Exercise 6.5   Following are three informal outlines. Each begins with a thesis statement followed by two or more subpoints that could become the main ideas of body paragraphs. Read the outlines; then add one more subpoint to each.

1. Malls not only provide a place to shop, but they have become popular entertainment centers as well.

    a. They provide teenagers a place to hang out.

    b. They provide endless subjects for people watchers.

    c. They provide . . .

2. The behavior of some moviegoers is enough to drive me from the theater to the nearest video store.

    a. Some moviegoers do not make their children behave.

    b. Some moviegoers disturb others by leaving their seats frequently.

    c. Some moviegoers litter the theater.

    d. Some moviegoers . . .

3. Going to the movies is better in some ways than when I was a child, but in other ways it is worse.

    a. Better

        1. More theaters are available to choose from.

        2. A wider variety of snacks is available.

        3.

    b. Worse

    1. Moviegoers are not as considerate as they used to be.

    2. Not as many good shows for children are made.

    3.

Exercise 6.6   Following are two thesis statements. For each of them, list two to four main ideas that could be developed into the body paragraphs of an essay.

1. Although people look for many qualities in a good friend, the quality I admire most in my best friend is a sense of humor.

2. Everyone knows you cannot cure the common cold, but while you are waiting for one to go away, try my method to make yourself comfortable.

ARRANGING YOUR ESSAY'S DETAILS

Not only should you choose specific details, but you should arrange them logically. Logical arrangement of details will help give your essay unity and coherence. The thesis is your central idea. To support your thesis, break it down into subpoints, which are the main ideas of your body paragraphs. Then support each subpoint or main idea with specific details. If you follow this logical plan from *thesis* to *topic sentence* to *major* and *minor supporting details,* your essay will be unified and coherent.

Example 1 on page 167 shows a thesis statement and an informal outline of the main ideas suggested by the thesis statement. The following formal outline adds supporting details and gives you a clearer picture of how the writer will support the thesis.

THESIS: A good weight-training program should concentrate on how to build and tone the muscles in four major parts of the body.

    I. The muscles of the chest: pectorals

       A. How we use these muscles

       B. Type of training

 Major details

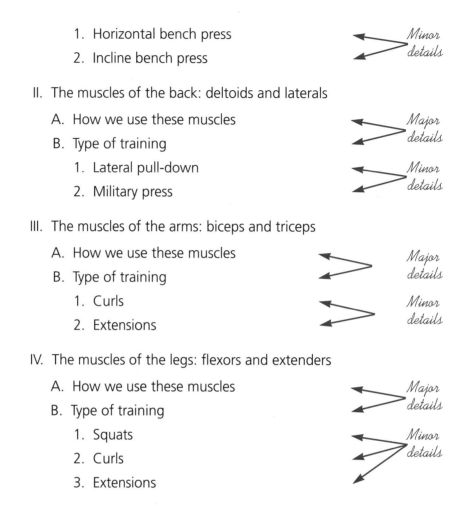

1. Horizontal bench press — *Minor details*

2. Incline bench press

II. The muscles of the back: deltoids and laterals

    A. How we use these muscles — *Major details*

    B. Type of training

       1. Lateral pull-down — *Minor details*

       2. Military press

III. The muscles of the arms: biceps and triceps

    A. How we use these muscles — *Major details*

    B. Type of training

       1. Curls — *Minor details*

       2. Extensions

IV. The muscles of the legs: flexors and extenders

    A. How we use these muscles — *Major details*

    B. Type of training

       1. Squats — *Minor details*

       2. Curls

       3. Extensions

This outline shows that the writer will support the thesis by telling readers which muscles to train, what these muscles help them do, and which exercises help build and tone each muscle. The details are now more specific, and the outline has helped the writer to arrange them logically so that readers will be able to follow the writer's organizational pattern. Someone else writing on the same topic might choose to arrange the details differently or choose different details. How you support a thesis is up to you, as long as your details are specific and are arranged logically.

Exercise 6.7   Choose one of the informal outlines in Exercise 6.5 and add major and minor supporting details so that your outline looks like the preceding expanded outline.

THINKING IT OVER

Test your recall of this chapter's concepts by completing the following statements. If you cannot complete a statement, look back through the chapter to find the answer.

1. You must provide readers with _____ to support your main idea.

2. The types of _____ and levels of _____ you look for in reading should also be present in your writing.

3. _____, _____, and _____ are the types of details explained in this chapter and in Chapter 5.

4. _____ details are specific and descriptive.

5. Your details should also appeal to your readers' fine _____.

6. Not only should you choose specific details, you should arrange them _____.

7. Just as details within a paragraph support the topic sentence, the main ideas and details of each paragraph should support an essay's _____ _____.

8. Choose one of the Thinking First questions at the beginning of the chapter to answer on the following lines:

_____

_____

_____

TOPICS FOR WRITING

1. Choose one of the topics below, or make up your own topic. Then plan and write an essay.

   Advantages or disadvantages of shopping with others

   Money-saving tips for shoppers

   Shopping habits of men or women

   A favorite store and why you like it

   A store that has benefited or harmed your community

   Clothes as a form of rebellion or self-expression

2. Imagine you had to buy one gift for each member of your family and you had only $25 to spend for all the gifts. Write an essay explaining what you would buy and why.

Checklist for Revision

As you revise and edit your essay, check for the following.

1. Have you determined the major divisions of your essay?

2. Do your paragraphs have clearly stated main ideas?

3. Have you supported your main ideas with enough concrete details?

4. Do the main ideas and details within paragraphs support your essay's thesis?

5. Are your details logically arranged?

6. Have you found and corrected your errors?

REFLECTIONS ON READING AND WRITING

As you read "Shopping with Children," were you able to follow Theroux's ideas? Did you have any trouble finding the thesis? What examples of concrete details can you find in the essay? What have you learned, either from Theroux's essay or from this chapter, that you will apply to your writing?

Chapter 7

Organization I:
Unity and Coherence in
Reading and Writing

THINKING FIRST

- *How do writers organize their ideas?*
- *Does the way details are organized guide my reading?*
- *How can I write well-organized paragraphs and essays?*

*G*ood writing is unified and follows certain recognizable patterns. As you begin to understand the way a paragraph or essay is organized, you can see relationships among ideas. Your reading comprehension improves because you are better able to follow the development of an idea from introduction to conclusion. Your writing skill increases when you are able to organize your ideas in meaningful patterns your readers can follow.

In the process of writing do you ever ask yourself, "How can I organize my details? What should come first, next, last?" In the process of reading do you ever get lost in details, unsure of what follows next or why, and wonder, "What am I missing?" To answer these questions, this chapter explains two principles of organization you should look for in your reading and practice in your writing: *unity* and *coherence*.

BACKGROUND CHECK

Before reading the following excerpt, check your knowledge and assumptions about intelligence.

1. What does the word *intelligence* mean to you? What examples can you give?

2. Can people be intelligent in some ways and not in others? What examples can you give?

3. Can you think of a recent event in the news or in your life where intelligence, or the lack of it, influenced the outcome?

4. Based on your survey of the title, author information, and first two paragraphs, what do you expect to follow?

5. What else do you know or think about the topic?

The Different Ways of Being Smart
Sara Gilbert

In this excerpt from Chapter 5 of Sara Gilbert's Using Your Head, The Different Ways of Being Smart, *Gilbert categorizes kinds of intelligence. Her thesis, or central idea, is that many kinds of intelligence exist and that each of us is "smart" in one or more ways. As you read the excerpt, try to discover how each paragraph supports its own main idea, and how all the paragraphs together support Gilbert's central idea.*

VOCABULARY CHECK

unique (2)	one of a kind
spectrum (2)	range
conscientious (3)	thorough
symbols (13)	something that represents something else
intently (13)	with deep concentration
persistent (13)	refusing to give up
tycoons (14)	wealthy and powerful businesspersons
merits (14)	earned value

Book smarts, art smarts, body smarts, street smarts, and people
smarts: These . . . labels . . . describe the various forms of intelligence
and their use. As you might imagine, psychologists and other re-
searchers into the nature of intelligence have come up with more formal terms for the types that they have isolated. One set of labels in
common use is: convergent, divergent, assimilating, and accommo-
dating. The converger and assimilator are like our book-smart person;
the diverger, like our art-smart; and the accommodator, like our street-
smart and people-smart. . . .   1

Whatever categorization we use, we will find some overlap within
any individual. In fact, there are probably as many answers to the
question "What are the different ways of being smart?" as there are
people in the universe, because each of us is unique. We can't be
typecast; we each have a wide spectrum of special talents.   2

Still, you probably know well at least one person whose talents
generally fall into each of our categories. Keep those people in mind
as you read through the detailed descriptions of them. . . .   3

At first it might seem that each of those types must call on very
different sorts of abilities to be smart in his or her own ways. But
in fact, each of the categories of intelligence on our list must use
the same ingredients . . . learning ability, memory, speed, judgment,
problem-solving skill, good use of language and other symbols, and
creativity. Also, the thought processes that go on inside the heads of
people with those varying kinds of smarts include the same steps:
planning, perceiving, imaging, remembering, feeling, and acting.   4

Intelligence expresses itself in different forms, in part because of
the differing physical qualities born and built into each person's body   5

and brain, and in part because of the values and motivations that each person has learned.

However, the fact that each kind of smarts makes use of the same   6
steps means that anyone can learn or develop skills in any or all of the categories. . . . Let's take a closer look at the many ways of being smart.

A *book-smart* person is one who tends to do well in school, to   7
score high on tests, including intelligence tests. He or she is likely to be well-organized, to go about solving problems in a logical, step-by-step fashion, and to have a highly developed language ability. Another label for a book-smart person is "intellectual," meaning someone who uses the mind more to *know* than to feel or to control, and a book-smart person is especially proud of having knowledge. That knowledge may range from literature through science to math, but it is probable that it is concentrated in one area. Research shows that different knowledge areas occupy different clusters in the brain, so that someone whose connections for complicated calculations are highly developed may have less development in the areas controlling speech and writing.

Although as we've said, current research indicates that learning   8
centers may be scattered throughout both hemispheres of the brain, the activities of the "logical" left side are probably most important in the lives of book-smart people. Book-smart people may also be creative: Many mathematical or scientific problems could not be solved, for instance, without creative insights, but the primary focus of a book-smart person is the increase of knowledge.

Art-smart people, on the other hand, rely primarily on creativity.   9
They create music, paintings, sculpture, plays, photographs, or other forms of art often without being able to explain why or how they chose a particular form or design. They are said to be "right-brained" people, because it appears that the control centers for such skills as touch perception and intuition—the formation of ideas without the use of words—lie in the right hemisphere. Artistic people tend to take in knowledge more often by seeing, hearing, and feeling than by conscientious reading and memorizing.

An art-smart person may not do too well in school, not because   10
he or she is not bright, but because of an approach to problem solving that does not fit in well with the formats usually used by teachers and tests. A book-smart person might approach a problem on a math test logically, working step-by-step toward the right answer, while an art-smart person may simply "know" the answer without being able to demonstrate the calculations involved. On a social studies exam, the book-smart person will carefully recount all the facts, while the more artistic one may weave stories and fantasies using the facts only

as a base. In both cases, it's a good bet that the book-smart student will get the higher grade.

People who are serious about becoming artists, of course, may   11
need to absorb a great deal of "book knowledge" in order to develop a solid background for their skills. There are other overlaps, as well: People with great musical ability, for instance, also tend to be skilled at mathematics, perhaps because of brain-cell interactions that are common to both processes. And in order to make use of any talent, art-smart people must have good body control as well.

The people we're calling *body smart* have a lot of that kind of   12
body control. Most of them start out with bodies that are well put together for some kind of athletics—they may have inherited good muscular development for a sport like football, or loose and limber joints for gymnastic-style athletics. Or they may be people whose hands are naturally well coordinated for performing intricate tasks.

But although the physical basis for their talent may come from   13
their genes and from especially sensitive brain centers for motor control, to make use of their "natural" skills they must be able to observe accurately—to figure out how a move is made or an object is constructed—and they must think about how to do it themselves. This thinking involves a complex use of symbols that enables the brain to "tell" another part of itself what to do. In other situations, such as school, a body- smart person is probably best able to learn through some physical technique: In studying for an exam, for instance, he or she will retain information by saying it out loud, acting out the facts, or counting them off with finger taps. Although athletes or the manually talented are often teased as being "dumb" in schoolwork, that is not necessarily an accurate picture. To be good in using physical talents, a person must put in a lot of practice, be able to concentrate intently, and be stubbornly persistent in achieving a goal. And those qualities of will and self-control can also be put to good use in more "intellectual" achievements.

Persistence is also an important quality of *street-smart* people.   14
They are the ones who are able to see difficulties as challenges, to turn almost any situation to advantage for themselves. As young people, they are the ones who are able to make the most money doing odd jobs, or who can get free tickets to a concert that others believe is completely sold out. As adults, they are the business tycoons, for instance, or the personalities who shoot to stardom no matter how much or little talent they have. A street-smart student may do well in the school subjects that he or she knows count for the most and will all but ignore the rest. When taking exams, street-smart people are likely to get better grades than their knowledge merits be-

cause they can "psych out" the test, and because, when facing a problem or question they can't answer, they are skilled at putting on the paper something that looks good.

To be street smart in these ways—to be able to achieve highly individualistic goals and to be able to get around obstacles that totally stump others—a person must draw upon a wide scope of mental powers. It takes excellent problem-solving ability, creative thought, good planning and goal setting, accurate perception, persistent effort, skill with language, quick thinking, and a strong sense of intuition.   15

Intuition plays a major role in *people smarts* as well. This kind of intelligence allows a person to sense what others are thinking, feeling, wanting, and planning. Although we might tend to put this sort of skill down as basic "instinct," it actually relies on higher activities of the brain. People smarts rely on very accurate and quick perceptions of clues and relationships that escape the notice of many, and they include the ability to analyze the information taken in. A people-smart student can do well in school simply by dealing with individual teachers in the most productive way: Some can be charmed, some respond well to special requests for help, some reward hard work no matter what the results, and so forth. The people-smart student figures out easily what is the best approach to take. People with these talents also achieve well in other activities, of course—they become the leaders in clubs, and organizations, and they are able to win important individuals, like potential employers, over to their side. They would probably be typed as right-brained people, like artists, but their skill with language, both spoken and unspoken, is one that draws heavily on the left side.   16

Have you been able to compare these types with people you know in your class, family, or neighborhood? Of course, no individual is actually a type: People with any one of the kind of smarts that we've described also have some of the others. . . .   17

THINKING CRITICALLY

Main Idea

1. What is Sara Gilbert's thesis? Is it stated or implied?

Details

2. According to Gilbert, what are the different ways of being smart?

Organization

3. Explain how the details support Gilbert's thesis.

Purpose, Audience, Tone

4. Who is Gilbert's audience? What words or phrases in the excerpt help you determine the audience?

Inferences and Conclusions

5. Based on Gilbert's statement, "Anyone can learn or develop skills in any or all of the categories," what inference can you make about a person who says, "I'm no good at math"?

Making Connections

Which of Gilbert's categories best describes you? Do you see yourself in more than one category? Are you intelligent in ways that Gilbert does not describe? Write a paragraph in which you describe your kind of intelligence.

UNITY IN PARAGRAPHS

Unity means *oneness* or *wholeness*. Animal rights activists are *united* in their efforts to protect animals from being exploited. Environmental activists are *united* by their common goal to save the environment. Members of professional, political, and social organizations are *united* by shared beliefs, values, and goals. The sentences of a paragraph are *united* when they all work together to make and support a main idea. When one or more sentences or details within a paragraph do not support the main idea, then unity is interrupted and the paragraph strays from its topic.

When you read, think of the essay, article, or chapter you are reading as a unified piece of writing. Read it one section or paragraph at a time. Read for ideas: the main idea and the details that support it. Ask yourself, "What connects these ideas?" Try to discover a unifying principle, sometimes called the *controlling idea*. A repeated word or phrase may provide a clue. For example, Gilbert's unifying principle is *different ways of being smart.* This idea is stated in the title and repeated in the first sentence in the phrase *various forms of intelligence.* As a reader you should ask yourself, "What are Gilbert's ways, and how do they differ?" This question pinpoints the details you should look for as you read.

As a writer, you must strive for unified paragraphs. Having a topic sentence is a sure way to begin. Select only the details that support your topic sentence. Edit your paragraph for any off-topic sentences and either delete them or rewrite them so that they are on topic. The next two paragraphs each contain a sentence that keeps them from being unified. Find the off-topic sentences before reading the explanation that follows the paragraph.

PARAGRAPH 1

Ellen Barkin, who starred in *Man Trouble,* had two problems that had to be accommodated during the filming of the picture. Jack Nicholson also starred in the film. Barkin is allergic to dog dander. If she gets near a dog, she may have a runny nose, watery eyes, and other unpleasant reactions. The scenes had to be shot in such a way that Barkin did not come into contact with the dog. For example, he does not appear in the car with her or in the same room. Another problem that had to be accommodated is that Barkin did not know how to drive, yet the script called for her to drive a car. She took lessons and learned enough to be able to do the scenes. Neither her allergy nor lack of driving skill proved to be a problem that could not be solved.

PARAGRAPH 2

If you would like to get fit and are thinking about joining a health club or gym, you should also consider the advantages of a membership in a hospital wellness center. Unlike some health clubs or gyms, wellness centers hire only trained staff members who have degrees or other certification in fields such as nutrition and fitness. These people are qualified to assess your level of fitness and design a safe program for you that is based on the results of a blood test, a stress test, and your doctor's recommendation. In fact, you cannot even join a wellness center without your doctor's approval. Some health clubs serve as meeting places for young singles. Another advantage of wellness centers over health clubs and gyms is that they offer services other than fitness training, such as nutritional counseling, stress reduction seminars, and weight-loss classes. At a health club or gym you may be left on your own after your first visit, but at a wellness center, someone monitors your progress and continually updates your program as your fitness level increases. Surprisingly, a wellness center membership may cost you a lot less than a membership in a health club or gym, and that is another advantage.

In paragraph 1, the sentence, "Jack Nicholson also starred in the film" is off-topic because the paragraph is about Ellen Barkin, not Jack Nicholson. In paragraph 2, the unity is disrupted by the sentence, "Some health clubs serve as meeting places for young singles." This paragraph is a comparison of wellness centers and health clubs or gyms on the basis of their fitness advantages, not on their social advantages.

To stick to the point in your reading, find the author's unifying principle or controlling idea. To write unified paragraphs, state your main idea and do not stray from your topic. In addition, experiment with finding a controlling idea. State this idea in your topic sentence. Then repeat it or state it in different words one or more times within your paragraph.

Exercise 7.1   Read the following paragraphs and evaluate them for unity. If you find any sentences that do not stay on the point, cross them out. Be able to explain your results.

1. Count Dracula is a character who continues to appeal to filmgoers. Many actors have played him, each one adding something different to the role. In *Nosferatu,* a silent film of the 1920s, Max Shreck plays Dracula as a supernatural being having a ratlike appearance. Frankenstein is another character who appeals to filmgoers. In 1931, Bela Lugosi portrayed Dracula as an attractive, cultured man whose genteel manner barely concealed his violence. Christopher Lee's performances in the 1950s emphasized Dracula's sex appeal. George Hamilton was the first to make us laugh at Dracula in *Love at First Bite,* a cult favorite. The 1970s gave us an updated version of *Nosferatu* in which Klaus Kinski combines aspects of the Shreck and Lugosi roles. Frank Langella is a sensitive Dracula who falls in love with a "liberated" woman. Lon Chaney plays the Wolfman as an ordinary fellow fallen on bad times. Every decade has its re-creation of the old and popular vampire legend.

2. U.S. politics has always been a two-party system, but change seemed possible with the campaign of Ross Perot in the 1992 presidential election. Perot is a Texas billionaire who ran for president as the nominee of the Independent party, a third party that has never

aroused much interest or support. During the week of the Democratic National Convention, Perot announced that he would not run. Barbara Jordan and Jesse Jackson, both Clinton supporters, addressed the convention. But Perot rejoined the campaign, debated the other two candidates, then lost the election to Bill Clinton. The successful campaign of an Independent proved, however, that the Republicans and Democrats would have to do some serious overhauling to win back the support they lost to Ross Perot.

3. Although being a dental hygienist may not be everyone's idea of the perfect job, Kelly would not want to do anything else. For a brief time, she had thought she wanted to be a court reporter. One reason she likes her job is that she can schedule her hours so that she works four days a week and is off in the afternoons. This allows her to be at home when her children arrive from school. Because she does not work on Fridays, she has a three-day weekend. Another reason Kelly likes her job is that the work is challenging and pleasant. For example, cleaning children's teeth is a challenge because Kelly has to find ways to distract the children so that they will let her do what she needs to do without making a fuss. Kelly's work is pleasant because just about everyone likes the way his or her mouth feels after a cleaning, and they compliment Kelly on what a good job she does. But Kelly's best reason of all for liking her job is that she gets to be with her family while she is at work. After all, the dentist Kelly works for is her dad, and her sister is his receptionist.

Exercise 7.2   Write a unified paragraph about an event or experience of your choice. Think about the event or experience. What happened? What did you do? Was it pleasant or unpleasant? To find a controlling idea for your paragraph, think of one word or a short phrase that describes either how you felt or what the process was like. Whatever your controlling idea is, select details that reflect that idea. Make sure your topic sentence states your controlling idea. To help you get started, use the following example as a guide.

Event or experience:	Registering for classes
Controlling idea:	Hectic
Topic sentence:	Registering for classes this semester was a hectic process for me.

COHERENCE PATTERNS IN PARAGRAPHS

Cohere means *to stick together.* A paragraph has *coherence* when it is so well organized that the details flow smoothly and the relationship among the details is clear. Coherence can guide your reading if you become aware of the author's chosen pattern: the type of order or arrangement of details. To give your own paragraphs coherence, choose a pattern that is appropriate for your topic. Although you can organize details in many ways, these three basic patterns are good choices: *time order, emphatic order,* and *spatial order.*

Time Order

Another name for time order is *chronological order,* and it is helpful for organizing details according to a time sequence. Suppose you are reading a textbook chapter on human reproduction that explains what happens during pregnancy. After making some notes, you decide to write a paragraph in which you summarize what you have read. Because pregnancy occurs over a nine-month period, you arrange your details into three 3-month periods. Your informal outline might look like this:

1. The first three months

    a. Little increase in size.

    b. Embryo becomes a fetus.

2. The next three months

    a. Fetus becomes larger.

    b. Heartbeat and movement occur.

3. The last three months

    a. Fetus continues to grow.

    b. Fetal movements increase.

    c. Body prepares itself for birth.

When using time order, help your readers follow your ideas by beginning some of your sentences with signal words and phrases that serve as *time markers,* such as *first, next, third,* and *finally;* times of day, such as *at 10:30;* or phrases that indicate time of day, such as *this morn-*

ing. Time order signals help readers to understand when you have finished explaining one step or stage and have moved on to another. Time markers also help you identify and follow patterns in your reading. In the following paragraph, transitional words and phrases that serve as time markers are underlined for you.

Flood

At first, the rain fell slowly. We thought it was just another summer storm. Then the rain began to come in torrents, drenching everything in sight. For days, it rained. Our doormats and flowerpots washed away. The dog's outdoor water bowl overflowed and was swept down the street, along with the neighbors' garden hoses, garbage cans, and various kinds of debris. By the end of the week, the water was over the threshold, soaking the carpets. We moved what furniture we could upstairs. The rest, we raised on blocks to keep it dry. Over the weekend, the rain slowed, then stopped. By Sunday afternoon, the water had begun to recede. On Monday, everyone on our block was busily assessing damages and cleaning up.

This paragraph traces a sequence of events through one week. Time markers help you follow the rain's progress as it leads to flooding conditions.

Emphatic Order

Sometimes writers arrange details in their order of importance, especially if one detail is clearly more important than another, if they want to save the best suggestions for last, or if they want to emphasize the conclusion. Suppose you have learned from experience that cramming for a test does not work, and you write a paragraph that explains an effective way to study for an exam. You may think that the most important thing students can do to ensure success is to review periodically. You might save this suggestion for last and conclude with tips on how to make periodic review easier. Use *words of emphasis* to signal your readers when another important idea is coming or to show a progression of ideas from least important to most important. Words and phrases such as *equally important, the most important of all, major* and *minor,* and *of primary concern* are helpful signals for readers and may improve the coherence of your paragraphs. Remember to pay attention to these words in your reading also. In the following paragraphs, words of emphasis are underlined.

> The power of television news to capture the public's attention became apparent in the 1960s. In 1963, the nation was gripped by horror and grief at the assassination of President Kennedy; the event and its aftermath kept the nation riveted to the television for days. Other major events, though reported in newspapers and magazines as well, were likewise widely and instantaneously experienced on television. Several incidents occurred in 1968 alone: the first expedition to set foot on the moon, the assassination of Senator Robert F. Kennedy, the riots at the Democratic National Convention, and North Vietnam's Tet offensive—television coverage of which brought into American homes bloody images from a war that previously had seemed quite remote.
>   Each of these events, seen over several days by a huge section of the American public, became part of a shared set of experiences, all seen through the eye of television. Since then, television has become the primary source of news information for a large section of the American public, with newspapers, magazines, and radio assuming supplemental roles. . . .

The excerpt explains how television became the primary, or most important, source of news information because of a progression of several televised major events that began with the assassination of President Kennedy.

Spatial Order

Spatial order describes the location of people or things. Writers use spatial order to create images in readers' minds of the places they want them to visualize. For example, in a detective novel, a writer might use spatial order to describe a crime scene. In a history textbook, a writer might use spatial order to describe a battle scene. Words or phrases such as *in front, behind, near, north, on the left,* and *down* signal placement or location. When you encounter these spatial markers in your reading, try to visualize the scene they describe.

To write about a place, try to re-create the scene. Imagine yourself in that place. Tell readers what would be in front of them, behind them, on either side of them, directly overhead, and beneath their feet if they were to stand in the same spot as you. Use spatial markers to signal a reader where to "look" in his or her mind's eye. The following excerpt is from the first paragraph of "Home," a chapter in *Lake Wobegon Days* by Garrison Keillor. Spatial details provide a description of Lake Wobegon, a Minnesota town. The order of details creates a view of the town that you would see by looking or walking in the direction the writer suggests. Spatial details and the words that signal their order are underlined.

> The town of Lake Wobegon, Minnesota, lies on the shore against Adams Hill looking east across the blue-green water to the dark woods. From the south, the highway aims for the lake, bends left by the magnificent concrete Grecian grain silos, and eases over a leg of the hill past the SLOW CHILDREN sign, bringing the traveler in on Main Street toward the town's one traffic light, which is almost always green. A few surviving elms shade the street. Along the ragged dirt path between the asphalt and the grass, a child slowly walks to Ralph's Grocery, kicking an asphalt chunk ahead of him. It is a chunk that after four blocks he is now mesmerized by, to which he is completely dedicated. At Bunsen Motors, the sidewalk begins. A breeze off the lake brings a sweet air of mud and rotting wood, a slight fishy smell, and picks up the sweetness of old grease, a sharp whiff of gasoline, fresh tires, spring dust, and, from across the street, the faint essence of tuna hot-dish at the Chatterbox Cafe. . . .

The spatial details in this paragraph help you to visualize the imaginary town of Lake Wobegon. The order of details leads you on a visual trip through the town by following the highway south to Main Street, then along Main Street where your eyes travel down the dirt path beside the street and to the sidewalk. You *see* the town through Ralph's Grocery, Bunsen Motors, and the Chatterbox Cafe. Sensory details such as the breeze and smells of mud, rotting wood, fish, grease, gasoline, tires, and spring dust complete the picture. The order of spatial details gives them coherence. They draw you into Garrison's image of Lake Wobegon just as the arrangement of colors, shapes, and figures in a painting draws you into the picture.

Coherence comes with practice. You may have to revise a paragraph several times to make the ideas flow smoothly and to make one sentence lead logically to the next. Whether choosing patterns for your paragraphs or trying to identify patterns in your reading, let your guides be the main idea and the type of support chosen. Figure 7.1 illustrates three choices for main idea, type of support, and coherence pattern for the topic "my typical day at work."

FIGURE 7.1	MAIN IDEA	TYPE OF SUPPORT	COHERENCE PATTERN
Choosing Coherence Patterns	My typical work day consists of the things I do before lunch and after lunch.	Details that explain what the duties are and *when* you do them	Time order
	A typical work day for me is filled with several important tasks.	Details that explain what the tasks are and their order of *importance*	Emphatic order
	My typical work day is easy because of the way my office is arranged.	Details that explain *where* everything is	Spatial order

Exercise 7.3

Read the following three paragraphs and decide whether the details are organized according to *time order, emphatic order,* or *spatial order.* Underline words or phrases that help you decide, and then write your answer beside each paragraph.

——————

1. When interviewing for a job looking your best is important. Wear a conservative outfit, stick to neutral colors, and avoid fashion fads. Let the interviewer run the show. Answer questions clearly and completely; stick to the point and do not ramble. Not only should you dress carefully and follow the interviewer's lead, but you should refrain from doing anything that may be out of place. Do not smoke even if the interviewer offers you a cigarette. Let your actions show that you know the difference between a social situation and a business situation. Most important, be yourself. You have heard this many times, and it is still good advice. The interviewer wants to know who you are, not who you *think* you are.

_____   2. It is easy to get a part-time job at my college. Whether you would like to work as an office assistant or a tutor, following these steps is important. First you have to qualify. Financial aid is not available to everyone. To find out whether you qualify, go to the financial aid office and fill out the form. Next you will be given a list of job openings. Before accepting the first one on the list, you will need to find out what each job pays, whether the hours conflict with your schedule, and what the duties are. Once you have selected the right job for you, you are ready to go to work. The whole process, from application to first day on the job, may take several days. Following the steps in the right order may save you a lot of time.

_____   3. The "new" theater at the Peabody Arts Center is not new. It is a reconstructed opera house brought over from Europe and assembled piece by piece. Once you get past the modern lobby and walk into the theater itself, it is like stepping into another world. If you are sitting about halfway down the aisle in the center of your row, you can look directly overhead and see an immense crystal chandelier suspended above you. In front of you are rows of red plush–covered seats, then the orchestra pit, then the stage flanked on either side by heavy red velvet curtains. When they are closed, you can see the initials PAC. The intertwined letters measure several feet from bottom to top, and they are embroidered in gold and silver thread. To the left, right, and in back of you are more rows of seats. Follow the rows to the end in each direction; then let your gaze travel up the walls, which are decorated with ornate wallpaper. Carved columns support balcony areas on three levels. No matter where you look, the view is sumptuous, reflecting the elegance of another age.

Exercise 7.4   Revise for coherence the paragraph you wrote for Exercise 7.2. Add signal words to help readers follow your organization.

THINKING ABOUT PROCESS

Unity and coherence are organizing principles that can guide both your reading and writing processes.

1. A controlling idea unites the main idea and the details that support it. In your reading, try to identify an author's controlling idea. Add selecting a controlling idea to your prewriting strategy.

2. Transitional words and phrases can signal an author's coherence pattern. If you identify *time order, emphatic order,* or *spatial order* in your reading, then you will know how the details are linked and may have a better chance of following them.

3. During your drafting process, experiment with coherence patterns. Revise your paragraphs and essays to improve your choice of transitions and to eliminate any details that are off topic.

UNITY AND COHERENCE IN ESSAYS

Just as the sentences of a paragraph must flow smoothly and be logically related, so must the paragraphs of an essay. What ties introductory, body, and concluding paragraphs together are your thesis, your controlling idea, and the transitional words and phrases within and between paragraphs. The following extract from the beginning of "Vocabulary Building," a chapter from Jess Stein's *The Word-a-Day Vocabulary Builder,* illustrates how the author uses a thesis and transitional words and phrases to achieve coherence between paragraphs.

1

In borrowing so freely, the English language did just what we do as individuals to increase our personal vocabularies. [When we see something strange or experience something new, either *Thesis* we take the name for it that someone else—whether a foreigner or not—is using or, on the basis of some real or fancied resemblance, we take an old word and apply it in a new situation.] This gives it a new meaning and us a new word.

Kangaroo is an <u>example</u>. Captain Cook first saw a <u>kangaroo</u> during his exploration of the South Pacific (1768–1771). *Relates* No European language had a name for this animal, much less *back to:* an idea of it. It was a very strange and exciting thing. There- *"We take* fore, it *had* to be talked about at once and that meant it had *the name* to have a name. <u>There is a story</u> that when Cook asked a na- *. . . that* tive what the animal was, the native, in his own tongue, said, *someone* "I don't understand you." Since that statement sounded *else is* something like <u>"kangaroo,"</u> Cook mistook it for the crea- *using"* ture's name and forthwith called it that.

2

Repetition of a key word or term

Though Cook does not tell <u>the story</u> himself, it is a very old story and may very well be true. Nobody has ever found any word in any known Australian native language that describes the beast and sounds like <u>kangaroo</u>. But then, according to the story, that wasn't what the native really said anyway. And the story certainly illustrates a common event in conversation. A asks B a question, which B doesn't understand. B gives A an answer, which A doesn't understand, but thinks he or she does. Both go along under the impression that they have communicated with each other.

3

Repetition of a key word or term

At any rate, *kangaroo* is now the animal's name in English. A word that had never appeared in any European tongue before the latter part of the seventeenth century, and has never been traced to any Australian dialect, is now as fixed in the language as if it could be traced back to Latin. It's accepted as much as *wolf* or *rabbit* or any other name for an animal. . . .

4

These paragraphs are tied together by one controlling idea: how English borrows from other languages. Stein develops his thesis by the extended example of how *kangaroo* became part of the English language: Captain Cook adopted the word he thought he heard an Australian call the animal now known as a kangaroo. Three types of transitions help achieve coherence in Stein's paragraphs:

1. Signal words that establish a relationship between paragraphs (example)

2. Repetition of a word, phrase, or idea in one paragraph that is mentioned in the previous paragraph (story)

3. Repetition of a key word or term throughout the passage (kangaroo)

The word *example* in the first sentence of Stein's second paragraph signals that an idea mentioned in the previous paragraph will now be illustrated. In the first sentence of the third paragraph, the phrase "the story" repeats the phrase "there is a story" from the previous paragraph. This transition indicates that the third paragraph will tell readers more about "the story." Throughout the four paragraphs, Stein's repetition of the word *kangaroo* lets readers know that the example continues and keeps their attention focused on the controlling idea: how the English language borrows words.

Suppose you had written this thesis statement.

> Malls not only provide a place to shop, but they have become popular entertainment centers as well.

Imagine also that you had begun writing an informal outline using the following two subpoints.

> 1. They provide teenagers a place to hang out.
>
> 2. They provide endless subjects for people watchers.

With a little rewriting, you could use these sentences as the topic sentences of your first and second body paragraphs following your introduction. To achieve smooth transitions between paragraphs, you could add a signal word or phrase to your topic sentences as shown in the following paragraphs.

> If you visit a shopping mall on any weekend, you will probably see more people milling, or should I say "malling," around than buying. The mall is a place to hang out. For some, it is a

Transition signals that an example follows to illustrate one way the mall functions as an entertainment center

Transition indicates that another example of the mall as entertainment center follows

Thesis

Circles indicate repetition of key ideas

place to exercise. For many, the mall is a cheap way to spend an evening. Malls not only provide a place to shop, but they have become popular entertainment centers as well.

For example, the mall is a popular hang-out for teenagers. Teenagers looking for an afternoon or evening's entertainment will find it at their local mall. Even if they don't have any money, they can hang out in a video arcade and watch their friends play "World Heroes," or they can roam the aisles of Waldenbooks and see what's new in fiction. If the mall has a food court, they can get a cheap meal at a Taco Bell, Chik-fil-a, or Sbarro. They might even take in a movie, check out the new clothes in their favorite stores, or indulge a popular pastime, people watching.

Endless subjects for the people watcher stroll the mall, providing another source of entertainment. Mall walkers keep up a steady pace in their Reeboks and warm-up suits. This group includes men and women, old and young—anybody who wants a good aerobic workout in a safe, stimulating, temperature-controlled environment. . . .

To complete the essay, you could add more examples of "subjects" for the people watcher, then one or more paragraphs that explain other ways in which the mall is an entertainment center.

Each time you revise your essay, you should seek ways to improve the coherence of your paragraphs. For example, in the preceding essay, you might use "entertainment" or a related concept, such as "pastime" or "recreation," as a controlling idea to repeat throughout the essay. You as a writer are free to organize your essay any way you like and select whatever examples, facts, or reasons you think will support your thesis. Of course, not everyone is familiar with the large shopping malls characteristic of sprawling suburban areas. Where do city dwellers shop, and where do urban teenagers hang out with their friends? In your neighborhood or community, where do people go for entertainment and what do they do? Let knowledge and experience shape what you write.

Whatever you read, look for transitions and let them guide you through the details. Whatever you write, remember to keep your audience in mind. Smooth transitions between paragraphs will give your essay coherence and help your readers keep up with you.

STUDY TIP: *Good writing takes time. Make a study schedule that allows you plenty of time to draft and revise papers before they are due. Do not procrastinate. Writing at the last minute guarantees that the result will be less than your best.*

Exercise 7.5   Examine Sara Gilbert's essay on pages 174–178 for the three types of transitions listed below. Find and mark them in the text; then share your results with the rest of the class.

- Signal words to establish a relationship between paragraphs
- Repetition in the first sentence of a paragraph, a word, phrase, or idea mentioned in the previous paragraph
- Repetition of a key word or term throughout the essay

Exercise 7.6   Revise an essay you are working on to improve organization and coherence. To improve organization, try making an outline of what you have written so far. An outline may help to reveal weak spots in your development. For example, you might find that a paragraph consists of one or more general statements with no examples to support them. To improve coherence, read the first sentences of your paragraphs and determine whether transitions are missing, or decide how you can improve on the transitions you have.

THINKING IT OVER

Test your recall of this chapter's concepts by completing the following statements. If you cannot complete a statement, look back through the chapter to find the answer.

1. _____ and_____ are two organizational principles to look for in reading and practice in writing.

2. A _____ _____ is a unifying principle that connects main ideas and details.

3. _____ means oneness or wholeness.

4. In a paragraph that has _____, the details flow smoothly and the ideas "stick together."

5. Another name for _____ _____ is chronological order.

6. _____ details tell you the location of people or things.

7. When details are arranged in order of importance, they are said to have _____ _____.

8. Transition words such as *first, next, third,* and *finally* are also called _____ _____.

9. _____ of a key word or term is one type of transition that helps writers achieve coherence.

10. Choose one of the Thinking First questions at the beginning of the chapter to answer on the following lines:

_____

_____

_____

TOPICS FOR WRITING

1. Practice your paragraph skills by choosing one of the following topics:

   a. Using *time order,* write a paragraph on one of these topics: a typical day on campus, a typical day at work, or a typical weekend.

   b. Using *emphatic order,* write a paragraph on one of these topics: why you like a certain magazine, why you admire a certain person, or why you do or do not support a certain elected official.

c. Using *spatial order*, write a paragraph in which you describe one of the following: your workplace, a city park, the objects on a shelf or desktop, or the people or things in a photograph or painting.

d. Make up your own topic and use a coherence pattern of your choice.

2. Select one of your returned essays or an essay in progress to revise for unity and coherence. Eliminate any off-topic details and rewrite one or more paragraphs using coherence patterns of your choice.

Checklist for Revision

As you revise and edit your paragraph or essay, check for the following.

1. Are the topic and focus clear in your topic sentence/thesis statement?

2. Have you supported the main idea/thesis with enough concrete details?

3. Have you checked your paragraph/essay for unity and coherence?

4. Have you used appropriate transitions?

5. Have you found and corrected your errors?

REFLECTIONS ON READING AND WRITING

Reflect on your reading of Sara Gilbert's "The Different Ways of Being Smart." Were you able to determine the thesis? Did you understand the categories? Could you place yourself and others you know in these categories? Applying what you have learned from this chapter, explain what gives Gilbert's essay unity and coherence.

Chapter 8

Organization II: Patterns in Reading and Writing

THINKING FIRST

- *What is an organizational pattern?*
- *How can I recognize patterns in my reading?*
- *How can I use patterns in my writing?*

The seasons of the year are one of the first things you learn in school. Think back to when you learned the seasons. Why were they easy to remember? Could it be because there are only four of them, and each one has characteristic weather patterns and holidays associated with it? Moreover, the seasons divide the year into four parts. This part-to-whole relationship is only one of many organizational patterns you probably already recognize although you may not yet have names for them.

Organizational patterns describe ways of thinking logically about a subject. Ideas that are related are much easier to understand and remember than random, isolated facts. In reading, patterns help you see how ideas are related. In writing, patterns help you organize your details in meaningful ways. Narration, description, sequence, process, classification and division, comparison and contrast, definition, and cause and effect are some common organizational patterns. If you think about them, you will probably realize that you have been using these patterns your whole life.

If you tell a bedtime story to a child, or relate a series of events such as what happened in a car accident, you are using *narration*. When you explain someone's physical appearance or special qualities, you are using *description*. When you count, dial a telephone number, or read a map, you are following a *sequence*. If you have ever used a recipe or followed directions to complete a task, you have used a *process*. If you take something apart or put it together, you are using *division*. *Classification* has taught you that a rose is a type of flower, and a crow is a kind of bird. Selecting a car, buying a home, choosing an outfit—all require you to *compare and contrast*. What does success mean to you? To answer this question, you must use *definition*. Have you ever had to explain why you were absent from class, or why you did not have an assignment in on time? If so, then you used *cause and effect*.

The point is that our minds work in logical ways. We seek connections among events and look for relationships among ideas as we try to make sense of our world. Because we do this automatically, why not take advantage of an innate skill?

This chapter explains how to identify organizational patterns in your reading and use them in your writing. As a reader, you are better able to follow ideas when you can fit them into a logical framework. As a writer, you are better able to organize your details when you choose an appropriate pattern to serve as your framework. The more patterns you know, the more choices you have.

BACKGROUND CHECK

Before reading the following essay, check your knowledge and assumptions about intelligence.

1. List as many words or phrases you can think of that mean *intelligence.*

2. Without mentioning names, describe someone you know who is intelligent. What makes this person intelligent? For example, what is he or she able to do?

3. What qualities do you want in a mate? Would you classify intelligence as very important, somewhat important, or not important at all?

4. Based on your survey of the title, author information, and first two paragraphs, what do you expect to follow?

5. What else do you know or think about intelligence?

Intelligence

Isaac Asimov

The late Isaac Asimov wrote numerous articles, essays, and books, both fiction and nonfiction, on a wide variety of subjects. The Foundation, *for example, is one of his best-selling science fiction novels. In the following essay, Asimov explores the concept of intelligence.*

VOCABULARY CHECK

complacent (2)	self-satisfied
bents (2)	inclinations
hastened (3)	hurried
pronouncements (3)	formal opinions, judgments
oracles (3)	predictions
foist (4)	impose
indulgently (6)	with leniency or tolerance
raucously (6)	rough sounding, harsh

What is intelligence, anyway? When I was in the army I received a kind of aptitude test that all soldiers took and, against a normal of 100, scored 160. No one at the base had ever seen a figure like that, and for two hours they made a big fuss over me. (It didn't mean anything. The next day I was still a buck private with KP as my highest duty.)   1

All my life I've been registering scores like that, so I have the complacent feeling that I'm highly intelligent, and I expect other people to think so, too. Actually, though, don't such scores simply mean that I am very good at answering the type of academic questions that are considered worthy of answers by the people who make up the intelligence tests—people with intellectual bents similar to mine?   2

For instance, I had an auto-repair man once, who, on these intelligence tests, could not possibly have scored more than 80, by my estimate. I always took it for granted that I was far more intelligent than he was. Yet, when anything went wrong with my car I hastened to him with it, watched him anxiously as he explored its vitals, and lis-   3

tened to his pronouncements as though they were divine oracles—
and he always fixed my car.

Well, then, suppose my auto-repair man devised questions for an   4
intelligence test. Or suppose a carpenter did, or a farmer, or, indeed,
almost anyone but an academician. By every one of those tests, I'd
prove myself a moron. And I'd *be* a moron, too. In a world where I
could not use my academic training and my verbal talents but had to
do something intricate or hard, working with my hands, I would do
poorly. My intelligence, then, is not absolute but is a function of the
society I live in and of the fact that a small subsection of that society
has managed to foist itself on the rest as an arbiter of such matters.

Consider my auto-repair man, again. He had a habit of telling me   5
jokes whenever he saw me. One time he raised his head from under
the automobile hood to say: "Doc, a deaf-and-dumb guy went into a
hardware store to ask for some nails. He put two fingers together on
the counter and made hammering motions with the other hand. The
clerk brought him a hammer. He shook his head and pointed to the
two fingers he was hammering. The clerk brought him nails. He picked
out the sizes he wanted, and left. Well, doc, the next guy who came
in was a blind man. He wanted scissors. How do you suppose he asked
for them?"

Indulgently, I lifted my right hand and made scissoring motions   6
with my first two fingers. Whereupon my auto-repair man laughed
raucously and said, "Why, you dumb jerk, he used his *voice* and asked
for them." Then he said, smugly, "I've been trying that on all my customers today." "Did you catch many?" I asked. "Quite a few," he
said, "but I knew for sure I'd catch you." "Why is that?" I asked. "Because you're so goddamned educated, doc, I *knew* you couldn't be
very smart."

And I have an uneasy feeling he had something there.   7

THINKING CRITICALLY

Main Idea

1. What is Isaac Asimov's thesis?

Details

2. According to Asimov, why has he always had the feeling that he is
   intelligent?

3. According to Asimov, what kinds of questions are easy for him to answer? What kinds of questions would he find difficult?

Organization

4. Asimov defines intelligence by using a special kind of example called an *anecdote*. An anecdote is a brief story about someone or something that makes a point. In which paragraphs does Asimov's anecdote begin and end?

Purpose, Audience, Tone

5. What is Asimov's purpose? For a clue, reread the first sentence.

Inferences and Conclusions

6. What are aptitude tests supposed to measure? What does Asimov suggest that they really measure?

7. Asimov says he took it for granted that he was more intelligent than his auto-repair man, yet he always took his car to this man. Why?

Making Connections

The point of the auto-repair man's joke is that there is a difference between being educated and being smart. Do you agree or disagree and why? Define *educated* and *smart*.

AN OVERVIEW OF THE PATTERNS

An organizational pattern provides a logical, meaningful framework for ideas that enables readers to see how they are related. Organizational patterns represent ways people think. It is natural in conversation, for example, to compare things, define terms, explain how something works, list steps or stages in a process, give examples, and trace a sequence of events. Writers, too, naturally resort to these common patterns to organize their thoughts. For example, in Asimov's essay the title and first sentence are strong clues that he plans to define intelligence. Although *definition* is Asimov's overall pattern, *narration* is the pattern in paragraphs 5 and 6. It is quite common for writers to combine patterns because different ones work better for some purposes or kinds of information than others. The following list briefly explains the common organizational patterns.

- **Narration**   This pattern explains an incident or series of events that are significant in an author's life or that an author believes will be significant to readers.

- **Description**   This pattern is rarely used alone. It is almost always used in combination with other patterns. Writers describe people, places, and objects by appealing to readers' senses of sight, hearing, smell, taste, and touch, and by providing examples. Description enables readers to see things from a writer's point of view.

- **Sequence/process**   Sequences explain the *time* and *order* of events. You can trace sequences through dates, time periods, or consecutive numbers. Processes explain either how to do something or how something happens. You can follow processes through steps or stages. Sequence and process often work together.

- **Comparison/contrast**   Objects or ideas are analyzed either according to the ways they are alike (comparison) or the ways they are different (contrast). Usually similarities *and* differences are considered.

- **Division/classification**   *Division* explains how the parts of something relate to the whole. *Classification* establishes categories into which items can be sorted according to shared characteristics. These patterns often work together.

- **Cause and effect**   This pattern helps explain *why* things happen (the reasons or causes) and their consequences (results or effects). These patterns often work together.

- **Definition**   This pattern provides either a brief explanation or an in-depth analysis of the meaning of a word, term, or idea.

See Figure 8.1 for a list of transitional words and phrases that can help you identify the patterns. See also Figure 8.2, which lists purposes for using the patterns in your writing and possible essay topics for which the patterns are appropriate. The first topic listed after each pattern is for a personal essay. The second topic is for an academic essay.

PATTERNS	TRANSITIONS THAT IDENTIFY THEM
FIGURE 8.1 **Organizational Patterns with Transitions**	
Narration	after, later, during, meanwhile, suddenly, once, never, following, last
Description	for example, to illustrate, such as, for instance, used with sensory details
Sequence/process	first, next, then, after, before, now, later, trace, following, step, stage, method, procedure, how to
Comparison/contrast	like, unlike, similar, different, as, as if, however, in contrast, yet, but, on the other hand
Division/classification	part, type, group, category, class, member, branch, section, segment, kind
Cause and effect	reason, result, because, thus, since, therefore, consequently, due to
Definition	for example, to illustrate, such as, means, is defined, can be seen as

NARRATION

Narration is a pattern of organization screenwriters, television writers, speech writers, news reporters, fiction writers, and even textbook writers use to relate a series of events. In a biology textbook, for example, you may read a narrative account of what happens to the food you eat as it is digested, processed, and excreted. When you watch a movie or television program, or read a book or a newspaper article, you become involved in the unfolding series of events that make up a story. You, too, use narration as part of your everyday conversation whenever you tell someone about something that has happened to you, especially if it involves a series of events or small incidents that make up one major event.

Narration is a story-telling pattern. A narrator is one who tells a story. Whether a story is fact or fiction, certain rules apply. These rules are simply readers' expectations. For example, when a story begins, you expect to know *who* the people involved are, *what* happens to them, *where* the story takes place, *when* it happens, *why* it happens, and *how*

FIGURE 8.2

Organizational Patterns for Thinking and Writing

PATTERN	PURPOSE	ESSAY TOPICS
Narration	To relate an event or series of events leading to an outcome	An award or special recognition you received; a myth of your own modeled after a Greek myth (humanities)
Description	To create a vivid mental picture	A person you will never forget; the view from the pulpit of Chartres Cathedral (humanities)
Sequence/process	To explain how to do something or how something occurs	How you overcame a difficult situation; the steps involved in getting a bill enacted into law (U.S. government)
Division/classification	To explain parts of a whole or to sort into categories	Types of restaurants in your community; the division of labor within a Kibbutz (sociology)
Comparison and contrast	To explain similarities and differences between two subjects	The car you own now versus the car you want; how Freud's and Jung's personality theories differ (psychology)
Cause and effect	To explain reasons, results, or both	The positive or negative effects of an important choice you had to make; the causes and prevention of AIDS (biology)
Definition	To define a term either to clarify its meaning or to suggest a new meaning	Your definition of a good friend; what are *fractals?* (math)

everyone is affected. You also expect to follow the story, and you may look for clues that signal the sequence of events. As a reader, you usually expect some point to the story, an answer to the question, "Why has this happened?" or, "What does this mean?"

As a writer, you probably should not deliberately set out to write a narrative essay and then attempt to think of a story that will fit into this pattern. Instead, choose narration only if your topic would be especially effective if developed as a narrative. For example, a topic such as "my first date" might work very well as a narrative essay. You could describe the date as an event telling who you were with, where you went, how you felt about it, what he or she said or did, how the date ended, and whether you ever saw your date again. To organize your essay, try breaking up the event into time periods. For example, if you are writing about a first date, you could describe your anticipation *before the date,* what you did *during the date,* and how you felt *after the date.* To come up with a thesis or central idea for your essay, think of what the date meant to you—for example, what it taught you about yourself, other people, or the dating process.

Exercise 8.1   Read the passage below, and answer the following questions about its organizational pattern.

Speaking in front of the class was the worst thing I ever had to do. I   1
can still remember the first time. The teacher, Mrs. Kavanaugh, told us
we had to memorize and recite a poem of our choice. I chose William
Wordsworth's "Daffodils."

On the day we were to recite, Mrs. Kavanaugh asked for volun-   2
teers. No one made a move. She then said we would go in alphabeti-
cal order. My last name began with C, so I didn't have long to wait. By
the time it was my turn, my hands were shaking and my throat was
dry. I walked mechanically to the front of the class. When I tried to
open my mouth, my lips stuck to my teeth. Still, I managed to get
through the first verse of my poem by staring out the window while I
recited. Then I made the mistake of making eye contact with my classmates. I froze. I couldn't remember the next line. A few students
chuckled and shifted nervously in their seats. Ollie Knight whom I
hated and who hated me laughed out loud. "That's enough," Mrs.
Kavanaugh said to Ollie, and she told me to sit down. But I ran out of
the room, red-faced, choking back tears.

1. What is the narrative about?

_____

2. What happens? Briefly list the events and the outcome.

_____

_____

_____

3. What transitions help you follow the narrative?

_____

_____

_____

DESCRIPTION

Describing comes naturally to people. Description is a familiar means of self-expression you use whenever you want to tell a friend about a movie you have seen, a book you have read, a person you care about, or a place you have been. When you visit the doctor, he or she asks you to describe your symptoms. A prospective employer will ask you to describe your previous work experience. In all these exchanges, the people you are talking with can ask questions to clarify anything they may not understand. Readers, however, have only an author's words to go on. To make use of an author's descriptions, look for sensory details and try to visualize what is being described. In addition, determine the reason behind the description by reading for a controlling idea.

To write good descriptions of your own, use sensory details to create mental pictures for your readers. Spend time observing your subject directly. For example, if you are writing about a place, go there and take notes on what you see. Then use your observations in your writing. If you are describing something from memory, visualize it and observe that image just as you would if you had the real thing in front of you. Images you recall from memory may not be as clear as direct observations, but you can sharpen your visual memory. To develop a writer's eye, begin paying closer attention to your surroundings than before.

Exercise 8.2   Read the paragraphs below, and then answer the questions that follow.

> Carnivorous plants are those that get nourishment by trapping and di-   1
> gesting insects. Specially modified flowers or leaves may produce an
> odor or have a color that is attractive to insects. In some species a
> sticky coating on the petals holds the insect in place while the flower
> closes around it, trapping it inside the flower. The plant's juices con-
> tain a digestive acid.
>
> Carnivorous plants grow in many parts of the world and come in   2
> many varieties. One jungle species has a flower that is almost 3 feet in
> diameter. Two carnivorous plants that grow in bogs in the northeast-
> ern part of the United States are the *pitcher plant* and the *sundew.*
> These plants are easy to recognize.
>
> The pitcher plant looks exactly like a small pitcher that has a nar-   3
> row neck widening to a larger base. Mature plants can be 3 to 5
> inches tall. The "pitcher" is dark rusty red with darker vertical stria-
> tions. It has a base of dark green leaves.
>
> The sundew has a flower that looks much like a daisy with shorter,   4
> fatter petals. In the mature plant, the flower rises from a clump of
> dark greenish-brown leaves on a stem about 10 to 12 inches tall. The
> stem curves down at the top so that the flower hangs down.

1. What is the author describing?

   _____

2. What is the controlling idea?

   _____

3. Can you find at least one detail that appeals to each sense (sight, hearing, taste, smell, and touch)? List them on the following lines.

   _____

   _____

SEQUENCE/PROCESS

Sequence and process may work together, or they may work separately. *Sequence* refers to the order in which things happen, such as the chain of events that resulted in a car accident. *Process* refers to a method, how to do something. The "how to" may involve steps that have to be carried out in a certain order, in which case a sequence of steps is also a part of the process.

Writers use *sequence* patterns in many ways. In a history book, for example, you may read about the events that preceded the Persian Gulf War, or the important legislation that resulted during a certain U.S. president's term of office. Writers use the sequence pattern in diagrams to trace various biological processes such as the circulation of the blood as it passes through veins and arteries into every part of the human body. Your job is to recognize and be able to follow the sequence so that you know what happens and when. Numbers may alert you to a sequence. The numerals (1, 2, 3), ordinal numbers (first, second, third), and dates and times that proceed from past to present or early to late can signal a sequence pattern. Consider the description in the following paragraph.

> What happens during the nine months of pregnancy? During the first three months cells divide to become an embryo. The embryo becomes a fetus. At this stage, size increases little, but much differentiation of tissue occurs. The next three months show more activity. The fetus becomes larger, it has a heartbeat, and its first movements occur. In the last three months of pregnancy, the fetus continues to grow. Its movements increase as it prepares itself for birth.

This paragraph traces a few of the events that occur during the nine months of pregnancy. The sequence develops through three stages, each lasting three months. Details tell you what happens at each stage.

A *process* is a procedure, method, or way of doing something. The process pattern appears in many types of writing, including academic writing. For example, setting up a budget or establishing credit are two processes you might read about in a business course. In a biology course you read about processes in nature such as photosynthesis in plants or digestion in humans.

Processes are of two types: the *how-to process* provides steps or directions to follow that lead to a desired outcome. Ways to take notes, plan a speech, use a piece of equipment, and assemble a child's toy are examples of how-to processes. When reading about such a process, your goal is to identify and understand the steps so that you can repeat the process on your own.

The *informational process* describes what happens under certain conditions. How an automobile is assembled, how bills are enacted into laws, how cells reproduce, and how the actions of wind and water erode soil and rock to form canyons are examples of informational processes. Obviously, you cannot duplicate these processes on your own. They are complex processes that result from the actions of many people or forces working together. When reading about such a process, your goal is to identify the stages of the process, trace the order in which the stages occur, and determine what happens at each stage.

If you decide to write about a process, make sure you are familiar with it either from reading about it, observing it, or doing it. In your introductory paragraph, make clear to your readers why the process is important to you and should be important to them. Identify and explain each step or stage of the process, and the expected outcome. A good prewriting strategy is to outline the steps of the process. Figure 8.3 is an example of an outline that could be used for an essay on how to set up a home office.

Exercise 8.3   As you read each paragraph, try to follow its pattern of organization. Then complete the items that follow the paragraph.

1. Born in Massachusetts in 1804, Elizabeth Palmer Peabody was precociously literate. She founded two schools and was a confidante of such writers as William Ellery Channing, Ralph Waldo Emerson, and Nathaniel Hawthorne (who married her sister, Sophia). In 1839 Peabody opened a Boston bookshop that quickly became a notable center of American letters and reform and the place from which

FIGURE 8.3

**Sample
Outline for an
Essay that
Explains a
Process**

Thesis: If having a convenient work space has always been your goal,
            then follow these four steps to create a home office.

I.   Decide how you will use your office

   A. for study
   B. for job-related work
   C. for managing the household, paying bills, and other tasks

II. Choose a place for your office

   A. a spare room
   B. an area of another room, such as utility room, bedroom, or
       kitchen
   C. a "portable" office such as a cart or table on wheels
   D. a closet that can be converted to an office space

III. Select the furniture you will need

   A. desk or table
   B. chair
   C. lamp or other light fixture
   D. bookcase
   E. storage space

IV. Arrange your equipment and supplies

   A. equipment

       1. computer and printer
       2. fax machine
       3. telephone and answering machine

   B. supplies

       1. paper, pens, pencils, paper clips, and other items
       2. books and reference materials

The Dial was published. She was a sympathetic observer of the doings at Brook Farm, where she frequently taught. After 1845, Peabody devoted herself chiefly to education, writing a widely adopted history textbook and founding one of the earliest kindergartens in the United States. She was also a popular lecturer and donated most of her fees to further the education of Native Americans. She died in Jamaica Plain, Massachusetts, in 1894.

From *A More Perfect Union: Documents in U.S. History*, Vol. I, 3d ed., Paul F. Boller, Jr., and Ronald Story, Houghton Mifflin Co., 1992.

   a. What is the main idea?

      _____

   b. Does the paragraph explain a sequence of events, a process, or both? Explain your answer.

      _____

      _____

   c. List the events (or steps in the process) that support the main idea.

      _____

      _____

      _____

   d. List any transitions that help you identify and follow the pattern.

      _____

2. The **envelope system** of budgeting gets its name from the fact that exact amounts of money are placed into envelopes for purposes of strict budgetary control. If you wish to use the envelope system, at

the start of a budgeting period, place in an envelope money equal to the budget estimate for each expenditure classification. Write the classification name and the budget amount on the outside of the envelope. As expenditures are made, simply record them on the appropriate envelope and remove the proper amounts of cash. When an envelope is empty, funds are exhausted for that classification. This technique works well in controlling expenditures for variable expenses such as entertainment, personal allowances, and food. It may be a good way for younger children to learn to budget allowances. Of course, the envelopes must be safeguarded to prevent theft.

From *Personal Finance,* 4th ed., E. Thomas Garman and Raymond E. Forgue, Houghton Mifflin Co., 1994.

a. What is the main idea?

_____

b. Does the paragraph explain a sequence of events, a process, or both? Explain your answer.

_____

_____

c. List the events (or steps in the process) that support the main idea.

_____

_____

_____

d. List any transitions that help you identify and follow the pattern.

_____

COMPARISON/CONTRAST

Suppose you are having a conversation with someone and you are describing an attractive outfit you saw, or a new car, or a friend's house. You might compare it to something known and similar, or you might contrast it with something known but different. Comparison and contrast are so much a part of everyday conversation that you can probably come up with examples that you have recently used, read, or heard.

Writers use the comparison/contrast pattern because it clearly and simply explains the new or unfamiliar by comparing or contrasting it with the familiar. However, you should know several more things about this pattern.

1. The word *comparison,* to many people, implies a consideration of both similarities and differences. But it is possible to write about similarities only or differences only.

2. A comparison or contrast usually involves only two subjects or classes of objects—for example: two cars, two movies, two hotels, two colleges, two children, two pets, two CD players.

3. The comparison has a point. That point may be either to simply distinguish one object from another or to prove that one is better than or has advantages over another.

Furthermore, writers make comparisons in one of two ways. In a *point-by-point* comparison, the similarities or differences are explained one at a time, for example: object A has this, so does object B; A has that, so does B; A has these, B has those. In a *subject-by-subject* comparison, however, the writer says everything there is to say about one object before moving on to the next one, for example: A has this, that, and these; B has this, that, and those.

Read the next paragraph and identify the two subjects being compared, the ways they are different or similar, and the type of comparison that is being made.

When recent high school graduates arrive on college campuses and begin taking classes, one of the first things they learn is that college is not like high school. First of all, high school teachers have close relationships with students and are likely to interact with them outside the classroom in sports and club activities. In college, the relationships are not as close. Although some professors get involved in extracurricular activities, many do not. College professors are less accessible than high school teachers. The college professor has office hours, which he or she may not always keep. High school teachers, however, are confined to one classroom, where they can usually be found before and after school and in between classes. Second, the work load in college is greater than in high school. Students have more reading to do in college, the reading is more difficult, and homework is usually assigned every day, in every class. In high school, much of the work is done in class. Many students have homework only two or three nights a week. Finally, students have greater freedom in college. What students do between classes is their business. When they do not have a class scheduled, they neither have to be on campus nor account for their whereabouts. High school students, with few exceptions, must remain on campus during school hours.

This paragraph is a point-by-point comparison of high school and college. They are compared according to the ways in which they *differ:* relationships with teachers, workload, and amount of freedom students have. In the next example, the paragraph is rewritten to show how it would look as a subject-by-subject comparison.

When recent high school graduates arrive on college campuses and begin taking classes, one of the first things they learn is that college is not like high school. In high school, teachers have close relationships with students and are likely to interact with them outside the classroom in sports and club activities. They are accessible to students because they are often confined to one classroom, where they can usually be found before and after school and in between classes. Second, much of the work in high school is done in class. Many students have homework only two or three nights per week. Third, high school students have little freedom. With few exceptions, they must remain on campus during school hours. In college, on the other hand, relationships with professors are not as close. Although some professors get involved in extracurricular activities, many do not. College professors may be less accessible than high school teachers. The college professor has office hours, which he or she may not always keep. Second, the work load in college is greater than in high school. Students have more reading to do in college, the reading is more difficult, and homework is usually assigned every day, in every class. Finally, there is greater freedom in college. What students do between classes is their business. When they do not have a class scheduled, they neither have to be on campus nor account for their whereabouts.

In this paragraph the points of contrast are the same, but you get all the details about high school before you get any details about college. Does it matter whether a writer compares point by point or subject by subject? Generally speaking, no, although a writer's choice of a method may be influenced by his or her purpose. For example, a writer may choose a subject-by-subject comparison believing that the subject discussed last may leave a lasting impression on the reader.

If you were to draw maps of the paragraphs, they might look like the ones in Figure 8.4.

> **STUDY TIP:** *Idea maps, such as the ones in Figure 8.4, are diagrams that illustrate idea relationships. Mapping is a useful study aid for reading because it requires you to determine how ideas are related. Then you can arrange them in a format that both expresses their relationship and is meaningful to you. Mapping is also useful as a prewriting strategy. Like clustering, it offers a more visual alternative to outlining.*

Exercise 8.4   As you read each paragraph, try to follow its pattern of organization. Then complete the items that follow the paragraph.

1. There are some striking differences in political outlooks between men and women. In the 1950s, women were more often Republican, partly because under Eisenhower the Republicans were seen as the party of peace. This situation is now reversed. Women tend to be more liberal than men and to favor the Democratic party and the causes for which it stands. Women were 9 percent less likely than men to say that civil rights laws were strong enough. . . . This is a typical indicator of a difference in outlook that many people have called the **gender gap**. Other Gallup polls have consistently shown that a significantly higher percentage of women than men

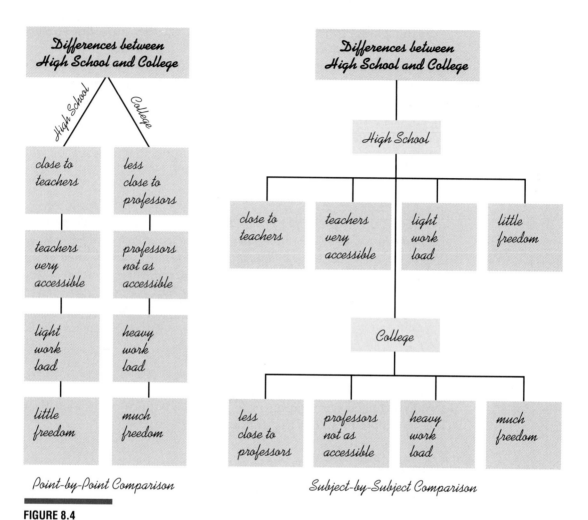

Point-by-Point Comparison

Subject-by-Subject Comparison

FIGURE 8.4

Idea Map

favor stricter gun control. Women are more likely than men to favor increased health care spending, and men are more likely to favor increased defense spending.

From *American Government*, 3d ed., Paul E. Johnson et al., Houghton Mifflin Co., 1994.

a. What is the main idea?

_____

b. What is being compared/contrasted?

_____

c. What are the similarities/differences?

_____

_____

_____

d. What kind of comparison is it?

_____

e. List any transitions that help you identify and follow the pattern.

_____

2. A distinction is traditionally made between organic and inorganic compounds. **Organic compounds** are compounds containing the element carbon, and usually hydrogen. They include methane, propane, glucose, and millions of other substances. These compounds are called organic because it was once (incorrectly) believed that they could be formed only by living organisms. **Inorganic compounds** are all the other compounds; these include water, calcium

sulfate, ammonia, silica, hydrochloric acid, and many more. In addition, some very simple carbon compounds, particularly carbon dioxide and the carbonates (which include chalk, or calcium carbonate), are treated as inorganic compounds even though they are formed by living organisms. . . .

From *General Chemistry*, 2d ed., P. W. Atkins and J. A. Beran, Scientific American Books, 1990.

a. What is the main idea?

_____

b. What is being compared/contrasted?

_____

c. What are the similarities/differences?

_____

_____

_____

d. What kind of comparison is it?

_____

e. List any transitions that help you identify and follow the pattern.

_____

3. Arachnids [spiders, scorpions, and ticks, for example] are often wrongly referred to as insects, but they have many differing characteristics. For example, arachnids lack antennae, mandibles, wings, and compound eyes, while, perhaps most obviously, they have four

pairs of legs, not three, as in insects. Also, instead of the three body divisions of insects (head, thorax, and abdomen), arachnids have only two regions—the anterior cephalothorax, or prosoma, and the posterior abdomen, or opisthosoma.

From *The Encyclopedia of Insects,* Christopher O'Toole, ed., Andromeda Oxford Ltd., 1993.

a. What is the main idea?

_____

b. What is being compared/contrasted?

_____

c. What are the similarities/differences?

_____

d. What kind of comparison is it?

_____

e. List any transitions that help you identify and follow the pattern.

_____

DIVISION/CLASSIFICATION

Division is a pattern for analyzing a subject by dividing it into parts. Classification is a pattern for analyzing a subject by identifying it as a member of a group having shared characteristics. To identify a pattern of division, look for a part-to-whole relationship. To identify a pattern of classification, look for the various categories into which a large number of things can be sorted. Like sequence and process, division and classification often work together.

A dolphin, for example, is classified as a mammal because it has the characteristics shared by other members of that group. A textbook explanation of the characteristics of a dolphin that places it in the category *mammals* is organized by classification. Another paragraph, however, describing the parts of the dolphin's digestive system, such as the stomach and intestines, is organized by division.

The parts that make up a whole (division) and the characteristics that distinguish a group (classification) are idea relationships that you will encounter frequently in your reading, especially in the sciences. In the next paragraph find the main idea and identify the part-to-whole relationship. What is being divided and how?

> Although a computer is a complicated piece of machinery, it has three basic parts: *input device, processor,* and *output device.* The input device consists of a keyboard, mouse, or modem. Input devices allow you to enter, access, and send information. The processor is the part of the computer that you cannot see. Inside the computer is the hard disk, an electronic memory, and storage system. When you input information, it is processed through this system and converted into a special electronic language that can be saved and stored. The output device consists of a screen or printer. The screen allows you to see the information that you have either entered or accessed. Whatever you enter shows up on the screen. Similarly, when you want to get information out of the computer, you call up the file on screen. To get a copy of your file on paper, you then use the printer.

The main idea is that a computer has three basic parts. The part-to-whole relationship is that of the computer to its parts. The parts are the *input device, processor,* and *output device.* Additional details tell you how each part functions.

In the following paragraph, identify what is being classified and how.

> The students who attend community colleges represent different age groups. Many are recent high school graduates. These students are seventeen to nineteen years old and are attending college for the first time. Most of them plan to transfer to a four-year college when they graduate. The largest group are the adult learners, in their twenties and thirties. Some are attending college for the first time, others are returning students who dropped out of college earlier in life to work, raise families, or for other reasons. Most of them are in college to improve their skills so they can advance in their careers or change jobs. A few are older students in their forties or fifties. Students in this age group may have lost their jobs and need retraining. Others may be looking for career changes or self-fulfillment.

In this paragraph, community college students are classified by age. They are sorted into three groups: recent high school graduates, adult learners, older students. The characteristics that distinguish each group include the age range and reason for attending college.

Exercise 8.5   As you read each passage, try to follow its pattern of organization. Then complete the items that follow the passage.

1. Two kinds of benefits motivate people to participate in politics. First, some people seek *direct benefits* of political participation, benefits that derive from the act of participation itself. At one time, for example, political candidates paid people to cast votes for them. The money was a direct benefit. Today, for most people, the direct benefits of voting are less tangible. People feel psychologically rewarded when they vote. Similarly, they might join an interest group or participate in a protest because they are stimulated by being part of the group.

   Other people hope for *indirect benefits* from participation. These are benefits that depend on the actions of others, which are inherently uncertain. Policy influence, for example, is an indirect benefit. Because political decisions are *collective decisions* made by huge groups of people, an individual can rarely claim to have had a measurable effect. People who are motivated by indirect benefits believe that the chance that their contribution might make a difference is great enough to outweigh the costs of participation.

   From *American Government,* 3d ed., Paul E. Johnson et al., Houghton Mifflin Co., 1994.

   a. What is the main idea?

b. What is being divided/classified?

_____

c. What are the parts/categories?

_____

_____

_____

d. What are the characteristics of each part/category?

_____

_____

_____

e. List any transitions that help you identify and follow the pattern.

_____

2. The necessary calories come from three main sources of nutrients: carbohydrates, fats, and proteins. **Carbohydrates** are sugars or more complex substances, and they are the body's main source of energy. They include starches and sugars found in bread, potatoes, and cereal grains, as well as in fruits and vegetables. **Fats** are concentrated sources of energy derived from animals and plants, including liquid oils (such as corn oil and olive oil) as well as fats of solid texture (such as butter or fat seen in meat), which are found plentifully in such foods as butter, margarine, shortening, salad oils, cream, most cheeses, mayonnaise, salad dressing, nuts, meat, and bacon. **Proteins** are a group of organic compounds that are essential for the growth and repair of muscle tissue and for increasing resistance to

disease, and they are found in meat and milk products, such as poultry, fish, milk, cheese, eggs, bread, and cereal. Carbohydrates and proteins have about the same calorie value, while fats have more than twice as much.

From *Consumer Economic Issues in America*, E. Thomas Garman, Houghton Mifflin Co., 1991.

a. What is the main idea?

_____

b. What is being divided/classified?

_____

c. What are the parts/categories?

_____

_____

_____

d. What are the characteristics of each part/category?

_____

_____

_____

e. List any transitions that help you identify and follow the pattern.

_____

3. Even smiles can vary as people learn to use them to communicate certain feelings. Ekman and his colleagues categorized seventeen types of smiles, including "false smiles," which are aimed at convincing another person that enjoyment is occurring; "masking smiles,"

which hide unpleasantness; and "miserable smiles," which indicate a willingness to endure unpleasantness. They called the smile that occurs with genuine happiness the *Duchenne smile,* after the French investigator who more than a hundred years ago first noticed the difference between spontaneous, happy smiles and posed smiles. A genuine, Duchenne smile includes contractions of the muscles around the eyes (which creates a distinctive wrinkling of the skin around the eyes) as well as of the muscles that raise the lips and cheeks. Very few people can voluntarily contract the muscles around the eyes when they pose a fake smile, so this feature can often be used to discern "lying smiles" from genuine smiles (Ekman, Friesen, & O'Sullivan, 1988). In a study of people watching films by themselves, the Duchenne smile was highly correlated with subjective reports of positive emotions, as well as with EKG recordings of a pattern of brain waves related to positive emotions. Other types of smiles were not (Ekman, Davidson, & Friesen, 1990).

From *Psychology,* 3d ed., Douglas A. Bernstein et al., Houghton Mifflin Co., 1994.

a. What is the main idea?

    _____

b. What is being divided/classified?

    _____

c. What are the parts/categories?

    _____

    _____

    _____

d. What are the characteristics of each part/category?

_____

_____

_____

e. List any transitions that help you identify and follow the pattern.

_____

CAUSE AND EFFECT

Causes are the reasons behind events; they explain *why* or *how* events happen. *Effects* are the results of events; they explain *what* happens, or the *outcome.* Suppose you fail an algebra test. The failing grade is an *effect,* the result or outcome of something else. Why did you fail? There may be several causes, as the following paragraph demonstrates.

> Yesterday my instructor returned my algebra test. Unfortunately, I failed it, but at least I know why. For one thing, I did not study enough. Another reason is that I got nervous. Most important, I made some careless errors. I guess I'm not really surprised that I did so poorly.

In this paragraph, failing the test is the effect. The causes are not enough study, nervousness, and careless errors. The causes are identified by the transitions *for one thing, another reason,* and *most important.*

If you were to draw a map of the paragraph, it might look like the one in Figure 8.5.

Read the next paragraph and try to identify causes and effects.

> My alarm did not go off this morning. As a result, I did not have time for breakfast, so I had to leave home hungry. Then I was late to class. As if that were not bad enough, I left my books at home. All in all, it was a disastrous morning.

In this paragraph, several effects result from a single cause: the alarm did not go off. The effects are no time for breakfast, arriving late to

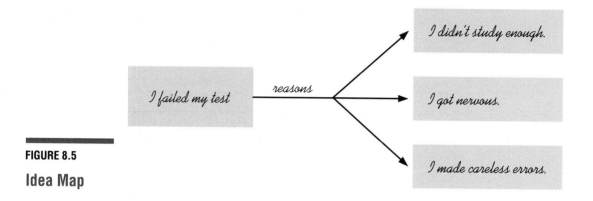

FIGURE 8.5

Idea Map

class, and leaving books at home. Transitions that signal these effects are *as a result, then,* and *as if that were not enough.*

If you were to draw a map of the paragraph, it might look like the one in Figure 8.6.

To identify causes and effects in your reading look for these transitions: *why, reason, cause, result, because, therefore,* and *consequently.* Use transitions in your writing to help readers identify your causes and effects. In addition, ask yourself these questions about your reading:

1. What happened? (effect)

2. Why or how did it happen? (cause)

3. What are the clues? (transitions)

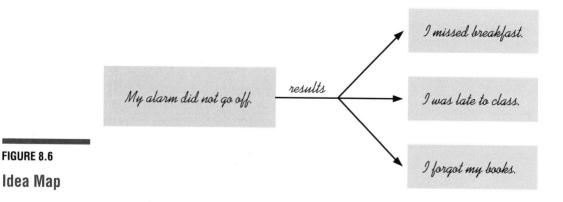

FIGURE 8.6

Idea Map

To brainstorm causes and effects for writing, ask yourself these questions:

1. What happened? What would I like to happen? What do I think will happen? (effects)

2. Why or how did, or could, or will it happen? (causes)

3. What are my clues for readers? (transitions)

Exercise 8.6

As you read each paragraph, try to follow its pattern of organization. Then complete the items that follow the paragraph.

1. Even though sellers are generally receptive to complaints, many consumers do not complain. Most commonly, people do not complain because they think complaining will not be worth their time, because they think that complaining will not do any good, and because they do not know how or where to complain. Many consumers do not complain because they believe the benefits of complaining will not exceed the costs.

From *Consumer Economic Issues in America,* E. Thomas Garman, Houghton Mifflin Co., 1991.

a. What is the main idea?

_____

b. What effect is explained?

_____

c. What are the causes that produce this effect?

_____

_____

_____

d. List any transitions that help you identify and follow the pattern.

_____

_____

2. There are many reasons why public speaking can be frightening. Speaking before large groups of people, where one is the center of attention, is not an everyday occurrence for most people. We may feel strange and uncomfortable when we confront it. Moreover, the importance of communication in such moments is usually great; much depends on how well we express our ideas. This element of risk, combined with the feeling of strangeness, can explain why many people dread public speaking. The important thing is not to be too anxious about your apprehension. Accept it as natural, and remind yourself that you can convert these feelings into positive energy. . . .

From *Public Speaking*, 3d ed., Michael Osborn and Suzanne Osborn, Houghton Mifflin Co., 1994.

a. What is the main idea?

_____

b. What effect is described?

_____

c. What are the causes that produce this effect?

_____

_____

_____

d. List any transitions that help you identify and follow the pattern.

_____

3. Why do obese people gain so much weight? The body maintains a given weight through a combination of food intake and energy output (Keesey & Powley, 1986). To become obese, a person must consume more calories than the body can _metabolize,_ or burn up; the excess calories are stored as fat. The body constantly metabolizes calories, and this metabolic level increases during activity. Because women tend to have a lower metabolic rate than men even when equally active, they tend to gain weight more rapidly than men when eating the same number of calories (Ferraro et al., 1992).

From _Psychology,_ 3d ed., Douglas A. Bernstein et al., Houghton Mifflin Co., 1994.

a. What is the main idea?

_____

b. What effect is described?

_____

c. What are the causes that produce this effect?

_____

_____

_____

d. List any transitions that help you identify and follow the pattern.

_____

DEFINITION

Many writers define words, terms, concepts, and qualities in context. Whole essays have been based on the definition of a single word, such as John Stuart Mill's essay "On Liberty." Textbook writers in particular define words and terms that have specialized meanings within their disciplines. Writers use two kinds of definitions: functional and extended. *Functional definitions* are relatively short and to the point. Their purpose is to define a word or term necessary to your understanding of a topic or concept. Functional definitions occur throughout textbook chapters and other informational material. Often the word or term to be defined is highlighted with a special color or different type of print. In the preceding sentences, for example, the explanation that follows the italicized term *functional definitions* is itself a functional definition.

Extended definitions are much longer. The essay that begins this chapter is a good example. Often the purpose in writing an extended definition is to go beyond what is usually meant by the term. The writer may challenge our ideas about what the term means or define it in a new way. Intelligence, for example, is a topic that causes controversy. Asimov knew this when he wrote the essay. He knew that readers had different assumptions about what it means to be intelligent. His essay gives his particular slant on the concept.

Definitions, whether functional or extended, have two characteristics. They tell what general class of things the object or idea being defined belongs to, and they explain the characteristics that distinguish it from others in the class.

Read the following paragraph to determine what is defined, what class it belongs to, and what its characteristics are.

> A **cleaver** is a cutting tool. It has a large, wide, rectangular blade with a sharp edge. It is used for separating meat from bone and for chopping. Cooks and butchers use the cleaver.

Cleaver is the term defined. It belongs to the class *cutting tools*. It has the following characteristics: a blade that is large, wide, rectangular, and sharp; its uses are separating meat from bone and chopping; those who use it include cooks and butchers.

In Asimov's essay, *intelligence* is the term defined. Asimov identifies several classes of intelligence: aptitude, academic training, and verbal talent. He concludes that intelligence is more than these. Knowledge gained from experience and hands-on knowledge such as that of the auto-repair man are also kinds of intelligence. Asimov asks, "What is intelligence, anyway?" and implies that we are all intelligent in some ways and not in others. Intelligence, he says, "is a function of the society I live in."

When reading definitions, identify the class and characteristics of the object or idea defined. When writing definitions, use examples, make comparisons, or describe situations that illustrate what you mean.

Exercise 8.7   As you read each paragraph, try to follow its pattern of organization. Then complete the items that follow the paragraph.

1. Fruits protect dormant seeds and aid in their dispersal. A **fruit** is a

   mature ovary. . . . As seeds develop after fertilization, the wall of the

   ovary thickens. A pea pod is an example of a fruit, with seeds (ma-

   ture ovules) encased in the ripened ovary. Some fruits, such as ap-

   ples, incorporate other floral parts along with the ovary. Peas and

   apples are both simple fruits, meaning they develop from a single

   ovary. Aggregate fruits, such as raspberries, come from several

   ovaries that were part of the same flower. A pineapple is an example

   of a multiple fruit, one that develops from separate flowers.

   From *Biology*, 3d ed., Neil A. Campbell, Benjamin/Cummings Publishing Co., 1993.

   a. What is the main idea?

   _____

   b. What term is defined?

   _____

   c. To what class of things/ideas does it belong?

   _____

    d. What are its characteristics?

_____

_____

_____

    e. List any transitions that help you identify and follow the pattern.

_____

2. . . . Love is something you do: the sacrifices you make, the giving of self, like a mother bringing a newborn into the world. If you want to study love, study those who sacrifice for others, even for people who offend or do not love in return. If you are a parent, look at the love you have for the children you sacrificed for. Love is a value that is actualized through loving actions. . . .

From *The 7 Habits of Highly Effective People,* Stephen R. Covey, Simon and Schuster, 1989.

    a. What is the main idea?

_____

    b. What term is defined?

_____

    c. To what class of things/ideas does it belong?

_____

    d. What are its characteristics?

_____

_____

_____

e. List any transitions that help you identify and follow the pattern.

_____

3. The potent stimulant *caffeine* is probably the world's most popular
psychoactive drug (Gilbert, 1984). It occurs in coffee, tea, chocolate,
and many soft drinks. Caffeine decreases drowsiness, makes thought
more rapid (Goodman-Gilman et al., 1990), increases the capacity
for physical work, and raises urine production. At high doses it in-
duces anxiety and tremors. Tolerance develops to caffeine's effects,
and it can induce physical dependence (Evans & Griffiths, 1992;
Griffiths & Woodson, 1988). Withdrawal symptoms—including headaches, fatigue, anxiety, shakiness, and craving—begin to appear
twelve to twenty-four hours after abstinence, peak at about forty-
eight hours, and last about a week (Silverman et al., 1992).

From *Psychology*, 3d ed., Douglas M. Bernstein et al., Houghton Mifflin Co., 1994.

a. What is the main idea?

_____

b. What term is defined?

_____

c. To what class of things/ideas does it belong?

_____

d. What are its characteristics?

_____

_____

_____

e. List any transitions that help you identify and follow the pattern.

_____

THINKING ABOUT PROCESS

Patterns are a necessary part of your thinking, reading, and writing. All three processes require you to see relationships and make connections among ideas.

1. Patterns are merely descriptions of the characteristic ways people think.

2. Organized ideas are easier to understand and remember than random, unconnected thoughts.

3. The transitions that link ideas are the clues to a writer's organizational pattern. Some transitions signal more than one pattern; for example, sequence, process, and narration all use time markers. However, a sequence is an order; a process is a method; and a narration is an account or story. Transitions alone are not enough to identify a pattern; you must also recognize the pattern's characteristics.

 ## THINKING IT OVER

Test your recall of this chapter's concepts by completing the following statements. If you cannot complete a statement, look back through the chapter to find the answer.

1. _____ _____ describe ways of thinking logically about a subject.

2. A _____ explains a significant incident or series of events.

3. _____ enables readers to see things from a writer's point of view.

4. _____ explains when and in what order events occur.

5. _____ explains methods or procedures.

6. To explain similarities and differences, use the _____ pattern.

7. The _____ pattern describes a part-to-whole relationship.

8. Writers use _____ to sort items or ideas into categories.

9. _____ and _____ are reasons and results.

10. You can use _____ to explain the meaning of a word, term, or idea.

11. Choose one of the Thinking First questions at the beginning of the chapter to answer on the following lines:

_____

_____

_____

TOPICS FOR WRITING

Write an essay on a topic of your choice or select a topic from the following list.

1. Write a *narrative* essay about an event that has a special meaning for you.

2. Write a *descriptive* essay about a place you like to visit, a favorite room in your house or apartment, or a favorite possession.

3. Write about a *process* that you have either observed or done. For example, you could explain how to study for a test, how to buy a used car, or how to prepare for a job interview.

4. Write an essay in which you *compare and contrast* two teachers, two friends, two places to live, two schools, two types of automobiles, or any two subjects of your choice.

5. Using *division* or *classification,* write an essay on a topic such as: ways to save money, cassette tapes or CDs in your collection, the types of students at your college, or the neighborhoods in your town or city.

6. Write a *cause and effect* essay about an issue you think is important or about a behavior you think is either desirable or objectionable.

7. Write an essay in which you *define* a term such as intelligence, a good friend, a good (or bad) parent, a good (or bad) student, a hero, or any term of your choice.

Checklist for Revision

As you revise and edit your essay, check for the following:

1. Do you have a clearly stated thesis?

2. Have you supported the thesis with enough concrete details?

3. Have you checked your paragraphs for unity and coherence?

4. Does your essay have a recognizable organizational pattern?

5. Have you used appropriate transitions?

6. Have you found and corrected your errors?

REFLECTIONS ON READING AND WRITING

Chapters 7 and 8 give you two views of intelligence: Isaac Asimov's view that intelligence is the result of academic aptitude and common sense, and Sara Gilbert's view that people possess five kinds of intelligence. Reflect on these two views. Do they contradict each other? Do Asimov's academic aptitude and common sense compare to any of Gilbert's categories? How has your reading of both selections influenced your own view of intelligence?

Chapter 9

Purpose, Audience, and Tone in Reading and Writing

THINKING FIRST

- *What do the terms* purpose, audience, *and* tone *mean?*
- *How can I determine a writer's purpose, audience, or tone?*
- *Should I consider purpose, audience, and tone in my writing?*

ecause writers have a wide range of choices to make from selecting a topic to choosing an organizational pattern, no two people writing on the same topic are ever likely to make exactly the same choices. The opinions expressed, the facts presented, the examples given, the points emphasized, and the attitudes revealed generally differ among writers. To a large extent, purpose, audience, and tone account for these differences.

Several chapters so far have explained some of the skills that enable you to think critically about reading and writing. For example, finding implied main ideas or discovering an author's organizational pattern require you to make inferences from details and transitions. Choosing an organizational pattern for your own writing requires you to think critically about your topic and determine the most appropriate way to organize your details.

Being able to determine an author's purpose, audience, and tone not only will help you to think critically about reading, but will also enable you to think critically about ways to apply these skills to your writing. An author's *purpose* is his or her reason for writing. The *audience* consists of readers, real or imagined, and an author makes certain assumptions about what readers know, need, or want to know. *Tone* is the author's expressed attitude or feeling toward the topic and is revealed through word choice.

As explained in Chapter 1, purpose, audience, and tone are so interdependent that they may seem to be the parts of one decision-making process. For example, purpose and tone influence the selection of details and organizational pattern, and they work together to create an overall effect and to provoke an intended response from the audience.

This chapter explains purpose, audience, and tone so that you can recognize them in your reading and make choices based on them in your writing. As you read this chapter, keep three definitions in mind:

1. A *purpose* is a reason for writing.

2. The *audience* consists of those for whom writing is intended.

3. A *tone* is an expressed attitude or feeling.

BACKGROUND CHECK

Before reading the following essay, check your knowledge and assumptions about teaching and learning.

1. What do grades mean to you? For example, do you think your grades reflect your knowledge?

2. If you could suggest one thing that would improve teaching and learning, in your opinion, what would it be?

3. Do failing grades serve a useful purpose? Why or why not?

4. Based on your reading of the title, author information, and first two paragraphs, what do you expect to follow?

5. What else do you know or think about the topic?

In Praise of the F Word

Mary Sherry

Mary Sherry is a teacher from Minnesota. This essay appeared in Newsweek's *"My Turn" column.*

VOCABULARY CHECK	
semiliterate (1)	having limited knowledge
impediments (4)	barriers
composure (6)	calm
perceive (8)	understand, become aware
conspiracy (11)	plot

Tens of thousands of 18-year-olds will graduate this year and be handed meaningless diplomas. These diplomas won't look any different from those awarded their luckier classmates. Their validity will be questioned only when their employers discover that these graduates are semiliterate. 1

Eventually a fortunate few will find their way into educational-repair shops—adult-literacy programs, such as the one where I teach basic grammar and writing. There, high-school graduates and high-school dropouts pursuing graduate-equivalency certificates will learn the skills they should have learned in school. They will also discover they have been cheated by our educational system. 2

As I teach, I learn a lot about our schools. Early in each session I ask my students to write about an unpleasant experience they had in school. No writer's block here! "I wish someone would have had made me stop doing drugs and made me study." "I liked to party and no one seemed to care." "I was a good kid and didn't cause any trou- 3 ble, so they just passed me along even though I didn't read well and couldn't write." And so on.

I am your basic do-gooder, and prior to teaching this class I blamed   4
the poor academic skills our kids have today on drugs, divorce and other impediments to concentration necessary for doing well in school. But, as I rediscover each time I walk into the classroom, before a teacher can expect students to concentrate, he has to get their attention, no matter what distractions may be at hand. There are many ways to do this, and they have much to do with teaching style. However, if style alone won't do it, there is another way to show who holds the winning hand in the classroom. That is to reveal the trump card of failure.

I will never forget a teacher who played that card to get the   5
attention of one of my children. Our youngest, a world-class charmer, did little to develop his intellectual talents but always got by. Until Mrs. Stifter.

Our son was a high-school senior when he had her for English.   6
"He sits in the back of the room talking to his friends," she told me. "Why don't you move him to the front row?" I urged, believing the embarrassment would get him to settle down. Mrs. Stifter looked at me steely-eyed over her glasses. "I don't move seniors," she said. "I flunk them." I was flustered. Our son's academic life flashed before my eyes. No teacher had ever threatened him with that before. I regained my composure and managed to say that I thought she was right. By the time I got home I was feeling pretty good about this. It was a radical approach for these times, but, well, why not? "She's going to flunk you," I told my son. I did not discuss it any further. Suddenly English became a priority in his life. He finished out the semester with an A.

I know one example doesn't make a case, but at night I see a   7
parade of students who are angry and resentful for having been passed along until they could no longer even pretend to keep up. Of average intelligence or better, they eventually quit school, concluding they were too dumb to finish. "I should have been held back," is a comment I hear frequently. Even sadder are those students who are high-school graduates who say to me after a few weeks of class, "I don't know how I ever got a high-school diploma."

Passing students who have not mastered the work cheats them   8
and the employers who expect graduates to have basic skills. We excuse this dishonest behavior by saying kids can't learn if they come from terrible environments. No one seems to stop to think that—no matter what environments they come from—most kids don't put school first on their list unless they perceive something is at stake. They'd rather be sailing.

Many students I see at night could give expert testimony on un-   9
employment, chemical dependency, abusive relationships. In spite of
these difficulties, they have decided to make education a priority. They
are motivated by the desire for a better job or the need to hang on to
the one they've got. They have a healthy fear of failure.

People of all ages can rise above their problems, but they need to   10
have a reason to do so. Young people generally don't have the maturity to value education in the same way my adult students value it. But
fear of failure, whether economic or academic, can motivate both.

Flunking as a regular policy has just as much merit today as it did   11
two generations ago. We must review the threat of flunking and see
it as it really is—a positive teaching tool. It is an expression of confidence by both teachers and parents that the students have the ability
to learn the material presented to them. However, making it work
again would take a dedicated, caring conspiracy between teachers
and parents. It would mean facing the tough reality that passing kids
who haven't learned the material—while it might save them grief for
the short term—dooms them to long-term illiteracy. It would mean
that teachers would have to follow through on their threats, and parents would have to stand behind them, knowing their children's best
interests are indeed at stake. This means no more doing Scott's assignments for him because he might fail. No more passing Jodi because
she's such a nice kid.

This is a policy that worked in the past and can work today. A   12
wise teacher, with the support of his parents, gave our son the opportunity to succeed—or fail. It's time we return this choice to all students.

THINKING CRITICALLY

Main Idea

1. What is Mary Sherry's thesis? Is it stated or implied?

Details

2. Which paragraph contains an extended example of a teacher who played "the trump card of failure"?

3. According to Sherry, what is the result of passing students who have not mastered the work?

Organization

4. What is the essay's organizational pattern? List the transitions that help you identify the pattern.

Purpose, Audience, Tone

5. Do you think Sherry's purpose is to inform readers about students' lack of skills, persuade readers to revive the policy of flunking, or entertain readers with interesting stories about students? Use evidence from the essay to support your answer.

6. Who is Sherry's intended audience: parents, teachers, students, or more than one of these groups? Use evidence from the essay to explain your answer.

7. Would you describe Sherry's tone as uncaring, critical, or angry? What words and phrases help you identify the tone?

Inferences and Conclusions

8. Would Sherry agree or disagree with flunking a high school senior who had not mastered the skills in an algebra course? Use evidence from the essay to support your answer.

Making Connections

Sherry says her students have no trouble writing about an unpleasant experience. Write about an unpleasant experience you have had either in high school or in college. What happened? What did you do about it?

PURPOSE AND AUDIENCE IN READING

The writer's purpose is his or her reason for writing about a particular subject. Sometimes you will find a direct statement of purpose near the beginning of an essay or in the introduction to a chapter. Often, however, writers do not state the purpose directly. Instead, you may have to infer the purpose. To find the writer's purpose you need to know what the kinds of purposes are and what questions to ask to find them.

Writers usually have one of three common purposes: to inform, to persuade, or to entertain. If the purpose is to *inform*, the writer's goal is to explain or teach. Writers with this purpose in mind give you mainly facts and information. If the purpose is to *persuade*, the writer's goal is to convince you of something or influence your thinking. Writers seeking to persuade have an opinion to promote, which they may or may not support sufficiently with facts. If the purpose is to *entertain*, the writer's goal may be to amuse you, to arouse some other emotion, to excite your imagination, or simply to express a feeling. Writers with this purpose in mind use descriptive details that appeal to your senses and may write fiction or nonfiction. The following examples illustrate the three purposes.

1. The city of Orlando has done much to promote its Lynx System both to make citizens aware that the bus service exists and to encourage them to ride rather than drive on overcrowded highways. Some buses are painted bright colors, for example, hot pink, electric green, and stoplight yellow. Artists have painted designs on the buses. One bus displays a jungle scene with huge tropical flowers. Another sports the Orlando Magic logo. Still another shows a stylized silhouette of a lynx, the animal the bus system was named after. Bus stops throughout the city are identified by signs painted with a pink paw print.

2. If you live in an apartment, you should consider paying for a garbage pickup service. For a small fee you can leave your garbage outside your door, and someone will pick it up on designated days. Although you may think it is no trouble to carry your garbage to the dumpster in the parking lot, the fact is that if, like many people, you wait until 10:00 P.M., when it is dark, you may be putting yourself at risk. Also, most people are in a hurry in the morning, and it is easy to forget to take out the garbage. If you had a service that came once or twice a week and all you had to do was set the bags outside the door, you would be less likely to let the garbage accumulate in the kitchen, drawing insects and creating an unpleasant odor. Think about it. Wouldn't it be nice to be relieved of this hassle?

3. In the days before smoking was banned in public buildings, Francine, an attorney, took her last thoughtful drag of cigarette smoke, exhaled, and stubbed the butt out in an ashtray that was already overflowing. Looking around for the wastebasket and not finding it, she carried the ashtray into her paralegal's office and dumped the contents into the large trash-filled receptacle on the floor beside the desk. "Hey!" cried the paralegal, "That's my purse."

The first paragraph informs readers about the way Orlando has attracted attention to its bus system. Facts about the buses support the main idea. In the second paragraph, the goal is to persuade readers to hire a garbage collection service. The writer's opinions about tenants and their habits support the main idea. The third paragraph entertains readers by relating a humorous incident. The paralegal's comment and the writer's choice of words such as *drag* and *receptacle* make some readers chuckle. The purposes in these paragraphs are fairly obvious. Sometimes, however, you may have difficulty finding the writer's purpose. To determine whether the purpose is to inform, entertain, or persuade, ask yourself three questions.

- What does the writer want readers to know and why?

- Who is the intended audience?

- What response does the writer expect from the reader?

Often you can determine the purpose from a stated main idea. Suppose a paragraph begins with the sentence, "Attitudes can act as barriers to communication." You can tell from this sentence that the writer's purpose is to inform you of the ways attitudes prevent communication. If a main idea statement contains words like *should, must, ought, necessary,* or *essential,* the writer's purpose may be to persuade, as in this sentence: "We should all discontinue the wasteful practice of bagging groceries in paper and plastic." The writer states an opinion in this sentence. The persuasive word *should* and the value judgment *wasteful* suggest that the writer wants to convince you to stop using paper and plastic bags for your groceries.

Figure 9.1 compares purposes, the details that support them, the responses writers expect from readers, and a few typical sources where you are likely to find writing that achieves these objectives. Please note that the figure makes a general comparison only. As you become a more experienced reader, you will find that the categories overlap a great deal. For example, although descriptive details are a common feature of writing for entertainment, writers who seek to inform or persuade may also make use of description, as in the paragraph about the Lynx bus service on page 243.

FIGURE 9.1

The Writer's Purpose

WRITER'S PURPOSE	SUPPORTING DETAILS	EXPECTED READER RESPONSE	MOST COMMON SOURCES
Inform (to instruct or explain)	facts, examples, and other kinds of information	to understand or be able to apply information gained	textbooks, periodicals, journals, instruction manuals
Persuade (to influence or convince)	mostly opinion with facts carefully chosen to persuade the reader to support writer's opinion, emotional language	to be convinced or moved to take action	newspaper editorials, essays and articles, advertising copy, political tracts, appeals for money, membership, and contribution to causes
Entertain (to express or arouse feeling, excite imagination)	descriptive details, facts used for their entertainment value	to experience pleasure, both emotionally and intellectually	fiction and nonfiction: novels, poems, stories, essays

Exercise 9.1   Read the following sentences. Then determine whether the author's purpose is to inform, persuade, or entertain. Be able to explain your answer. The first one is done as an example.

1. In the 1995 NBA playoffs, the Houston Rockets defeated the Orlando Magic in a clean sweep victory.

   The purpose is to inform readers of who won the playoffs.

2. Every woman should do a monthly self-examination of her breasts because early detection of cancer increases her chances for survival.

   _____

3. When asked how she stayed so slim, the fashion model replied, "I follow a three-step plan: no food, no food, and no food."

   _____

4. Did you know that some tomatoes, which are picked green, are gassed to make them red before you buy them at the grocery store?

   _____

5. Students who are attending college on sports scholarships should prepare for careers in fields other than sports because so few make it to the professional leagues.

   _____

6. Congress says a law against flag burning will make people more respectful of the flag, but as Barbara Ehrenreich points out in a *Time* essay, apparently Congress thinks that the only way to show respect for something is to refrain from setting it on fire.

   _____

7. The Southside Mall needs more and better lighting in its parking garage because everyone knows that well-lighted places are a deterrent to crime.

   _____

8. The bodies of fireflies, or lightning bugs, contain phosphorous, which causes them to glow so they can attract mates.

   _____

9. Louise Erdrich's novel *Tracks* is about Fleur, a descendent of the Chippewa Indians.

   _____

10. The best way to quit smoking is to become a nonsmoker.

_____

As you know, main ideas are not always stated. But if you can infer the main idea, you can probably determine the writer's purpose. For one thing the topic, what the selection is about, and the source, where it comes from, may contain clues. If the topic is the human circulatory system and the source is a biology textbook, you can conclude that the purpose is to inform you about the circulatory system. A letter from NOW (the National Organization of Women) about its current lobbying efforts may have the purpose of persuading you to join or to contribute money. A humorous magazine essay about "paranoid packaging" is written to entertain. Of course a writer may have more than one purpose, for example to inform you of harmful experiments cosmetics companies perform on animals _and_ to persuade you to boycott their products. Usually, however, an overall purpose will dominate.

Exercise 9.2 Read each topic and its source and decide whether the purpose is to inform, persuade, or entertain. Write your choice on the line provided. The first one is done as an example.

1. A section in your biology textbook on the Krebs cycle

   The purpose is to inform.
   _____

2. An editorial urging you to vote no on an upcoming referendum

   _____

3. A letter from your insurance company explaining new benefits for policyholders

   _____

4. A magazine advertisement from the American Dairy Association explaining the benefits of drinking milk

   _____

5. A movie review in your local newspaper

_____

6. A book that tells about the care and training of a certain breed of dog

_____

7. The biography of a popular film star

_____

8. A pamphlet in your doctor's office advising you to lower your fat intake

_____

9. "We Real Cool" from a collection of poems by Langston Hughes

_____

10. A journal article about ways to increase reading comprehension

_____

The *intended audience* and the *expected reader response* are two more keys to the writer's purpose. Students are the audience for textbook writers. These writers expect students to be able to understand and apply concepts after reading about them and practicing with them. The general public is the audience for newspapers. News reporters and columnists expect a variety of outcomes from readers. Reporters expect readers to know the facts after reading about current events: what happened to whom, where, how, and why. Some columnists are social critics who want readers to respond by changing their behavior. Others are humorists who want to make readers laugh. Still others are political commentators who assume readers will support or reject certain programs, policies, or candidates.

Some magazines have a specific audience in mind. *Sports Illustrated* appeals to sports enthusiasts of all kinds. *Golf Digest* appeals to golfers. The intended audience of *Modern Maturity* is senior citizens; teenaged girls are the intended audience for *Seventeen,* and children are the audience of *Owl* and *Chickadee.* For just about every interest you can imagine a magazine is probably written for people who share that interest. Obviously the purposes of those who write for any magazine are to inform and entertain readers on topics that interest them. Some may seek to persuade readers as well. Most of us read magazines for fun and information. So writers expect that we will learn something, perhaps even use the information they give us. They also expect us to have a pleasant reading experience.

Have you ever picked up a magazine, leafed through it, and decided that it was not for you? If so, then you recognized that you were not a member of that magazine's intended audience. You are, however, the intended audience for much of the reading that you do in college. For some reading, particularly in English courses where you may be required to read both the fiction and nonfiction works of many authors, on many topics, written for many audiences, determining the writer's purpose may be your key to interpreting these works.

Exercise 9.3   Working on your own or with a partner, identify the audience for each source listed. If you are not familiar with some of the materials on the list, ask your librarian for help. The first one is done for you.

1. *Catholic Digest*

   This magazine appeals to a religious group: Catholics.

   _____

2. *USA Today*

   _____

3. *Journal of Reading*

   _____

4. General Colin Powell's autobiography, *My American Journey*

   _____

5. Your college catalog

   _____

6. A law textbook

_____

7. *Popular Mechanics*

_____

8. *Ebony* magazine

_____

9. *Shape* magazine

_____

10. *Journal of Popular Culture*

_____

DETERMINING YOUR PURPOSE AND AUDIENCE

Now that you are in college, you write to answer test questions, to complete exercises and assignments, and perhaps even to fill out application forms for scholarships, financial aid, or part-time jobs. Before you graduate, you will probably write a résumé, or summary of your work and other experience, which you will submit along with job applications. In the workplace you may have to write reports or take the minutes of a meeting. In your personal life you may write letters to friends and relatives, to the editor of your local newspaper, or even to your state representative or senator. In each of these situations, your purpose is clear.

In each case you want something—for example, a good grade, a good job, a promotion, or a favorable response. Your purpose should be just as clear before you begin writing an essay. One way to determine a reason for writing is to ask yourself, "Why am I writing this?" Most of the time your answer will reveal one of two reasons: *to inform* or *to persuade.*

If your purpose is to inform readers, you need to tell them something about your topic that will educate or enlighten them. Perhaps you work as a host or hostess in a popular restaurant. To some people it may look as if you have an easy job. You greet people when they come in, take their names if they do not have a reservation, show them where to wait, and then seat them when their table is ready. However, this job may involve more than people think. You may decide to write an essay to inform your readers that being a restaurant host or hostess is not as easy as it looks.

If your purpose is to persuade readers, you will want to influence them so that they change their opinions or behavior. Perhaps you are concerned about the environment, and you believe everyone should begin to do what is necessary to help preserve the world for future generations. For example, you want people to recycle cans and newspapers, discontinue their use of aerosol sprays, and boycott products that come in nonrecyclable, nonbiodegradable containers. You may decide to write an essay to persuade readers to take these steps.

Remember that writers often have more than one reason for writing. In the process of *informing* readers that a job might involve more than appears on the surface, you may find yourself *persuading* them not to consider taking this job unless they first find out what is involved. In order to *persuade* readers to recycle cans and newspapers, you may first have to *inform* them that a problem exists.

Less often your purpose may be to entertain readers. For example, you may decide to write a humorous essay such as "Wait Divisions" in Chapter 5 or "Shopping with Children" in Chapter 6. In both essays the writers are poking fun at two everyday activities: waiting and shopping. Although their primary purpose is to entertain readers, the writers of these essays are also commenting on two of life's common frustrations. Waiting wastes time and raises tempers. Shopping with children, as every parent knows, can lead to arguments and hurt feelings. Tom Bodett and Phyllis Theroux remind us in their lighthearted essays to see the humor in both situations.

Exercise 9.4   Read each paragraph below and decide whether the purpose is primarily to *inform, persuade,* or *entertain.* Underline words or phrases in each paragraph that help you determine the writer's purpose.

1. From his broad, flat bill to his webbed feet, the furry duck-billed platypus is an odd animal. Awkward on land, he is a graceful swimmer. Shrimp are the platypus's favorite food, but you might wonder how he ever finds them because he swims with his eyes closed. Electric sensors on his bill can detect the tiny electric current given off

by the movement of the shrimp's tail. Not only do the receptors in the platypus's bill help him find dinner, but they help him navigate too. Flowing waters create electric fields through which the platypus glides with ease.

2. NASA's space station, which was first proposed in 1984, is still not finished. So far $40 billion has been wasted on what would amount to a spaceship construction site, an observation platform, and a manufacturing plant for chemicals. Caught in the budget crunch, NASA first scaled down the space station's functions to one, a research lab for studies in weightlessness. Then in May 1991 the space station was cut from NASA's budget. Officials are fighting to restore the space station when what they should do is cancel it. From that first walk on the moon, we are still light years away from the regular space flights that NASA had predicted. It is time to put that flight of fancy to rest and spend the money on a more down-to-earth science we can put to use.

3. "Canned hunts," that's what they're called, and what they are is an excuse for people who call themselves hunters to shoot exotic, often endangered, animals at as much as $3,500 a pop. Often the animals are drugged or chased out of cages into a fenced-in open area where they are trapped. Some sport that is. The real tragedy is that a lot of money is to be made in this grisly business. Exotic animal "preserves" are springing up in some states; these are the wildlife supermarkets where hunt organizers shop. Canned hunts are currently under investigation, but progress is slow because of weak and ambiguous laws. Legitimate hunters and sportsmen should deplore canned hunts and demand that their legislators become involved in this issue.

4. When it comes to mate selection, do you believe in true love or propinquity? Those who believe in true love believe that love happens only once and that just one "right" person exists for everyone. Those who believe in propinquity believe that anyone can fall in love with any number of people, and that the "right" person may be the one who is the most available at the time. Propinquity means closeness or nearness in a physical sense. Two people sitting next to each other in a movie theater have propinquity. One reason so many people marry the girl or boy next door is propinquity. So when you are looking for a mate, chances are you will select some-

one from your own neighborhood, someone you went to school with, or someone you met at work. Other factors that play a role in mate selection are physical appearance, race, nationality, age, educational level, socioeconomic status, religion, personality characteristics, and shared interests. In other words, you are probably going to marry someone very much like yourself; most people do.

5. They tell me that an old sow-hog taught me how to walk. That is, she didn't instruct me in detail, but she convinced me that I really ought to try.

It was like this. My mother was going to have collard greens for dinner, so she took the dishpan and went down to the spring to wash the greens. She left me sitting on the floor, and gave me a hunk of cornbread to keep me quiet. Everything was going along all right, until the sow with her litter of pigs in convoy came abreast of the door. She must have smelled the cornbread I was messing with and scattering crumbs around the floor, so, she came right on in, and began to nuzzle around.

My mother heard my screams and came running. Her heart must have stood still when she saw the sow in there, because hogs have been known to eat human flesh.

As for the sow, poor misunderstood lady, she had no interest in me except my bread. I lost that in scrambling to my feet and she was eating it. She had much less intention of eating mama's baby, than Mama had of eating hers.

With no more suggestions from the sow or anybody else, it seems that I just took to walking and kept the thing a-going.

From *Dust Tracks on a Road,* Zora Neale Hurston (1942), Harper Collins Edition, 1991.

Like other writers you can write for one of two possible audiences, a general one or a specific one. Most of the time in college, you will write for your classmates and your instructor. What assumptions can you make about them? First of all, they are part of your college community, so they share your interests, concerns, and problems as a college student. Because they are also part of the larger community in which you live, they are members of a *general audience.* You can assume that they have shared many of your same experiences, that they may be aware of current events and of the social issues that affect everyone's lives. In addition, people of varying races, cultural backgrounds, nationalities, and ethnic groups are all part of a general audience in the United States today and are also part of your classroom audience. It is important to keep in mind that some of your readers will have had experiences that are very different from yours. You therefore cannot assume that readers will always know what you mean unless you explain it to them.

Sometimes you may write for a *specific audience*. Perhaps you have decided to write about a controversial topic—animal rights, for example—and you imagine that some of the people reading your essay will strongly disagree with you. To write effectively for this audience, you will have to know what their views are so that you can choose your evidence and develop your thesis to answer these views.

How you write about a topic will differ depending upon who the audience is and what your purpose is. In the following examples, the topic is the same, but the audiences are different. The topic is "competency testing, for college students." Notice how *purpose* and *audience* affect the writing.

Following is Example 1, a paragraph from a typical news article a journalist might write in response to a new state law requiring college students to take a competency test in math and English. The purpose of the article is to inform readers about the test. The general public is the audience.

EXAMPLE 1

Soon, all college students in our state will have to take a basic skills test. The test comes at a time when educators across the country are expressing concern about declining SAT scores and about complaints from employers that college graduates lack basic communication skills. The purpose of the test is to ensure that students who want to continue in college are able to demonstrate that they can read, write, and compute at a basic level. Students who fail one part of the test will have an opportunity to retake that part without having to repeat the whole test. Though the test is still in its experimental stages, eventually every student will have to take it in order to be eligible for an associate of arts degree and to continue his or her education. Students will have to pay a fee to take the test; however, the price has not yet been determined. . . .

The next two examples are possible letters to the editor of a local newspaper in a community where competency testing has been going on for some time. One writer defends the test and the other condemns it. Parents of college students are the specific audience for both letters, and the writers' purpose is to persuade them either to support or reject the test.

EXAMPLE 2

Dear Editor:

When I was in school you either learned, or else. The "or else" came in the form of a rap on your knuckles with the teacher's ruler. No one passed to the next grade who had not learned the lessons. I remember one boy in the sixth grade who was 18 years old. Eventually, he graduated and went on to earn a living and support his family like the rest of us.

I don't advocate a return to those times. I know that all students are entitled to the opportunity to continue their education, not just those who can afford the tuition. However, I think it's a shame that so many kids graduate from college who can't even spell.

After all these years of social promotion and lack of accountability on the part of schools and teachers, I'm glad that my child will have to take the state competency test. Maybe because of this test, he'll work harder in school and his teachers will feel obligated to help him succeed. I hope all parents will get behind the state's efforts to upgrade education and support the testing program.

A Concerned Parent

EXAMPLE 3

Dear Editor:

My daughter has always been a good student except in math. In high school she made mostly A's and B's. She has done well in her college courses too, but now her graduation is being delayed because she didn't pass the math part of the state competency test. She is spending another semester at the community college to brush up on her math skills so she can pass the test. I'm worried that she may never pass this exam because math is the one subject that has always given her trouble.

What a lot of parents do not realize is that students have to pay for this test, and in my case I am having to pay my daughter's tuition for another semester in college, which I had not planned on and which I can ill afford.

Not only does the test cause students needless anxiety, but it is very discouraging to them when they fail. How can one test be a measure of a person's ability, and why should one test determine whether a student gets to continue her education? Furthermore, the test is timed. When students are under that kind of pressure, it is no wonder that they do not do well. I am sure I am not alone when I say that I think the test is unfair. I urge parents to write their legislators opposing the test.

A Concerned Parent

The writers of Examples 1, 2, and 3 know their audiences. Each knows the extent to which his or her audience is informed about the topic; what additional information about the topic the audience needs; why the audience should be interested in or concerned about the topic; and what new information would enlighten the audience.

The writer of Example 1 assumes that some readers may know about the new competency test but that most of them do not. He also assumes that most of them are aware that educators are concerned about college graduates' declining performance. He probably thinks that they do not know what the test covers or that all college students will have to take it. Because many of the members of this writer's audience are parents, they are probably interested in or concerned about competency testing because their children will have to take the test if they expect to graduate from college. As a result of reading the article, parents may be inclined to encourage their children to succeed in those subjects that the test covers. Although some readers of the article undoubtedly may have heard that their state had established competency testing, they may not have realized that failing the test could delay or even prevent graduation. That students would have to pay a fee to take the test may also have struck some readers as new information. This writer states facts without making judgments, and the language is formal and unemotional.

The writers of Examples 2 and 3 are writing at a time when the competency test is an established fact. Therefore, they can assume that parents of college students, or students who want to go to college, are aware of the test, what it covers, its cost, and that it is required. These writers can also assume that although some members of the audience are in favor of the test, some oppose it. Both writers make judgments about the test. They rely on personal examples and opinions more than facts for their support, and their language is informal and emotional.

The writer of Example 2 believes that many parents remember the days when students did learn their lessons. She also believes that, like her, many of her readers take for granted that schools and colleges need reform. The test, she thinks, is an effort to improve education. She probably thinks that readers who do not support the test do not realize that it might have a positive effect on the state's education program. She is writing for an audience of readers whom she believes would support the state's testing program were they to see it as both encouraging students to work harder and teachers to provide more help.

The writer of Example 3, on the other hand, believes that those who favor the test do not realize its drawbacks. She cites the cost, the inconvenience and discouragement of having to take all or parts of the test more than once to pass it, the time limit, and the added cost of delaying graduation, all as hardships for students and, in some cases, for their parents. For some members of the audience, this additional information may be of some interest and concern particularly if they have college-age sons and daughters who have failed the test and encountered similar problems.

Both writers of Examples 2 and 3 hope their readers will take action either in the form of supporting the test or writing their legislators to complain about it. Both either know or have studied their audiences well enough to present facts and opinions that will appeal to their readers' interests.

In considering your audience's needs, good questions to ask are:

- What can I assume readers already know about my topic?

- What additional information about my topic do I think they need to have?

- Why should they be interested in or concerned about my topic?

- Can I tell them something new about my topic?

Exercise 9.5   Working with a partner, imagine that you live in a state that requires competency testing. As college students, you will have to take the test. Working through your student government association, you have decided to offer a prep session to help students get ready for the test. You have convinced a group of teachers to conduct the session and give a practice exam and exercises. You think all students who are planning to take the test ought to take advantage of the prep session. The session is free, but students do have to sign up in the student government office. Your job is to write an article for the campus newspaper to advertise the prep session. Before you write the article, decide who your audience is and ask yourself what their needs may be. As you think about what to say, generate evidence, such as *who* is eligible to attend the prep session, *what* it will cover, *where* it will be held and *when, why* students should attend, and *how* they should sign up. Keep your article brief, 200 words or fewer. Share your article with the rest of the class.

THINKING ABOUT PROCESS

Finding the main idea, identifying supporting details, and determining the meanings of words in context are basic *reading skills. Determining purpose, audience, and tone are more advanced skills.*

1. The main idea and details are usually what you notice first as you begin to think about what you have read. You may also have to look up difficult words or terms that you cannot define in context. By making inferences from the main idea, details, and author's choice of words you can usually determine purpose, audience, and tone.

2. Similarly, in writing, you will probably begin with what comes easiest to you. Some students are able to decide on a thesis soon after they select a topic and brainstorm for details. Then they may think about purpose, audience, and tone. Others begin with a topic and purpose. The purpose then guides all their other choices.

3. When you write, put yourself in the reader's place. Seeing yourself as a member of an audience may help you to become aware of your audience and their needs.

DETERMINING A WRITER'S TONE

The writer's tone is the writer's voice. Just as you have a tone of voice whenever you speak, so do writers whenever they write. Your tone is easy for your friends and others to interpret because what you say is accompanied by facial expressions and gestures. Also, the emphasis you place on words, the softness or loudness of your voice, and the attitude conveyed by your tone of voice—whether you sound angry, sad, or loving—all help others to read your moods and sense your feelings. Writers do not have all those advantages. Only through choice of words do writers reveal tone.

Some tones are obvious. If you read letters to the editor in your newspaper, you can easily determine the letter writer's tone. One may seem angry while another may seem respectful. Letters from good friends may have a friendly, considerate, or excited tone. Manuals explaining how to operate a piece of equipment or assemble a piece of furniture have a matter-of-fact tone. They get right to the point, telling you what to do and in what order. Textbooks have a serious tone, revealed in the use of technical terms or the precise terms of the discipline. Some textbooks may have an objective tone, one that does not take sides, if the writer's goal is to present all sides of an issue or problem, letting you decide how to respond. A humorous, or comic, tone, revealed either by the incidents themselves or the way a writer describes them, makes you laugh.

Other tones are less obvious. You may have to consider the writer's purpose, the main idea, the selection of details, and the words themselves to determine the tone. *Tone,* therefore, is the writer's attitude or feeling toward the subject that comes through in the words and details he or she selects. Purpose and tone work together. Often the writer's purpose determines the tone. Some writers' personalities so strongly influence the tone of what they write that readers identify them with certain tones. Rush Limbaugh and Andy Rooney, for example, both speak and write in characteristic ways. Limbaugh's tone is at times arrogant, outspoken, or impassioned. Rooney's tone is always amused, often astonished, and at times cynical. Sometimes it helps to know who the writer is and what he or she does or is interested in besides writing.

Mary Sherry writes from her experience as a teacher and a parent. As a teacher, she wants grades to reflect performance and a diploma to mean something. As a parent, she wants her son's education to prepare him for the future. She is critical of public schools because they have turned out graduates who are semiliterate: barely able to read and write. As such, they make poor candidates for employment. Sherry believes passing students who have not earned passing grades is in no one's best interests. The fear of failure, she says, is a positive teaching tool because it motivates students to try harder and to achieve. Her purpose is to persuade readers that flunking as a regular policy should be restored.

Sherry's critical tone is revealed by her choice of words. She refers to adult-literacy programs as "educational-repair shops" where graduates who were "handed meaningless diplomas" learn the skills "they should have learned in school." Sherry says our educational system has "cheated" students and employers and is guilty of "dishonest behavior."

Tone expresses feelings, and readers respond to tone with feelings. So another way to determine the writer's tone is to ask yourself how you feel about what you have read. Does it make you angry? Does it arouse your sympathy? Do you feel cheerful, lighthearted? Your emotional reaction may be a clue to the writer's tone. Figure 9.2 compares four different passages and their tones. The words that reveal each tone are underlined.

The underlined words in the first passage in Figure 9.2 express the writer's anger with the bats and with the contractor who cannot fix the house to keep them out. The second passage has an objective tone, as indicated by the underlined factual details and the absence of any emotional language. In the third passage the underlined details indicate that the writer is upset, or distressed. The fourth passage has a comic, or humorous, tone, as indicated by the underlined words and phrases. Figure 9.3 lists and defines words commonly used to describe certain tones.

Exercise 9.6   Read the following paragraphs. Then, from the choices given, select the word that *best* describes the writer's tone. Refer to Figure 9.3 if you need help with the definition of a tone word.

1. It is always wise to consider your resources before going out shopping. If you only expect to spend $10 or $20, there may be no problem. But an expenditure of hundreds of dollars might require an analysis of tradeoffs you might make among such factors as money, time, and energy. Make a long-range plan of the things you want to buy, and modify and add to it when necessary. Having an idea of how much you want to spend for an item is also useful, since you can tell a salesperson the price range that interests you.

   From *Consumer Economic Issues in America,* E. Thomas Garman, Houghton Mifflin Co., 1991.

   a. Optimistic

   b. Condescending

   c. Sympathetic

   d. Serious

FIGURE 9.2

Determining Tone

Something has to be done about these bats. The loathsome creatures are taking over. I'm at my wit's end. I can't keep the nasty things out of my house. That good-for-nothing contractor I keep hiring to find and plug the holes where they're coming in isn't worth what I pay him.

ANGRY

Numerous species of bats inhabit North America. They sleep during the day and are active at night. They are harmless to humans. Many species feed on insects, though some, notably the fruit bat, eat plants. The vampire bat is the only species that lives on the blood of animals. Though this bat harms livestock, it is not known to attack humans.

OBJECTIVE

It is sad that so many people fear bats. There is no reason to fear these poor little creatures. In fact, we should do all we can to protect them. Bats eat millions of mosquitoes and other annoying insects. Without bats, these bugs would multiply beyond control. It is too bad that more people do not build bat houses to attract bats.

DISTRESSED

How would you like to give birth to a child while hanging by your feet? Does a diet of fat, juicy insects appeal to you? Are you a party animal who stays out til dawn and sleeps in all day? Whether you can answer yes or no to these questions, you have to appreciate the life of the average Mexican split-tail bat.

COMIC

FIGURE 9.3

Tone Words and Their Definitions

ambivalent	uncertain, indecisive
amused	provoking laughter, amused, comical
angry	showing anger or rage
apathetic	indifferent, unconcerned
arrogant	displaying undeserved importance or pride
astonished	surprised
bitter	harsh and resentful
cheerful	full of cheer, happy
condescending	displaying a superior attitude

FIGURE 9.3

Tone Words and Their Definitions (continued)

comic	provoking laughter, amusing
compassionate	showing pity and sorrow for others' suffering
critical	judgmental, making an evaluation of worth
cruel	mean and vicious
cynical	scornful and bitterly mocking
depressed	downcast, sad
detached	unemotional, uninvolved, impersonal
distressed	upset, worried
earnest	deeply sincere
evasive	intentionally vague, unclear
formal	proper, conventional
gentle	kind
indignant	angry with feelings of injustice
impassioned	filled with passion, strong emotion
intense	deeply felt, profound
ironic	saying one thing but meaning another
irreverent	disrespectful
joyful	extremely happy
loving	expressing love
mocking	making fun of
nostalgic	looking to the past with longing
objective	unemotional, without prejudice
outraged	shocked and angry, morally offended
optimistic	positive, looking on the good side
outspoken	speaking without holding back, frank
pessimistic	negative, looking on the bad side
playful	humorous and full of fun
pompous	having inflated self worth
regretful	sorrowful, feeling loss or disappointment
reverent	respectful
sarcastic	ridiculing in a sharp and teasing way
satirical	using irony or sarcasm to attack or expose
sentimental	overly sensitive or emotional
serious	concerned, responsible
solemn	serious and dignified
somber	serious and gloomy
sympathetic	expressing compassion or shared feelings
uneasy	anxious, insecure
vindictive	seeking revenge, wanting to get even

2. Born on American soil in common with yourselves, deriving our bodies and our minds from its dust, centuries having passed away since our ancestors were torn from the shores of Africa, we, like yourselves, hold ourselves to be in every sense Americans, and that we may, therefore, venture to speak to you in a tone not lower than that which becomes earnest men and American citizens. Having watered your soil with our tears, enriched it with our blood, performed its roughest labor in time of peace, defended it against enemies in time of war, and at all times been loyal and true to its best interests, we deem it no arrogance or presumption to manifest now a common concern with you for its welfare, prosperity, honor and glory.

From Frederick Douglass's Address to the Louisville Convention (1883), *A More Perfect Union: Documents in U.S. History,* Vol. I, 3d ed., Paul F. Boller, Jr., and Ronald Story, Houghton Mifflin Co., 1992.

   a. Solemn

   b. Critical

   c. Formal

   d. Outspoken

3. People find it curious that those without homes would rather sleep sitting up on benches or huddled in doorways than go to shelters. Certainly some prefer to do so because they are emotionally ill, because they have been locked in before and they are damned if they will be locked in again. Others are afraid of the violence and trouble they may find there. But some seem to want something that is not available in shelters, and they will not compromise, not for a cot, or oatmeal, or a shower with special soap that kills bugs. "One room," a woman with a baby who was sleeping on her sister's floor, once told me, "painted blue." That was the crux of it; not size or location, but pride of ownership. Painted blue.

From "Homeless," *Living Out Loud,* Anna Quindlen, Ballantine Books, 1988.

   a. Indignant

   b. Sentimental

   c. Depressed

   d. Uneasy

4. Through the thicket, across the river, and deep, deep in the woods, lived a family of bears—a Papa Bear, a Mama Bear, and a Baby Bear—and they all lived together anthropomorphically in a little cottage as a nuclear family. They were very sorry about this, of course, since the nuclear family had traditionally served to enslave woymn, instill a self-righteous moralism in its members, and imprint rigid notions of heterosexualist roles onto the next generation. Nevertheless, they tried to be happy and took steps to avoid these pitfalls, such as naming their offspring the non–gender-specific "Baby."

From *Politically Correct Bedtime Stories,* James Finn Garner, Macmillan Publishing Co., 1994.

a. Bitter

b. Mocking

c. Cheerful

d. Earnest

SELECTING YOUR TONE

Your tone and choice of words can help readers determine your purpose and respond to the self that your tone reveals. As a writer, you have a voice. You can make the tone of your written voice sound different depending upon how you feel toward your topic and audience and the words you choose to express those feelings. Consider how being in a restaurant where a noisy child seated at the next table may affect people in different ways. A person who is also a parent and has been through the process of teaching young children how to eat in restaurants might sympathize with the parents of the noisy child and therefore not become annoyed with the child's behavior. Someone else might be very annoyed. Perhaps this person came to the restaurant with a date for a quiet, pleasant evening. He or she might feel that the parents of the noisy child are inconsiderate. If these two restaurant goers were each to write an essay about the experience, their essays would be quite different. One might write with an amused, sympathetic tone. The other might choose an angry, annoyed tone.

Tone is the attitude you convey through your choice of words. Read paragraphs A and B below. They are written on the same topic, "office thieves," but each has a different tone. In the first paragraph, the writer is amused. In the second, the writer is angry. In each paragraph the words, phrases, or sentences that help convey the tone are underlined.

PARAGRAPH A

Humorous words and phrases that mean stealing

Creates a humorous visual image

Office thieves are like those people who are always trying to bum a cigarette: a little annoying, basically harmless, but not criminals. You would think that an office manager would have something more important to do than to waste time crying over a pilfered paper clip. So what if someone lifts a legal pad, rips off a ream of paper, bags a box of number 2 pencils. Surely the office orders a surplus to cover these losses. Some managers guard the supply cabinet with their lives. Just try to get a ballpoint pen out of them if you have already used your allotted quota for the year. If more managers would realize that one of an employee's perks is free supplies and look the other way, then maybe fewer office thieves would steal a colleague's stapler with one hand while bumming a cigarette with the other.

An act that usually causes laughter

Humorous exaggeration

PARAGRAPH B

Words and phrases that suggest anger

"we" and "they" pronouns emphasize angry conflict

Strong term for office stealing— an angry exaggeration

Office thieves make life difficult for the rest of us. While we try to cut costs by making supplies last, the thieves are taking more than their share and costing us more. They are selfish, wasteful, and inconsiderate. To them, taking a box of pencils home for their own use is not stealing. Their attitude is that there are plenty more where those came from. A box of pencils costs about $8.50. A box of manila folders or a ream of paper costs around $18.00. Who do these thugs think pays for the supplies? The cost comes out of the office management budget. If we could cut consumption by eliminating the stealing, we might have more money left to upgrade some of the equipment we all have to use. We ought to punish the culprits by adding up the cost of their larceny and deducting it from their paychecks.

"us" against "them"

an angry exaggeration

"us" against "them"

Choosing the right tone for an essay does not have to be difficult. Although you should consider tone during the prewriting stage, you may not know what tone you want until you write your first, or rough, draft. Read your draft to yourself, or have someone read it to you. Try to recall how you felt as you wrote it. Were you sad, angry, amused, or did you have a different feeling? Also, how do you want readers to respond as they read your essay? Your purpose, what you expect of the audience, and your attitude toward your topic should influence your choice of an appropriate tone.

Exercise 9.7   Examine five pieces of writing and determine the *tone* of each: "It's OK to Be Different" on pages 65–68, and the paragraphs in Exercise 9.4. Is the tone of each piece of writing appropriate for its purpose? Why or why not? What could you add or change to make the tone more appropriate?

 ## THINKING IT OVER

Test your recall of this chapter's concepts by completing the following statements. If you cannot complete a statement, look back through the chapter to find the answer.

1. Understanding purpose, audience, and tone enables you to think _____ about reading and writing.

2. An author's _____ is his or her reason for writing.

3. The _____ consists of readers, real or imagined.

4. _____ is an author's expressed attitude or feeling as revealed by word choice.

5. Three common purposes are to _____, to _____, and to _____.

6. Audiences may be general or _____.

7. Two examples of tones are the _____ tone and the _____ tone.

8. Choose one of the Thinking First questions at the beginning of the chapter to answer on the following lines:

_____

_____

_____

TOPICS FOR WRITING

1. Write an essay in which your purpose is to *inform* readers about something you know, or have learned, or have read.

2. Write an essay in which your purpose is to *persuade* readers to take an action or to change an opinion.

3. Write an essay in which your purpose is to *entertain* readers with an amusing or interesting account of some event or situation.

Checklist for Revision

As you revise and edit your essay, check for the following:

1. Do you have a clearly stated thesis?

2. Have you supported your thesis with enough concrete details?

3. Do your paragraphs have unity and coherence?

4. Does your essay have a recognizable organizational pattern?

5. Have you used appropriate transitions?

6. Have you considered your audience's needs?

7. Will readers be able to determine your purpose?

8. Do your word choices create an appropriate tone?

9. Have you found and corrected your errors?

REFLECTIONS ON READING AND WRITING

Before reading this chapter, were you aware of writers' purposes and tones? What examples can you give? What have you learned from this chapter about purpose, audience, and tone that you can apply to your own reading and writing? What questions do you still have about purpose, audience, and tone?

Chapter 10

Inferences and Conclusions in Reading and Writing

THINKING FIRST

- *What are inferences and conclusions?*
- *How can I make inferences and draw conclusions?*
- *How do these skills help me in reading and writing?*

An inference *is an act of reasoning that leads you to draw a conclusion. A* conclusion *is a reasoned judgment or decision based on your inferences. An inference is also an interpretation of events or ideas based on available facts and the experience or opinions you bring to them as the following scenario illustrates.*

Imagine you are having trouble getting along with a roommate who has certain undesirable habits that you cannot accept. At first you try ignoring the behavior. Then you try talking about it with your roommate. As a last resort, you suggest that you both meet with a counselor, but

269

your roommate refuses. A couple of your friends offer suggestions, but because of experience you think nothing will work and that your roommate is unlikely to change. You also infer that the relationship has no future. As a result, you decide to move out.

In this scenario, your *opinions* are that your roommate's habits are undesirable and you cannot accept them. The *facts* are that you have ignored the behavior, talked to your roommate, and suggested seeing a counselor, but your roommate has refused. Based on these facts and opinions, your *inferences* are that nothing works, your roommate is unlikely to change, and the relationship has no future. Your *conclusion* is that you will move out, and this seems a reasonable course of action based on your inferences.

Making inferences and drawing conclusions are indispensable acts of daily living. For example, your decision to attend the college of your choice was a conclusion you reached based on inferences you made about your financial status, past performance in school, level of confidence, and many other factors. A diagnosis of an illness is a conclusion based on the inferences a physician makes from a patient's symptoms and examination results. The decision to hire someone is a conclusion based on inferences an employer makes from an applicant's qualifications, job history, and interview.

Making inferences and drawing conclusions are skills involved in the process we call logical, or critical, thinking, and they are as essential to the reading and writing processes as they are to everyday decision making. To think critically about reading and writing, you must be able to make inferences and draw conclusions. This chapter explains how to do both.

BACKGROUND CHECK

Before reading the following essay, check your knowledge and assumptions about the legal age for drinking.

1. If you drink, do you consider yourself a responsible drinker?

2. Do you think that, on the average, college students drink too much? Why or why not?

3. Are you in favor of lowering the drinking age to eighteen or keeping it at twenty-one? Explain your answer.

4. Based on your survey of the title, author information, and first two paragraphs, what do you expect to follow?

5. What else do you know or think about the topic?

Perils of Prohibition

Elizabeth M. Whelan

Whelan is president of the American Council on Science and Health. In this essay from Newsweek *she explains why we should lower the drinking age to eighteen.*

VOCABULARY CHECK

predicament (2)	unpleasant situation
moderation (2)	reasonableness
proscribe (3)	prohibit, forbid
disenfranchise (5)	to deprive of a right
dilemma (6)	problem
exacerbated (6)	made worse
anachronistic (6)	outdated
inevitable (7)	unavoidable
prudently (11)	wisely
abstinence (13)	refraining from

My colleagues at the Harvard School of Public Health, where I studied preventive medicine, deserve high praise for their study on teenage drinking. What they found in their survey of college students was that they drink "early and . . . often," frequently to the point of getting ill. 1

As a public-health scientist with a daughter, Christine, heading to college this fall, I have professional and personal concerns about teen binge drinking. It is imperative that we explore *why* so many young people abuse alcohol. From my own study of the effects of alcohol restrictions and my observations of Christine and her friends' predica- 2 ment about drinking, I believe that today's laws are unrealistic. Prohibiting the sale of liquor to responsible young adults creates an atmosphere where binge drinking and alcohol abuse have become a problem. American teens, unlike their European peers, don't learn how to drink gradually, safely and in moderation.

Alcohol is widely accepted and enjoyed in our culture. Studies show that moderate drinking can be good for you. But we legally proscribe alcohol until the age of 21 (why not 30 or 45?). Christine and her classmates can drive cars, fly planes, marry, vote, pay taxes, take out loans and risk their lives as members of the U.S. armed forces. But laws in all 50 states say that no alcoholic beverages may be sold to anyone until that magic 21st birthday. We didn't always have a national "21" rule. When I was in college, in the mid-'60s, the drinking age varied from state to state. This posed its own risks, with underage students crossing state lines to get a legal drink.   3

In parts of the Western world, moderate drinking by teenagers and even children under their parents' supervision is a given. Though the per capita consumption of alcohol in France, Spain and Portugal is higher than in the United States, the rate of alcoholism and alcohol abuse is lower. A glass of wine at dinner is normal practice. Kids learn to regard moderate drinking as an enjoyable family activity rather than as something they have to sneak away to do. Banning drinking by young people makes it a badge of adulthood—a tantalizing forbidden fruit.   4

Christine and her teenage friends like to go out with a group to a club, comedy show or sports bar to watch the game. But teens today have to go on the sly with fake IDs and the fear of getting caught. Otherwise, they're denied admittance to most places and left to hang out on the street. That's hardly a safer alternative. Christine and her classmates now find themselves in a legal no man's land. At 18, they're considered adults. Yet when they want to enjoy a drink like other adults, they are, as they put it, "disenfranchised."   5

Comparing my daughter's dilemma with my own as an "underage" college student, I see a difference—and one that I think has exacerbated the current dilemma. Today's teens are far more sophisticated than we are. They're treated less like children and have more responsibilities than we did. This makes the 21 restriction seem anachronistic.   6

For the past few years, my husband and I have been preparing Christine for college life and the inevitable partying—read keg of beer—that goes with it. Last year, a young friend with no drinking experience was violently ill for days after he was introduced to "clear liquids in small glasses" during freshman orientation. We want our daughter to learn how to drink sensibly and avoid this pitfall. Starting   7 at the age of 14, we invited her to join us for a glass of champagne with dinner. She'd tried it once before, thought it was "yucky" and declined. A year later, she enjoyed sampling wine at family meals.

When, at 16, she asked for a Mudslide (a bottled chocolate-milk-and-rum concoction), we used the opportunity to discuss it with her. We explained the alcohol content, told her the alcohol level is lower when the drink is blended with ice and compared it with a glass of wine. Since the drink of choice on campus is beer, we contrasted its potency with wine and hard liquor and stressed the importance of not drinking on an empty stomach. 8

Our purpose was to encourage her to know the alcohol content of what she is served. We want her to experience the effects of liquor in her own home, not on the highway and not for the first time during a college orientation week with free-flowing suds. Although Christine doesn't drive yet, we regularly reinforce the concept of choosing a designated driver. Happily, that already seems a widely accepted practice among our daughter's friends who drink. 9

We recently visited the Ivy League school Christine will attend in the fall. While we were there, we read a story in the college paper about a student who was nearly electrocuted when, in a drunken state, he climbed on top of a moving train at a railroad station near the campus. The student survived, but three of his limbs were later amputated. This incident reminded me of a tragic death on another campus. An intoxicated student maneuvered himself into a chimney. He was found three days later when frat brothers tried to light a fire in the fireplace. By then he was dead. 10

These tragedies are just two examples of our failure to teach young people how to use alcohol prudently. If 18-year-olds don't have legal access to even a beer at a public place, they have no experience handling liquor on their own. They feel "liberated" when they arrive on campus. With no parents to stop them, they have a "let's make up for lost time" attitude. The result: binge drinking. 11

We should make access to alcohol legal at 18. At the same time, we should come down much harder on alcohol abusers and drunk drivers of all ages. We should intensify our efforts at alcohol education for adolescents. We want them to understand that it is perfectly OK not to drink. But if they do, alcohol should be consumed in moderation. 12

After all, we choose to teach our children about safe sex, including the benefits of teen abstinence. Why, then, can't we—schools and parents alike—teach them about safe drinking? 13

THINKING CRITICALLY

Main Idea

1. What is Elizabeth Whelan's thesis? Is it stated or implied?

Details

2. According to Whelan, prohibiting the sale of liquor to responsible young adults causes problems. What are they?

3. According to Whelan, what is the result of banning drinking by young people?

Organization

4. What is Whelan's overall organizational pattern?

Purpose, Audience, Tone

5. Is Whelan's purpose to inform, persuade, or entertain? Explain your answer.

6. Who is Whelan's audience, and how can you tell?

7. Which word best describes Whelan's tone: objective, outraged, outspoken, or distressed? What words and phrases help you identify the tone?

Inferences and Conclusions

8. Whelan implies that binge drinking and alcohol abuse have become problems because U.S. teens, unlike European teens, do not learn to drink gradually, safely, and in moderation. Do you agree? Why or why not?

Making Connections

Whelan says we treat eighteen-year-olds as adults by letting them "drive cars, fly planes, marry, vote, pay taxes, take out loans and risk their lives as members of the U.S. armed forces." Therefore, she suggests, we ought to lower the drinking age. Not allowing eighteen-year-olds to buy a drink when they can legally do all these other adult activities is not realistic. Do you agree with this conclusion? Why or why not?

INFERENCES IN READING AND WRITING

First of all, you already possess the ability to make inferences, and, in fact, you use inferential reasoning every day. When you get up in the morning, you may look outside or watch the Weather Channel to see what the weather is going to be. Based on the forecast and your own observations, you make inferences about what to wear. In your classes, you may have to make inferences to complete many of your assignments and activities. For example, if you read Chapter 3 and successfully completed the exercises on finding implied main ideas, you used inferential reasoning to arrive at your answers. Remember that an implied main idea is one that is unstated. To find it, you have to make inferences from the details that *are* stated. In other words, you have to read between the lines. Determining the writer's purpose, audience, and tone as explained in Chapter 9 also requires some inferential reasoning.

The activities in several sections of each chapter of this book call for inferential reasoning: *Background Check, Thinking Critically,* and *Reflections on Reading and Writing.* If you have successfully completed many of these sections, you have been making good inferences, perhaps without knowing it. This chapter will help you bring that process out into the open. To start figuring out what you do when you make an inference, try this discovery exercise. Do not read the explanation that follows it until after you have completed the exercise.

Exercise 10.1   Read each passage and make as many inferences about it as you can.

1. A woman gets out of her car carrying a poodle. She enters a building. The sign on the building says Hawthorne Veterinary Clinic. What inferences can you make?

_____

_____

2. You wake up in the morning and the sky looks cloudy. Yesterday it rained. The weather forecast is for rain today. You have a long walk from the parking lot to class. What inferences can you make?

_____

_____

3. The room is clean. A diploma hangs on the wall. In the middle of the room is a long, padded table with a pillow at the head and a paper gown folded at the feet. What inferences can you make?

_____

_____

4. A man is walking down the street. He is shabbily dressed and has a day's growth of beard. He is carrying a bundle under his arm and is walking fast, looking over his shoulder. What inferences can you make?

_____

_____

5. You have a math test today. You have studied for the test and feel well prepared. You earned good grades on the last two tests. This test is on factoring, a concept you have had no trouble understanding. What inferences can you make?

_____

_____

The woman carrying the poodle may be taking it to the vet because it is sick. If the vet operates a boarding kennel, she may be leaving the dog while she goes on vacation. Or she may be there to pick up someone who is waiting for her and is taking the dog with her because she does not want to leave it in the car. All of these inferences are plausible, but without more information you cannot say for certain what the woman is doing or why.

In the second passage, the facts given would lead you to infer that it will rain. Because you have a long walk, another inference you can make is that you should take an umbrella. Still, weather predictions have been wrong. Although the facts support the inferences, they are still only predictions. Whether to take an umbrella or to take your chances is up to you.

The details in the third passage suggest a doctor's examining room: the diploma on the wall, the cleanliness, and the table with pillow and gown. Or it could be a laboratory or even a room in a college's health center. Without more facts your inference is only an educated guess.

About the man on the street: you might infer from his shabbiness and stubble that he is homeless, carrying a bundle of his possessions. Or perhaps he is a thief, and the bundle is something he has stolen; that could explain why he is walking fast and looking over his shoulder. On the other hand, maybe he is a computer programmer who worked all night on a project and is just now leaving the office to go home, carrying his jacket in a bundle. If he lives in a city, he may not have a car, and he may be walking fast and looking over his shoulder to find a taxi. Which of these inferences is most likely? Determining which is difficult because you do not have enough information.

In the fifth passage, enough facts are given to infer that you will do well on the math test unless, of course, the problems are harder than you expected.

By now it should be clear to you that inferences are no substitute for facts. They are helpful, but you need more information on which to base decisions, especially important ones.

So how did you arrive at your answers to Exercise 10.1? Your reasoning probably included steps such as these:

- Determine what facts are given.

- Use your experience.

- Start with the obvious, but consider other possibilities.

In the first passage, for example, you are given a woman carrying a dog into a building identified by a sign. Those are the facts. If you conclude that the dog is either sick or being taken to the kennel, you are inferring the obvious based on the facts and on your experience in similar situations. If you infer that the woman is entering the building for a reason having nothing to do with the dog, you are considering another possibility. Although it is an unlikely one, and therefore less valid, it is still a possible inference.

What purpose do those "other possibilities" serve, especially when they turn out to be less valid, or even invalid, inferences? For one thing they engage your imagination and open your mind to thinking creatively. Many of the world's greatest discoveries occurred as the result of accidents that prompted creative thinking. The more inferences you make, and the better able you are to evaluate their validity, the more likely it is that you will see all sides of an issue and thus reach an informed and reasonable conclusion or decision.

Exercise 10.2

Each passage is followed by three inferences, only one of which is valid. To find the valid inference, choose the one that is best supported by the facts in the passage. Circle your choice.

1. Your child does not want to get out of bed when you tell her it is time to get ready for school. Her forehead feels hot to the touch, and she coughs a few times.

    a. She has a cold.

    b. She may have a fever.

    c. She is pretending to be sick.

2. Terence bought a jacket in August. When he got home, he cut off the tags, threw away the receipt, and hung the jacket in the closet. By the time the weather cooled down enough for Terence to wear the jacket, it no longer fit because he had gained a few pounds. He took the jacket to the store for a refund, but the clerk said, "No refund without a receipt. Sorry." Terence was very angry and said he would never shop there again.

    a. Terence was right to be angry.

    b. Terence should have kept the sales slip.

    c. The store's policy is too strict.

3. Rita is trying to learn how to use a word-processing program. She has been at it for only three days, and she is having trouble remembering some of the commands. Whenever she hits the wrong key, she gets angry and says, "I'm never going to learn this stuff."

    a. The program is too hard.

b. Rita is not very bright.

c. She probably needs more time.

4. Chris scored a D on his economics test. This is the second low grade he has earned. At his college, he can withdraw without penalty if he does so before midterm. Chris has four weeks until midterm.

a. He should spend more time studying.

b. He should seek advice before doing anything.

c. He should withdraw from the course now.

5. Your neighbors have not picked up their newspaper in four days. You have not heard their children playing in the backyard pool, and at night the house is dark.

a. Someone in the family has died.

b. The neighbors have sold the house.

c. The neighbors may be on vacation.

THE DIFFERENCE BETWEEN DETAILS AND INFERENCES

At times you may confuse inferences with details. Details include stated facts, reasons, examples, and opinions. Inferences are the interpretations or predictions you make based on the details. Consider the following scenario.

> In an elementary school classroom, all the children are writing. The teacher has given them an assignment to write about a pet. One little boy writes a few words, wads up his paper, and pushes it aside. He does this two or three more times, then takes the wadded up pieces of paper to the trash can. When he sits down again, he tosses his pencil into the air and catches it. He looks around the room. He folds his arms and puts his head down on the desk. After a few seconds he shifts in his seat, takes out a clean sheet of paper, and begins to write. He writes for several minutes without stopping. He has a smile on his face.

In this paragraph, the writer tells you what happened without imposing an opinion. Why does the boy wad his paper? Is he unhappy with what he has written? Why is he smiling at the end? Has he thought of something to say? You could infer from this paragraph that the boy, like many people, has a hard time thinking of what to write. He makes false starts, wastes a little time, then finally gets down to business when an idea hits him. But those inferences come from you, not the writer. What you have done is to impose your own meaning on the writer's words. Most of the time writers do impose an opinion on the events they describe, as in the next paragraph.

> All of the students in Ms. Jones's class were writing about their pets. Jerry could not think of anything to say. He would start to write, wad up his paper, try again, until he had so many crumpled pieces of paper on his desk that he had to get up and throw them away before he could start again. What Ms. Jones should have known is that Jerry didn't have a pet. Like many children, he had never had a cat or a dog or an animal of any kind. He was truly at a loss for words. So he wasted time, rested his head on the desk, and tried to think of a way out of the situation. At last an idea came to him. His cousin had a little dog, which he played with when their families visited. He would write about Suzie's dog as if it were his own. When he began writing, he had a smile on his face.

When you read this paragraph, you have less room for interpretation. You know why Jerry cannot get started and you know why he is smiling. However, what other inferences can you make? The author says Ms. Jones *should have known* that Jerry, like many children, did not have a pet. From this you can infer that the author thinks Ms. Jones, perhaps all teachers, should know something about their students. You can make another inference from the phrase, "Like many children." If many children do not have pets, then the author probably thinks Ms. Jones's topic was not a good choice.

USING DETAILS TO MAKE INFERENCES

In a biology class you learn facts and concepts that you use as a basis for conducting experiments in your biology lab. Before an experiment, you make an inference, or prediction, about its outcome. To test your inference, you carry out the experiment. When you get the results, you then make more inferences about what the results mean. In a literature class, you make inferences to interpret the meaning of a character's actions or to find the theme of a short story. In a math class, making inferences may be one of the most important skills you use. To work out a word problem successfully, you start with what is given. What are the facts? What does the problem ask you to find? Based on those two pieces of information, you must infer the needed solution. Try these steps for making inferences from the details you encounter in your reading.

1. Read for the literal meaning: the main idea and supporting details.

2. Distinguish facts from opinions.

3. Look for clues in the details.

4. Do not infer anything you cannot support.

Exercise 10.3   Read the following textbook passages, then make inferences to answer the questions that follow them.

1. The sexual revolution has raised a number of important issues about the relationship between sex and satisfaction. Is having sex like adding butter to a sauce, does it make a crucial difference in satisfaction with the relationship? Or is sex more like the raisin on a cake? When the relationship as a whole is good, sex can top it off. But if the cake is a flop, no little raisin is going to rescue it.

   From *Social Psychology*, 2d ed., Sharon S. Brehm and Saul M. Kassin, Houghton Mifflin Co., 1993.

   a. What is the main idea?

   _____

   b. What details support the main idea?

   _____

   _____

   c. Are the details facts or opinions?

   _____

   _____

    d. What inference can you make from the last two sentences? What is the writer saying about the importance of sex in a relationship?

_____

_____

2. When you take out a loan to buy a condominium or house or when you refinance a mortgage, banks charge certain points or origination fees in addition to the cost of borrowing the money for fifteen or thirty years. Each point is equal to 1% of the total amount borrowed and is generally required in advance, unlike the mortgage payments. Depending on your financial situation, selecting the lowest interest rate advertised might not be your most economical choice.

From *Fundamentals of Mathematics,* Sandra Pryor Clarkson and Barbara J. Barone, Houghton Mifflin Co., 1994.

    a. What is the main idea?

_____

    b. What details support the main idea?

_____

_____

    c. Are the details facts or opinions?

_____

_____

    d. What inference can you make from the last sentence? Why might the lowest interest rate advertised not be the most economical choice?

_____

_____

3. The formation of one substance from another substance is called a **chemical change.** Chemical changes include the very complicated reactions that occur when food is cooked and the substances that contribute to its flavor and aroma are formed. The extraction of metals from their ores makes use of chemical changes, as does the production of synthetic fibers (for example, nylon, acrylics such as Orlon, and polyesters such as Dacron) from air, coal, and petroleum. Chemical changes occur during **chemical reactions,** in which one substance responds ("reacts") to the presence of another, to a change of temperature, or to some other influence. For example, the conversion of silica to silicon, the material used in the manufacture of microchips, is a chemical change brought about by a reaction between silica and carbon. Chemists respond daily to the challenge to discover the chemical reactions that produce a desired substance from other, more readily available starting materials.

From *General Chemistry,* 2d ed., P. W. Atkins and J. A. Beran, Scientific American Books, 1990.

a. What is the main idea?

_____

b. What details support the main idea?

_____

_____

c. Are the details facts or opinions?

_____

_____

d. Based on the authors' examples of chemical changes, what additional example of a chemical change can you think of?

_____

4. Sports is a form of popular culture that is deeply rooted in modern society. From neighborhood games to high school, college, and pro-

fessional sports, it is so pervasive in society that even a presidential debate had to step aside rather than compete for public attention and approval. During the 1992 presidential campaign, the timing of the World Series was a key to scheduling the debates, and no political party would have dared suggest preempting a game for a debate to pick the next president of the United States. In the midst of an important tennis playoff a few years ago, the CBS Evening News was delayed for several minutes. In a famous incident, Dan Rather stomped off the set. There was also the so-called Heidi incident of 1968. The New York Jets were leading the Oakland Raiders 32–29 with very little time left in the game when NBC cut away to begin the movie *Heidi*. The Raiders scored two touchdowns in the last nine seconds to win, and viewers in the Eastern time zone missed it. An extraordinary number of irate callers protested to NBC. As a result, NBC began a policy of broadcasting to the end of all football games. All of these incidents indicate the apparent economic and psychological value sports has for television.

From *Understanding Mass Communication,* 5th ed., Melvin L. DeFleur and Everette E. Dennis, Houghton Mifflin Co., 1994.

a. What is the main idea?

_____

b. What details support the main idea?

_____

_____

c. Are the details facts or opinions?

_____

_____

d. The concluding sentence states an inference the authors have made. In your opinion, is the inference valid? Explain your answer.

_____

_____

Inferences have much to do with logic. You make an inference based on what would seem logical given the details an author provides and given what you know about the topic from experience. The more concrete and better organized the details are, the more you are able to see how they connect and to make inferences from them. For example, one of the questions in Exercise 10.3 asks you to make up your own example of a chemical change. To do this, you must first know what a chemical change is. The authors provide both a definition and some examples. Did you have trouble thinking of your own example? Even if you did, imagine how much harder it would have been had the authors provided no examples from which you could make inferences to arrive at your answer.

The practice you get by making inferences from reading may influence some of the choices you make in writing. Remember that an inference is an interpretation or prediction. When you write about a significant event in your life, you are giving readers your interpretation of it. When you write about a way to improve grades you are making a prediction that grades will improve if readers follow your steps. You cannot make good inferences without sufficient information, and neither can your readers. The process you go through in making inferences from an author's details should make you aware of the necessity to improve your own selection and organization of details.

STUDY TIP: *You can make inferences to predict test questions. When you get ready to study for a test, put together all your notes, returned tests, handouts, and any other information you have. As you look these over, determine which facts stand out. What concepts, terms, or ideas are repeated in more than one place? Which ones has your instructor emphasized in class? You can infer that you are most likely to be tested on these kinds of information.*

THINKING ABOUT PROCESS

Reading everything the same way is inefficient. Different materials call for different strategies. For example, when reading a math word problem, the skill you will use the most is that of making an inference.

1. Word problems are like little puzzles. Some pieces are given, and some are missing. Your first step in working out a solution is to read the problem for the answers to two questions: What facts are given, and what am I asked to find? The answers to both questions are stated in the problem.

2. What is not stated, is how to solve the problem. Based on the facts given, you must make an inference to determine what operation (method) to use. Key words can help. For example, if the problem asks you to find a distance that is *twice as far,* these key words suggest that the operation to use is multiplication. *Decreased by* indicates subtraction, and *one half of* implies division.

3. When you arrive at an answer, you should check it for accuracy, but first you should make an inference. Based on what you think the solution *should* be, ask yourself, "Is my answer too great, too little, or does it seem about right?" Then verify your inference by using whatever procedure is appropriate.

CONCLUSIONS IN READING AND WRITING

A *conclusion* is a judgment or decision arrived at through reasoning. You have probably heard the saying, "don't jump to conclusions," which means do not make a judgment or decision based on faulty or insufficient evidence. A good conclusion is the result of a careful consideration of the available evidence. You can probably think of examples of good and bad judgments or decisions you have made.

What prompts someone to buy a car, begin or end a relationship, or look for a new job? Why do you like some people and not others? Why do you think certain actions or behaviors are good or bad? You make decisions and judgments such as these everyday. Some you arrive at quickly. Others take longer. For most people, important decisions require a lot of thinking, and some people like to ask others' opinions and advice before they decide. Are you quick to judge others? When you meet someone, do you generally go with your first impression, or do you reserve judgment until you know the person better? The decisions and judgments you have made are conclusions you have reached. Whether your conclusions are good depends directly on the evidence you have to consider and the inferences you can make from it.

You can apply the same principle to your reading and writing. As a reader, you should ask yourself, "What does the author conclude?" In addition, you must find the evidence, or details, that lead to the conclusion. As a writer, you should ask yourself, "How will I conclude my essay?" Also, you must make sure your details lead to your conclusion. Figure 10.1 lists some transitions writers use to signal readers that a conclusion follows.

Every aspect of the writing process presents choices for writers. How to conclude an essay or other piece of writing is another choice. The simplest type of conclusion is the summary statement or paragraph. The writer restates the thesis and main ideas in different words and draws a conclusion from them. For an example of this type of conclusion, see the last two paragraphs of Elizabeth Whelan's "Perils of Prohibition" on page 273.

Four of the introductory strategies explained in Chapter 4 also work well as concluding devices. Look for these in your reading and experiment with them in your writing.

1. End with an anecdote that reinforces your thesis.

2. End with a quotation and relate it to your thesis.

3. Use additional facts and figures to reinforce your thesis.

4. Ask one last revealing question that makes readers think about what you have said.

The following examples illustrate possible thesis statements and concluding paragraphs of essays for each of these devices:

EXAMPLE 1: END WITH AN ANECDOTE

Thesis: *Superstitions are of three major types: those that come from religious beliefs and practices; those that have a historical basis; and those that have cultural or national origins.*

FIGURE 10.1

Transitions Used to Signal a Conclusion

consequently	therefore	in summary
thus	finally	conclusively
in conclusion	to conclude	as a result

Concluding paragraph with anecdote bracketed:

[. . . A friend of mine accompanied me on a shopping trip recently. As we were walking down the street, talking and looking at the window displays, we suddenly had the choice of continuing on our path, which led directly under a ladder, or walking out of our way to avoid it. Without so much as a pause in the conversation, we walked around the ladder. In doing so, we did not stop to think that we were observing an age-old practice to ward off evil.**]** If you should catch yourself falling into an old superstitious habit, just remember that it probably has some religious, historical, or cultural significance.

EXAMPLE 2: END WITH A QUOTATION AND AN EXPLANATION

Thesis: *To prepare for an exam successfully, you need to first understand the material you want to remember; then use one of several common memory aids to help you study.*

Concluding paragraph with quotation and explanation bracketed:

. . . Someone once said, **[**"You cannot remember what you do not understand." Preparation alone is not enough, especially when your preparation consists of memorizing without understanding.**]** To make the best use of the tips we have explained, first determine what will be on your test. Next, review your lecture and textbook notes and any other materials until you are sure you understand them. Then apply the memory aids that work best for you.

EXAMPLE 3: USE ADDITIONAL FACTS AND FIGURES

Thesis: *The evidence is conclusive that smoking is a health hazard and that those who smoke should make every effort to kick the habit.*

Concluding paragraph with a fact and a figure bracketed:

. . . If you, like some smokers, still believe that the claims of tobacco use causing lung cancer, emphysema, and other diseases are largely exaggerated, talk to your doctor. Better yet, visit a hospital ward for emphysema patients. [Although you may not realize it, deaths from tobacco-related illnesses outnumber deaths from drug abuse two to one. In fact, more people die every year from smoking than from automobile accidents.]

EXAMPLE 4: ASK ONE LAST REVEALING QUESTION

Thesis: *Selecting a home computer is difficult unless you know exactly what you want your computer to do.*

Concluding paragraph with question bracketed:

. . . Selecting a computer for home use is no easy task because technology is changing so rapidly that your computer will be outdated almost as soon as you get your programs running. If you do not require "state-of-the-art" equipment, pick a model that will do what you want it to do and will last for several years. Consider all the jobs you normally use a computer for and buy one that does those tasks. [Two years from now, will you still be happy with your computer, or will you be kicking yourself for the extra money you spent on fancy features you have never used?]

You may also want to try these additional concluding strategies:

- Predict the future.
- Challenge your readers.

Predict the Future

Another way to conclude an essay is to point to some future outcome readers can expect as a result of what you tell them in your essay. For example, you might conclude the essay on a good weight-training program by telling readers what their bodies will look like if they follow your advice and approximately how long it will take to get it that way.

The following excerpt is from the concluding paragraph of Nikki Giovanni's essay ". . . And the Loser Is. . . ." In this humorous essay

Giovanni questions sports announcers who label a team "losers" before the game is over. She also feels that if more women were sports announcers, they might call the games differently.

> . . . Don't keep taking away from the effort on the field nor the effort in front of the TV screen. We just want to cheer. Since most teams are losers, as there is only one number one player, only one Super Bowl championship team, only one World Series winner, most teams and most fans have identified at one time or another with a loser. That's life. Most of us lose, too. And it's not the worst thing in the world to say, "Well done." At a certain level of excellence we are all the winners. And maybe the guys in the booth ought to think about that. Or maybe the women in the booth will be sure to mention it to them.

Giovanni's conclusion predicts the future of sports announcing when women take their place in the announcer's booth: more winners, fewer losers.

Challenge Your Readers

If you are writing persuasively about a topic, one of your purposes might be to get readers to change their behavior or to consider a better way of doing something. For example, suppose you write on the ineffectiveness of smoking and nonsmoking areas in restaurants and you argue that setting aside a nonsmoking area in a restaurant while maintaining a smoking area does not work because the smoke from one area will drift into the other. You conclude that we need legislation to prohibit smoking *anywhere* in restaurants and other public places in the interest of providing a truly smoke-free environment. Your conclusion might challenge readers who agree with you to write their representatives and demand more nonsmoking legislation.

Following is the conclusion from "Rock Lyrics and Violence against Women," an essay by Caryl Rivers. Rivers's thesis is that rock music that depicts violence against women sends a subtle message to its listeners that the violence is okay.

> . . . I think something needs to be done. I'd like to see people in the industry respond to the problem. I'd love to see some women rock stars speak out against violence against women. I would like to see disc jockeys refuse air play to records and videos that contain such violence. At the very least, I want to see the end of the silence. I want

journalists and parents and critics and performing artists to keep this issue alive in the public forum. I don't want people who are concerned about this issue labeled as bluenoses and bookburners and ignored.

And I wish it wasn't always just women who were speaking out. Men have as large a stake in the quality of our civilization as women do in the long run. Violence is a contagion that infects at random. Let's hear something, please, from the men. . . .

Rivers's conclusion challenges readers by asking them to do something about the violence against women that is expressed in some of the lyrics of rock music. Rivers also issues a special challenge to men to speak out.

Exercise 10.4   Choose any three of the chapter-opening essays from Chapters 1–9. Compare the ways these authors have concluded their essays, and then answer the following questions about each essay. Be able to explain your answers.

1. What concluding device has the author used?

2. Does the conclusion reinforce the thesis?

3. Is the ending effective?

THINKING IT OVER

Test your recall of this chapter's concepts by completing the following statements. If you cannot complete a statement, look back through the chapter to find the answer.

1. An inference is an act of _____ that leads you to draw a conclusion.

2. An inference can be an interpretation of events or ideas based on available _____ and the _____ or _____ you bring to them.

3. Inferences are also _____ you make based on an author's details.

4. A conclusion is a reasoned _____ or _____ based on your inferences.

5. Whether your conclusions are good depends directly on the _____ you consider and the _____ you make.

6. Two transitions writers use to signal readers that a conclusion follows are _____ and _____.

7. Two strategies for writing good introductions that can also be used for writing good conclusions are _____ and _____.

8. When your conclusion asks readers to change a behavior or take an action, the strategy you are using is _____.

9. Making inferences and drawing conclusions are skills involved in the process of _____ _____.

10. Choose one of the Thinking First questions at the beginning of the chapter to answer on the following lines:

_____

_____

_____

TOPICS FOR WRITING

Choose one of the topics below or make up your own topic.

1. Explain why you think the drinking age should or should not be lowered.

2. Agree or disagree with the reasons Elizabeth Whelan gives for lowering the drinking age.

3. Write about a fear or problem you have overcome.

4. Explain why students should reduce stress.

5. Explain what you think is the greatest problem facing young people today.

6. Write about your major, your career plans, and what you hope to accomplish.

Checklist for Revision

1. Do you have a clearly stated thesis?

2. Have you supported your thesis with enough concrete details?

3. Do your paragraphs have unity and coherence?

4. Does your essay have a recognizable organizational pattern?

5. Have you used appropriate transitions?

6. Have you considered your audience's needs?

7. Will readers be able to determine your purpose?

8. Do your word choices create an appropriate tone?

9. Does your essay have a good conclusion?

10. Have you found and corrected your errors?

REFLECTIONS ON READING AND WRITING

Reflect on your reading and writing skills. What are you doing well? What still needs improvement? To help you answer these questions, reflect on the choices for readers and writers explained in this book: main idea, details, organization, purpose, audience, tone, inferences, and conclusions. Of the strategies you have learned, which ones are you able to use with confidence? Explain one successful reading or writing experience you have had this term in any one of your classes.

Editing for Common Sentence Errors

*S*entence errors such as common mistakes in grammar, punctuation, and spelling, detract from your writing. Sentence errors call attention to themselves. If your paragraphs and essays contain errors, your readers will probably notice them and be distracted from your content. This is especially true of employers, many of whom believe that sloppy writing reflects on your job performance. A poorly written résumé or job application for example, could jeopardize your chances of getting the job you want. Therefore, you must always proofread a paper before handing it in. If you can find and fix your sentence errors, you may then have a better understanding of the kinds of errors you tend to make. Over time, you may be able to eliminate them. Sentence errors usually result from one or both of the following conditions.

1. Inconsistent application of the rules of Standard English

2. Forgetting to proofread for careless mistakes, and typographical errors.

To apply the rules of Standard English consistently, you may need to brush up on them. A handbook of English grammar, like a dictionary, is a tool every writer should never be without. If you do not have a handbook, check your college bookstore where you may find several to choose from.

To find your careless mistakes, proofread and edit your papers before handing them in.

EDITING FOR GRAMMAR

Become aware of the kinds of errors you most frequently make by carefully examining essays that have been graded and returned to you. Suppose, for example, that your essays often contain pronoun agreement errors. When you proofread, check every pronoun to make sure it agrees in number with the person or thing it stands for. Proofreading essays before you hand them in should help you find typographical errors and other mistakes.

Figure A.1 lists examples of some common grammatical errors and how to correct them. Read the figure, and find the type of mistake you most often make.

FIGURE A.1

Correcting Common Grammatical Errors

ERROR	EXAMPLE	CORRECTION
Fragment	When the lights went out.	Connect the fragment to an independent clause: "When the lights went out, we were plunged into darkness."
Comma splice	John felt his way around the room, he was looking for candles and matches.	Replace comma with period or semicolon: "John felt his way around the room; he was looking for candles and matches."

FIGURE A.1

Correcting Common Grammatical Errors (continued)

ERROR	EXAMPLE	CORRECTION
Run-on sentence	We waited for the lights to come back on after an hour we decided to call the power company.	Find the two independent clauses. Separate them with a period or semicolon: "We waited for the lights to come back on. After an hour we decided to call the power company."
Dangling modifier	Sitting in the dark, light came into the room from the full moon outside.	Who was sitting in the dark? After the comma that ends the modifier, insert the subject the modifier describes: "Sitting in the dark, we saw the light that came into the room from the full moon outside."
Pronoun-antecedent agreement	Someone remembered that they had a battery-operated radio.	*Someone* is singular, and it is the antecedent of *they*. Change *they* to either *he* or *she* to agree with *Someone*: "Someone remembered that *she* had a battery-operated radio."
Pronoun case	John and her went to look for the radio.	*Her* is one of the subjects of the sentence. *Her* is an objective-case pronoun. Change *her* to *she*, which is a subjective-case pronoun: "John and she went to look for the radio."
Subject-verb agreement	We heard on the news that people's lights was out all over the county.	Make the verb agree with the subject: "We heard on the news that people's lights were out all over the county."

FIGURE A.1

Correcting Common Grammatical Errors (continued)

ERROR	EXAMPLE	CORRECTION
Inconsistent tense	It was a power blackout, so we listen to the radio and waited for the lights to come back on.	Since the blackout took place in the past, all the verbs should be in the past tense. Make *listen* a past-tense verb: "It was a power blackout so we lis-tened to the radio and waited for the lights to come back on."
Inconsistent point of view	When the lights came back on, we had gotten so used to being in the dark that you had to ad-just your eyes.	*You* is inconsistent be-cause the point of view is first-person plural. Change *you* to *we* for a consistent point of view: "When the lights came back on, we had gotten so used to being in the dark that we had to ad-just our eyes."

EDITING FOR PUNCTUATION

When you are editing, check for correctly punctuated sentences. When you are drafting, and even when you are writing your final copy, leaving out commas and end punctuation marks is easy to do. Therefore, you need to proofread carefully.

EDITING FOR SPELLING

Spelling errors can interfere with the good ideas you are trying to com-municate. If you know you have a spelling problem, you need to use the dictionary when you write. Spelling errors may result from two major problems: not knowing the common rules of spelling and confusing the spelling of words that look or sound alike.

ANALYZING YOUR ERRORS

How much editing you have to do depends upon how many errors you usually make. If your only problem is a misspelled word now and then, one reading may be enough for you to find and correct your spelling errors. If you usually make several errors in grammar, punctuation, and spelling, you may have to do several readings: one for grammar, one for punctuation, one for spelling, and a final reading to see whether you missed anything. Figure A.2, on page 300 contains an editing checklist that will help you analyze your essays for errors. After you have analyzed several of your essays, you will be able to tell whether the errors you make are random or whether they fall into certain categories. Then you will know what you need to concentrate on when you edit.

FIGURE A.2

Your Editing Checklist

TYPE OF ERROR   **NUMBER OF ERRORS**

TYPE OF ERROR	ESSAY #1	ESSAY #2	ESSAY #3	ESSAY #4	ESSAY #5	ESSAY #6
Fragment						
Comma splice						
Run-on sentence						
Dangling modifier						
Pronoun-antecedent agreement						
Pronoun case						
Subject-verb agreement						
Inconsistent tense						
Inconsistent point of view						
Punctuation						
Spelling						
Other Error						
Other Error						

Acknowledgments

Chapter 1

Pages 3–5: "There Had Been a Death in the Family" by Mike Pride from *Newsweek*, February 10, 1986. Reprinted by permission of the author, the editor of the Concord (N.H.) *Monitor.*

Pages 16–17: From K. Seifert and R. Hoffnung, *Child and Adolescent Development,* Third Edition. Copyright © 1994 by Houghton Mifflin Company. Used by permission.

Chapter 2

Pages 40–42: "Spanglish Spoken Here" by Janice Castro with Dan Cook and Christina Garcia. Copyright © 1988 Time, Inc. Reprinted by permission.

Pages 55–56: Copyright © 1996 by Houghton Mifflin Company. Adapted and reprinted by permission from *The American Heritage Dictionary of the English Language,* Third Edition.

Chapter 3

Pages 66–68: "It's O.K. to Be Different" by Angie Erickson from *Newsweek*, October 24, 1994. All rights reserved. Reprinted by permission.

Pages 79–80: From *The Names: A Memoir* by Scott Momaday. Copyright © 1976 by N. Scott Momaday. Reprinted by permission of the author.

Pages 81–82: From Bernstein et al., *Psychology,* Fifth Edition. Copyright © 1994 by Houghton Mifflin Company. Used by permission.

Pages 85–86: From Barry L. Reece and Rhonda Brandt, *Effective Human Relations in Organizations,* Fifth Edition. Copyright © 1992

by Houghton Mifflin Company. Used by permission.

Pages 89–90: From E. Thomas Garman and Raymond E. Forgue, *Personal Finance,* Fourth Edition. Copyright © 1994 by Houghton Mifflin Company. Used by permission.

Chapter 4

Pages 96–100: Reprinted with the permission of Scribner, a division of Simon & Schuster from *Cheeseburgers* by Bob Greene. Copyright © 1985 by John Deadline Enterprises.

Pages 112–113: Joe Queenan, "I Married an Accountant," *Newsweek,* November 14, 1988. Used by permission of the author.

Page 114: Gregg Easterbrook, "Escape Valve" from *The New York Times,* December 26, 1981, page 23. Copyright © 1981 by The New York Times Company. Reprinted by permission.

Page 115: Elliott West, "Wagon Train Children," *American Heritage,* December 1, 1985, pages 90–91. Reprinted by permission of American Heritage Magazine, a division of Forbes Inc. © Forbes Inc., 1985.

Pages 116–117: Robert MacNeil, "The Trouble with Television," from a speech, "Is Television Narrowing Our Minds?" delivered at the Presidents Leadership Forum, SUNY, Purchase, November 13, 1984. Reprinted with permission from the March 1985 *Reader's Digest.*

Pages 119–120: Text excerpt, pages 295–296, from *How Did They Do That?* by Caroline Sutton. Copyright © 1984 by Hilltown Books. By permission of William Morrow & Company, Inc.

Index